Night Riders

IN BLACK FOLK HISTORY

Night Riders

IN BLACK

FOLK HISTORY

by Gladys-Marie Fry

THE UNIVERSITY OF TENNESSEE PRESS

Library of Congress Cataloging in Publication Data

Fry, Gladys-Marie, 1931–
  Night riders in Black folk history.

  Bibliography: p.
  Includes index.
  1. Slavery in the United States—Condition of slaves.
2. Negroes—Southern States. 3. Southern States—Race
question. 4. Folk-lore, Negro. I. Title.
E443.F89   301.44'93'0973   74–34268
ISBN 0–87049–163–6

To My Parents and Brother
OBELIA SWEARINGEN FRY, LOUIS EDWIN FRY, SR.,
LOUIS EDWIN FRY, JR.

*present links in a long Black family lineage,
dating back to 1684*

PREFACE

PROPHETICALLY, my collecting of slave reminiscences began in an old house on a cold and dreary Halloween night in Bloomington, Indiana. As a graduate student beginning the research for my dissertation, I had an uneasy feeling about the venture which the long walk from Indiana University's campus had not helped to erase. I felt I should do more library research; I had qualms about the number of people I had invited to my first group session; I wondered if my ancient tape recorder would hold up. Leaving the security of the library carrel was like cutting an academic umbilical cord. Here I was in the field—ready or not. My disquietude was not helped by the fact that it was dark and rainy and I was alone— and the house where my informants waited faced a cemetery.

The people I interviewed that evening were seven middle-aged, hard-working people from the local Black community, six of them women and the seventh the husband of my hostess. Most of them belonged to the Baptist church located a few blocks away. At my knock, the door opened on a large livingroom comfortably furnished in an eclectic style. The atmosphere was somber: dark reds and blues, and brownish walls. Everything was immaculate, but worn. On an overstuffed velvet sofa sat three of my informants. The other four and I faced them in a kind of informal semicircle.

At ten o'clock I was aware of the chimes from the University library tower. The interviews which had begun three hours earlier had not gone well. My questionnaire was unwieldly. I had too many questions and it took too much time to repeat the same questions and listen to the replies from each informant. The real problem lay in these replies, which were evasive, avoiding any relevant discussion of the slave system. In fact, three of the in-

vii

formants were anxious to disassociate themselves from any connection with slavery. All wanted to discuss the Black question today, exhibiting bitterness about their plight as Blacks. A full evening had already passed and all I had heard were superficial reminiscences about slavery "times," but no extended accounts about specific events or occurrences. I suddenly realized I had struck a solid wall of resistance. But why? I knew the slave experience is very much a part of Black oral tradition, so why wouldn't they talk to me—really talk, not just politely parry questions?

Suddenly there was a loud cracking noise that seemed to come from the unoccupied upstairs. It startled us. We all looked around and at each other. Then everybody smiled. "This old house is settling," somebody offered by way of explanation. "Well," I said, secretly relieved to shift the direction of the questioning, "this gives me a chance to ask if anybody knows any ghost stories?" Mrs. Smith, a short, pinchfaced woman who had previously said little, replied promptly with great feeling, "Don't you know the white man taught them all of that about ghosts. That was a way of keeping them down—keeping them under control." Then she described her grandmother's account of the overseer riding through slave quarters covered with a white sheet, tin cans tied to his horse's tail, in order to keep the slaves indoors at night. A trickle of stories about white manipulation of beliefs in conjuring, witches, and ghosts began to come. It was only the beginning!

CONTENTS

PREFACE   vii

PROLOGUE   3
  The Use of Black Oral Traditions as a Historical Source   3
  A Survey of Historical Source Material on Black
    Intellectual and Social Thought   10
  Field Work Methodology   29
  The Southern Character of Washington, D.C.   32
  Historical Materials on the District   33
  Nature of Black Oral Tradition in Washington, D.C.   35

1. THE PROBLEM OF SLAVE CONTROL   38
  Historical Background   38
  The System of Psychological Control   45

2. THE ROLE OF THE MASTER AND OF THE OVERSEER IN THE USE
    OF SUPERNATURAL SUBTERFUGE   59
  Circulation of Ghost Tales   63
  Haunted Places   66
  Masquerading as Ghosts   69
  Influence of Psychological Control on Black Narrative
    Tradition   73

3. THE PATROL SYSTEM   82
  Conditions Making a Patrol Necessary   82
  Composition, Compensation, Duties, and Powers   85
  Techniques of Surveillance   86
  Evolution of the Patrol System in Washington, D.C.   89
  General Ineffectiveness of the System   93
  Black Folk View of the System   102

4. THE RECONSTRUCTION KU KLUX KLAN   110
   Origin of the Klan   110
   Costume of the Klan   122
   Supernatural Practices   135
   Ante-bellum Patrol Duties Assumed by the Klan   147

5. THE KU KLUX KLAN IN THE EYES OF THE BLACK   154
   Black Folk View of the Klan   154
   Black Connections with the Klan   162

6. THE NIGHT DOCTORS: A FINAL PHASE IN THE PSYCHOLOGICAL
   CONTROL OF THE BLACK   170
   Historical Background and Genesis of Belief in Night
    Doctors   170
   Night Doctor Tradition in the Rural South   178
   Night Doctor Tradition in Washington, D.C.   182
   Apparel of the Night Doctors   188
   Kinds of Victims Sought   190
   Methods of Ensnarement and Abduction   192
   Conveyance of Victims and Manner of Death   197
   A Notorious Washington Night Doctor   202
   Legal Basis and Demise   207

EPILOGUE: The Preservation of Oral Stories in Black Culture   212

APPENDIX A: Biographies of Informants   216

APPENDIX B: WPA Informants   225

APPENDIX C: Texas Slave Narrative Informants   227

APPENDIX D: Tale Type Index   228
   Motif Index   228
   Classification of Superstitions   230

LIST OF WORKS CITED OR CONSULTED   232

ACKNOWLEDGMENTS   245

INDEX   247

ILLUSTRATIONS

following page 116

"Patterollers" or "night riders" checking a slave's pass
Slave quarters
Recording oral testimony of Blacks
The underground railroad
Black folk memory of kidnapping and other atrocities
A "visit" of the Ku Klux
The infamous William Burke
A joyous celebration of the Emancipation Proclamation
Disguises of the Ku Klux Klan
Control of Blacks by fear

Night Riders
IN BLACK FOLK HISTORY

PROLOGUE

The Use of Black Oral Traditions
as a Historical Source

DURING AND FOLLOWING the period of Black slavery in America, one of the means utilized by whites in controlling the Black population was a system of psychological pressure based on fear of the supernatural. The primary aim of such pressure was to discourage the unauthorized movement of Blacks, especially at night, by making them afraid of encountering supernatural beings. During slavery times this psychological control guarded against insurrection by discouraging nocturnal assembly; from the post-Civil War period to World War I, the method helped to stem the tide of Black movement from rural farming communities in the South to the urban industrial centers of the North. Originally practiced during slavery by masters and overseers dressed as ghosts, psychological control was later extended to the system of mounted patrols (or "patterollers") designed to monitor slave movement in antebellum days, the Ku Klux Klan of the Reconstruction era, and finally the night doctors. To their Black victims these groups were known as the night riders. Though they differed in disguises and stated aims, and even in point of time, all three adhered to a single cardinal purpose: the control of the Black through intimidation.

As will be seen in the following text, evidence of such practices is abundant in the reminiscences, genealogical data, and legends of oral tradition—a rich source of information in the study of Afro-American history. This oral tradition asserts that fear of the supernatural was a dominant factor employed by the whites in controlling the Blacks. This system evolved from inducing fear of

3

supernatural phenomena during the slavery-Reconstruction era to encouraging the body-snatching traditions of the post-Civil War period.

For many decades such apologists for slavery as Ulrich Phillips, Avery Craven, and James Randall created an aura of belief in slavery as a kind of romantic institution, portraying the Black as docile, superstitious, and mentally inferior. Philip A. Bruce reflects this point of view, emphasizing that Blacks are deeply ashamed of their superstition, yet, because it is so implanted in their nature, they are unable to resist its promptings.[1]

Folklore writings of the late nineteenth and early twentieth centuries also expressed this attitude. For at least the first thirty years of its existence the *Journal of American Folklore* mirrored the prevailing attitude toward the Black as inherently superstitious by publishing a number of articles on folk beliefs of the Southern Black, primarily concerning superstition and conjuring, to the neglect of other genres of Black folklore. John Hawkins' article "An Old Mauma's Folk-Lore" is typical, with its patronizing attitude toward the Black informant.

> Maum Sue being exceedingly superstitious, it occurred to me on a recent visit to the old homestead in lower South Carolina that some of her odd notions and practices might prove, if recorded, of general interest, especially since the young science of folklore is claiming everywhere so many devotees. She was plainly flattered by the mention of the subject. It delighted her to think that one so humble as she could say anything which would interest the ladies and gentlemen of the great North, of which she has only the very vaguest ideas. So willing was she, indeed, to "talk for publication," that the supply of material drawn from her rich store and poured out at my feet proved rather embarrassing from its very abundance. The following beliefs and customs must therefore be regarded only as specimens selected at random from this mine of ancient lore, and not, by any means, as a complete exhibit of its riches.[2]

Many contemporary historians have attacked these stereotypic ideas, particularly the theory, expounded principally by Stanley

[1] *The Plantation Negro As a Freedman* (New York, 1889), 120.
[2] *Journal of American Folklore*, 9 (April–June 1896), 129–31.

4

Elkins, that the Sambo-like personality (the feet-shuffling, head-scratching, docile Black) was an internalized trait produced by the unrestricted power of the slave master and unique to this country. Recognizing flaws in Elkins' methodology and lack of historical evidence, several Black writers have perceived his failure to understand the slave personality because of his neglect of Afro-American oral tradition. Condemning Elkins' thesis as "one of the most intellectually irresponsible of his generation,"[3] Sterling Stuckey observed that slave folklore "decisively repudiates that Negroes as a group had internalized Sambo traits, committing them, as it were to psychological marriage."[4] Ralph Ellison also denies the Sambo argument, asserting that his Black forefathers "by living their own lives and refusing to be destroyed by social injustice and white supremacy, real or illusory, made it possible for me to live my own life with meaning."[5] Looking at these people, Ellison concludes that another reality lies "behind the appearance of reality which they would force upon us as truth."[6] Perhaps John Blassingame touches the essence of the Sambo stereotype, however, as he explains why Southern whites needed this image to foster their own ends: "Without Sambo it was impossible to prove the essential goodness of Southern society."[7]

The actuality—that the Sambo image was a façade—can be learned not from folk knowledge, with which Elkins claims famil-

[3] "Through the Prism of Folklore: The Black Ethos in Slavery," *The Debate Over Slavery*, Ann J. Lane, ed. (Urbana, Ill., 1971), 245–68.

[4] "Twilight of Our Past: Reflections on the Origins of Black History," *Amistad* 2, John A. Williams, ed. (New York, 1971), 267.

[5] "A Very Stern Discipline," *Harper's* (March 1967), 83–84.

[6] *Ibid.* Some recent studies have also documented the existence of a viable Black community during slavery. Among these are: Earl E. Thorpe, "Chattel Slavery and the Concentration Camps," *Negro History Bulletin* (May 1962), 171–76; Mary Agnes Lewis, "Slavery and Personality," *American Quarterly* (Spring 1967), 114–21; Eugene D. Genovese, "On Writing the History of Black Slaves," *New York Review of Books* (Dec. 3, 1970), 34–42; Okon E. Uya, "The Culture of Slavery: Black Experience through a White Filter," *Afro-American Studies*, 1, no. 2 (1971), 203–209; "Life in the Slave Community," *Ibid.*, 1, no. 3 (1971), 281–90; "The Mind of Slaves as Revealed in their Songs: An Interpretative Essay," *Current Bibliography on African Affairs*, 5 (1972), Series 11, pp. 3–10.

[7] *The Slave Community* (New York, 1972), 139. For the most recent critique of the Elkins thesis, see Ann Lane, ed., *The Debate over Slavery* (Urbana, Ill., 1971).

iarity, but from Black oral tradition, of which he is obviously ignorant. For Sambo was not, as Elkins states, a part of the Black's own lore; he exists in neither slave narratives nor oral tradition as the typical plantation slave. Instead, Blacks themselves emphasize the slave dissemblers and the deceptions practiced on the masters.[8] Oral testimony provides ample evidence that slaves contrived all sorts of ingenious schemes to trick and deceive their masters. Aside from the tricks used to undermine the patrol system, chicanery and cunning were employed on a day-to-day basis to get choice food, easier work, uninhibited movement from one place to another, and uninterrupted secret assembly. Pranks were also executed simply to strike at the establishment, such as urinating in food served to the masters.

Wearing the mask and playing the game were commonly accepted mechanisms for survival during slavery. What whites saw was not an internalized Black Sambo image, as Elkins would have us believe, but a removable image, depending on the time, the audience, and the occasion. Had Elkins troubled to look at other areas, such as at folksongs and folktales, he could have seen a tough, vital personality whose inner core of stability endured in spite of overwhelming odds.[9] In fact, the freed Black performed remarkably well politically during Reconstruction, causing still another critic of Elkins to question the achievements of supposedly infantile Sambos. Obviously, Charles Joyner concluded, a few cracks existed in the so-called "closed" slavery system.[10]

Façade though the Sambo image might be, the preoccupation with the Black's superstitious beliefs was a two-sided affair—the assertions of the whites that appear in print, countered by the persistent, oral mumblings of the Black. What the Black said concerning the origin of the superstitions ascribed to him is the other side of the story, the side which constitutes a major facet in his folk history.

The universal acceptance of the supernatural has long been

[8] Stampp, 274–75.
[9] Stuckey, "Through the Prism of Folklore," 245–68.
[10] "Soul Food and the Sambo Stereotype: Foodlore from the Slave Narrative Collection," *Keystone Folklore Quarterly*, 15, No. 4 (Winter 1971), 171.

recognized as "the common heritage of humanity."[11] When the Black came to America from Africa it was only natural that he brought his cultural traditions with him, and they took firm root in American soil. Later, the supernatural aspects of these traditions were encouraged and adapted by white masters to provide the vehicle for psychological control of the Black. Significantly, even as this control was being exercised, the Black simultaneously not only believed in ghosts and other supernatural phenomena, but also realized that deception was being practiced by the whites.

Personal reminiscences, accounts of believed fact concerning past experiences,[12] provide the broad frame on which Afro-American history can be reconstructed. While reminiscences may relate incidents of general interest to a whole people, they are more often drawn from the unique experiences or impressions of a single individual. In contrast to legends, which are concerned with the unusual, reminiscences include the ordinary, as they relate the entire sequence of events, the sum total of an experience. If an isolated episode of a believed experience becomes structured and can stand alone as a complete narrative, it becomes known as a legend. When an informant describes an experience to which he was a first-hand witness, his reminiscences constitute a form of oral history,[13] and these verbally transmitted experiences enter the stream of oral tradition. Thus historical reminiscences and folklore blend and coalesce.

When a tradition persists within a family it constitutes a form of genealogical record, insofar as it relates oral accounts of the history

---

[11] George Lyman Kittredge, *Witchcraft in Old and New England* (Cambridge, Mass., 1929), 372.

[12] Because reminiscences must operate within the natural bounds of a conversational unit, like gossip and rumor, they must appear spontaneous, but are in fact structured by the strict rules of spoken intercourse. While not as stylized as a joke or a folktale, they nonetheless constitute a conversational narrative form which is in fact delivered as a performance while maintaining the appearance of unrehearsed, impromptu dialogue. The whole ritual system of practices, conventions, and procedural rules that govern the flow of talk is discussed by Erving Goffman in his essay "On Face Work," *Interaction Ritual* (Chicago, 1967), 37.

[13] For a full discussion of the relationship between folklore and history, see Richard M. Dorson, "Oral Tradition and Written History: The Case for the United States," *American Folklore and the Historian*, (Chicago, 1971), 129–44.

and descent of the family from one generation to another. Genealogies, in fact, are often the unconscious means by which reminiscences are retained within a given family. As a rule, in Black families the life of a particular relative may be remembered in detail. During the research for this book, when the social situation involved the presence of this relative in the family household for a long period of time, this particular figure became the focal point for all the traditions an individual informant remembered about a particular era.

Thus the slavery and post-Civil War reminiscences of Blacks constitute the beginnings of family sagas. Until recently almost nothing had been done by Blacks in the area of formal family histories based on genealogical evidence. The very nature of slavery, involving deliberately parted families, made it difficult to trace early family members. An important exception to this pattern is an article by Black folklorist Kathryn Morgan, "Caddy Buffers: Legends of a Middle Class Negro Family in Philadelphia." Centering on the life and experiences of the author's maternal great-grandmother, the article is based on reminiscences handed down within one family since the slavery period.

A more extended book, *Roots*, utilizing the techniques of oral history, is being completed by Alex Haley, who edited *The Autobiography of Malcolm X*. Relying heavily on interviewing elderly family acquaintances and on stories told by his maternal grandmother, Haley claims to have succeeded in tracing his family all the way back to an African village in Gambia.[14] This sobering discovery of direct and remembered family lineage over several hundred years may lead to more research in this area.

Certain traits were noticeable in the Black family genealogies investigated for the present book. Family history seldom could be traced beyond the third generation from the person interviewed. Even in rare instances in which the names of great-grandparents were known, little additional information could be provided. Another trait common to most Blacks interviewed was that seldom

[14] Hollie I. West, "Tracing Black Ancestors," *The Washington Post* (Washington, D. C.), Jan. 6, 1971.

were both the maternal and paternal grandparents remembered. Usually an informant remembered only one side of his ancestral descent, and generally only one ancestor on that side.

Orally transmitted folk legends form the hard core through which the Black tells of his historical experiences. As personal narratives believed to have been experienced by the informant or someone of his acquaintance, these legends relate encounters with "natural" and supernatural night riders. That they were all "told for true" is an important characteristic of these folk legends and is responsible for the unique personal quality which these traditions possess. Even in cases in which the narrator seemed skeptical of the veracity of a story learned from another source, he admitted that the original teller of the tale had believed it.

The term *memorat*, as used by folklorists, can be applied to these narratives because of the highly personal nature of the experiences they relate. As a body, this type of prelegend conforms to the definition of memorat as being belief tales which are not yet fully traditional. In becoming folk property, however, these personal narratives can acquire traditional aspects, often undergoing stylistic changes of detail. To a great extent these are ethnic belief tales which concentrate primarily on relating experiences of a particular group of people during a specified period. Their survival is not dependent upon being rooted in familiar local surroundings or upon repeated recitation. As to the latter, many of the persons interviewed prefaced their narrations by telling the collector that for want of an interested audience this was the first time in years that a particular episode had been told! People legends, as distinct from place legends, can flourish anywhere—city or country, North or South.

Why, then, do these legends cling so tenaciously to the Black folk mind in the absence of familiar neighborhood surroundings and without the benefit of repeated recital? First of all, these reminiscences are concerned with singularly uncommon events which are sufficiently unusual to be easily retained. The ghosts and apparitions created by the whites during slavery and post-Civil War days certainly provided the basis for many enduring narratives. Second, these legends serve the cultural function of preserving the

9

heroic exploits of a suppressed people. The theme in evidence is that the Black, though manipulated, overpowered, and mistreated, emerges to some extent as a culture hero. As has been indicated already, this particular picture of the Black is not a common one in the literature of history.

A Survey of Historical Source Material on Black Intellectual and Social Thought

Numerous observers, relying on limited documented material, have described the Black's social attitudes, beliefs, fears, and aspirations, but evidence contained in oral testimony has been almost totally disregarded. The matter of how the American Black viewed his own problems in the past, and how he explains his conduct and behavior in the present in accommodating to the dominant white culture, is still a neglected area in Black scholarship.

To meet this historical need, one must focus on slavery and the decade immediately following because this is the period during which the Black's general lack of literacy forced him to transmit his historical experiences by word of mouth. Vital questions include: What story does the Black tell about himself within the context of American historical development? Does his account differ from generally accepted sources now on record, and if so how? In terms of his private thoughts, feelings, and ideas, how has the Black reacted to the larger historical forces that impinged upon him, such as slavery, Reconstruction, and the Civil War? How does the Black assess his role in American history? What is his attitude toward the white man? To what extent does the Black feel that he was manipulated and controlled by the white man, and what aspects of his present-day belief in the supernatural does a Black trace to white origins? In short, what does the Black tell about his past, and what is the historical value of such accounts?

One reason these questions have not been answered to date is that until fairly recent times historians have neglected to fully utilize available sources of information. John Hope Franklin commented on this oversight, pointing out that collections of Black letters and slave narratives exist, as do Black newspapers, magazines, convention minutes, and protest petitions—all easily available yet consistently overlooked by historians.[15]

Printed slave narratives, as distinct from the recorded memoirs collected by the Work Projects Administration (WPA) and others, represent a unique and important body of American literature. They are unique because they depict conditions that have not been duplicated, and important because they give a first-hand view of historical events that have been either distorted or seldom considered by historians. Although scholars tend to disagree concerning which specific tract marked the official beginning of this genre,[16] most sources concur that the publication in 1900 of Booker T. Washington's *The Story of My Life and Work* brought it to a formal close.[17] The best of these narratives were written between 1830 and 1865 when the abolitionist movement was at its height, and they immediately became a popular type of antislavery literature.

As research sources, however, the quality of these narratives varies from accounts written by slaves themselves, such as the classic account by Frederick Douglass, *The Narrative of the Life of Frederick Douglass, An American Slave, Written by Himself*, to outright fabrications and fictionalized editions written in the time-honored tradition of "cashing in on a good thing." Charles Ball's autobiography, an example of this latter category, is entitled *Slavery in the United States: A Narrative of the Life and Adventures of Charles Ball, A Black Man, Who Lived Forty Years in Maryland, South Carolina and Georgia as a Slave*. Somewhere in between these extremes lies a body of historically questionable

[15] "New Perspectives in American Negro History," *Social Education*, 14 (May 1950), 196–200.

[16] Charles H. Nichols states in *Many Thousand Gone* that this genre began in colonial times with the publication of John Saffin's *Adam Negro's Tryall*, which was supposed to have been written as a response to an antislavery tract, *The Selling of Joseph*, by Samuel Sewall (Bloomington, Ind., 1963), ix–xi.

Arna Bontemps, among others, cites the publication in 1760 of Briton Hammon's "A Narrative of the Uncommon Sufferings and Surprising Deliverance of Briton Hammon, A Negro Man" as the first ex-slave narrative. See *Great Slave Narratives* (Boston, 1969), xii.

[17] Bontemps, ix.

accounts dictated to abolitionists who wrote down and edited the material, and it is this latter body of slave memories that have come under sharpest attack by historians. Ulrich B. Phillips observed that "ex-slave narratives in general, and those of Charles Ball, Henry Box Brown and Father Henson in particular, were issued with so much abolitionist editing that as a class their authenticity is doubtful."[18]

Authenticity and reliability are certainly valid considerations in historical evidence, but it should be recognized that abolitionists were very anxious to record ex-slave testimony as faithfully as possible, thus helping the slaves to write their own stories. The feeling was that the actual telling of their personal histories argued against the idea of Black inferiority.[19] In addition, abolitionists realized that fraudulent claims and exaggerations might damage their cause.[20] On the whole, the abolitionists were a group of dedicated, responsible, conscientious people who were not as inclined to distort the material as historians have generally assumed. In any case, these narratives should not be summarily dismissed; better that the obviously bogus autobiographies be set aside and the remainder be critically appraised in the light of corroborating evidence found in "accounts of travellers, newspaper advertisement, contemporary documents and letters."[21] Gilbert Osofsky describes this kind of search for historical truth:

> Narrators were subjected to detailed questioning by committees of knowledgeable people; letters were written to former masters and neighbors for corroboration. A tale so seemingly improbable as the life of Henry Bibb led to an extensive correspondence with white Southerners, all of whom verified Bibb's account—the improbable was the real. Solomon Northup's fantastic experiences were verified by a basketful of legal documents.[22]

Surely this genre constitutes an important source of historical material, not only in illuminating the Black experience, but in de-

---

[18] *Life and Labor in the Old South* (Boston, 1963), 219.
[19] Nichols, xii.
[20] William Loren Katz, *Five Slave Narratives* (New York, 1969), xix.
[21] Nichols, xii.
[22] *Puttin' On Ole Massa* (New York, 1969), 12.

12

tailing the day-to-day feelings and reactions of a neglected group. Nevertheless, these narratives were written by the articulate few and thus represent only a small portion of the total Black population of the period. What of the inarticulate multitude?

Many of the nonliterate slaves found a willing recorder of their oral testimony in William Still, a Black Philadelphian who apparently made his money from coal in the ante-bellum period. Still spent much of his time, however, in assisting fugitive slaves on the Philadelphia branch of the underground railroad. Elected secretary of the Vigilance Committee, reorganized on December 9, 1852, in order to aid runaway slaves more systematically, he helped ensure that records were kept of each individual assisted, an essential measure if relatives were to be reunited. Still published his collection of oral data in 1873 as *The Underground Railroad*, a volume that stands as one of the best contemporary sources concerning the memories and experiences of former slaves.[23]

The Underground Railroad is a compendium of information regarding the customs, practices, attitudes, and reactions of Blacks fresh from the slavery experience. Each runaway was carefully interviewed; as many as forty questions were asked, depending on the time available to the interviewer, before shipping the fugitive on to the next stop. The questions covered such facets of the slave's life as his age, place of former residence, skills, type of master, religion, reason for deciding to escape, and impressions of freedom. "These answers afforded the best possible means of seeing slavery in its natural, practical workings—of obtaining such testimony and representations of the vile system, as the most eloquent orator or able pen might labor in vain to make clear and convincing."[24] Still and his committee also included full contextual data, such as a thorough physical description of the respondent, his general manner, speech, hesitancy, or deliberation in answering certain questions.

Though the pattern of the book is not consistent because the author insists on randomly inserting historical miscellany (texts of

[23] Interview with Lawrence Reddick, Temple Univ., March 20, 1972.
[24] *The Underground Railroad* (New York, 1968), 273.

laws and documents relating to slavery), most sections begin with the actual text of the newspaper advertisement for an individual fugitive and are followed by a description of the interview itself, often in the full context of questions and answers. The sections usually conclude with letters, often in underground-railroad code, written by the runaways from their places of freedom—usually Canada. Addressed to the Vigilance Committee, the letters were, according to Still, "given precisely as they were written by their respective authors, so that there may be no apparent room for charging the writer with partial colorings in any instance."[25]

Yet another source of recorded contemporary accounts of slavery and the Reconstruction period is the Congressional testimony printed in thirteen volumes by the Government Printing Office in 1872. This testimony was gathered by a Joint Select Committee of Congress, formed to investigate the operation of the Ku Klux Klan not only in Washington, but throughout the South. Responding to public reaction against the political excesses of the Klan, Congress passed the Ku Klux Klan Act which created the Joint Select Committee to Inquire into the Condition of Affairs in the Late Insurrectionary States, formally organized the day the act became law (April 20, 1871). Chaired by Senator John Scott of Pennsylvania, the Committee's subcommittees held hearings in Georgia, Mississippi, South Carolina, and Alabama, with testimony from the latter two states comprising more than half the printed series.[26]

The volumes contain verbatim testimony, recorded by court transcribers, of questions and answers put to dozens of informants. Thus the question-and-answer context gives the over-all pattern of answers a great deal of meaning. For example, one can see the types of questions that were responded to fully, partially, or not at all, revealing to some extent individual attitudes toward a given topic. Certain basic questions concerning name, place of residence, occupation, age, and political identification were asked of all informants. Fortunately for this research, the designation "Colored" followed the names of Black informants, forestalling conjecture about race based on contextual comments.

[25] *Ibid.*, 39.
[26] Allen W. Trelease, *White Terror* (New York, 1971), 392.

Unfortunately, the material itself is uneven and unbalanced, not only from state to state—fewer Blacks were interviewed in Georgia and Alabama, for example—but within counties of a given state. Aside from the usual bias that enters into any interviewing situation, additional factors help to explain this unevenness. Some Congressional interviewers were more adept than others at asking questions and pursuing adequate responses from witnesses, often eliciting detailed responses concerning Klan costumes and operations. In other instances, Congressional interviewers stopped short of a complete answer by failing to probe a negative reply with appropriate questions. Also, most Blacks tended to give fuller responses to questions concerning the Klan's attempt at control through fear of the supernatural—possibly because they were the more frequent victims of this practice.

In spite of these obvious shortcomings, this Congressional testimony provides the best single source of written data available concerning the Reconstruction Ku Klux Klan. The fact that contemporary data were recorded from the point of view of the oppressed victims, as well as from that of the Klansmen, makes this material of extreme importance in providing a balanced view of the Reconstruction Ku Klux Klan. In fact, given the climate of fear in which testimony was taken (the Klan was still secretly operating in spite of the Ku Klux Klan Act, and there was nothing to prevent irate Klansmen from taking immediate revenge on what they termed "informers"), it is to the credit of the investigators that the information obtained is as full as it is.

Yet even granting the value of these various bodies of recorded oral testimony, gaps still exist in Black intellectual historiography, largely because of the difficulties involved in attempting to analyze and interpret human thought in the form of written or spoken records. Obviously, the social historian must also assume the role of philosopher—at best a difficult task, and in the case of the Black, monumental.

It should be noted that until this past decade scholars have concentrated primarily on documented sources of the nineteenth century, such as diaries, plantation records, and travel accounts. These were contemporary accounts by literate people who wrote their own versions of the historical events of the period, often in biased and subjective terms. On the other hand, the Black population, barred by various state laws after 1832 from acquiring even rudimentary literacy, left relatively few written records of their experiences.

Indeed, having explored this limited documentation, there came a time when most Black historians felt they had reached an impasse. In 1937, L. D. Reddick wrote that the topic of slavery as it existed in plantation records, papers, and slave masters' and travelers' impressions was nearly exhausted, unless new materials should be discovered.[27] Leo Hansberry complained as early as 1923 that too few social historians were attempting to write the social history of the Black; but with the appearance of Reddick's article, historians carefully began to re-examine new approaches. It is perhaps significant that the push for a new movement in historiography was led by Black historians, who repeatedly stated in various professional journals the need for additional historical sources to achieve a more balanced treatment of Black history. Their consensus was that the historical record of the slavery period could be completed only by presenting that institution from the Black's point of view. After all, they contended, "the best judges of the cruelty and the inhumanity of slavery were the ex-slaves who themselves were the victims of it."[28] In recognizing the inherent value of first-person testimony, these beliefs were, in essence, moving away from the historian's commitment to the documented, written word and proposing the utilization of another body of material to complete the historical record—oral traditions.

Thus attention is directed once more to the potential value of oral history. In the absence of literacy, the traditions of a people are transmitted by word of mouth from one generation to another. To the extent that they are collectively held and orally transmitted, they constitute a body of traditions known as folk history. The use by historians of such traditions serves the important function of supplementing the historical record by providing coverage of

[27] "A New Interpretation for Negro History," *Journal of Negro History*, 22 (Jan. 1937), 17–28.
[28] Informant Floyd Wardlaw Crawford, Feb. 9, 1964.

the lives of illiterate or semiliterate people who leave no formal record of their experience to balance written narratives.[29] To the extent that these people share a common heritage, ethnic background, experience, attitudes, and traditions, they constitute a homogeneous folk group.

The Blacks of slavery and Reconstruction times certainly comprised such a folk group, as a few historians began to realize in the late 1920s. Responding to the challenge to find new source materials for the study of Black history, investigators of the decade from 1929 to 1939 instituted several collecting projects designed to record the reminiscences of living ex-slaves. Perhaps the earliest attempt to obtain oral testimony for use as historical documentation was undertaken in 1929 by James B. Cade, historian and head of the Extension department of Southern University. His study grew out of a class assignment in United States history to interview ex-slaves and former masters throughout the state of Louisiana. Cade obtained approximately eighty-two interviews, which later became the basis for an article published in 1935.[30] Informants were queried about such things as food, clothing, housing facilities, working conditions, amusements, religious practices, educational opportunities, family life, and punishments. While this effort represented an important beginning, it was primarily devoted to a description of the outward forms of slavery, leaving the attitudes, emotions, reactions, and conduct within the slave system unconsidered.

The success of the Louisiana study prompted Cade to conduct a similar project in Madison and Leon counties of Texas from 1933 to 1938.[31] Utilizing his position as Extension Service director, Cade sent letters to coordinators of the Extension program at Prairie View asking faculty members to assign as a class project the questioning of Blacks regarding conditions during slavery and Civil War times. Each student was asked to interview at least three

---

[29] Richard M. Dorson, "Ethnohistory and Ethnic Folklore," *Ethnohistory*, 8 (Winter 1961), 12–30.

[30] "Out of the Mouths of Ex-Slaves," *Journal of Negro History*, 20 (July 1935), 294–337.

[31] The Louisiana slave-narrative material, the basis for "Out of the Mouths of Ex-Slaves," was destroyed. Conversation with James B. Cade, Aug. 14, 1969.

17

ex-slaves and to ask the same range of questions that had been used in the earlier study. Interviewers were instructed to record faithfully the language of the ex-slave and to retain with his personal testimony his name and present address. The Southern University archives house the results of this study: four hundred interviews with ex-slaves in thirteen states.[32]

A more in-depth study was begun in the same year as Cade's earlier study when the research staff of the Social Science Institute of Fisk University, under the direction of Ophelia Settle Egypt, recorded oral testimonies from one hundred ex-slaves residing in Tennessee and Kentucky during 1929 and 1930. Thirty-nine of these documents were distributed as a manuscript in 1945 and only recently published. The general value of these reminiscences as authentic source material is clearly set forth in the introduction:

> They tell what the slaves saw and remembered; how they, themselves, or others whom they knew lived through the drudgery of menial work and the fear of the impending precarious world; how the slaves met their basic needs of sex, hunger and rest, within the very narrow confines of the system. They represent essentially the memories of childhood experiences, and provide, in a measure, a personal history of the social world as recreated and dramatized by these slaves in the course of the telling. Taken as a whole, these autobiographies constitute a fabric of individual memories, which sheds interesting light on the mentality of the slave.[33]

Mrs. Egypt, a sociologist and trained interviewer, and Charles S. Johnson, chairman of Fisk's social science department during this period, initially conceived the project to collect contemporary data from the rural Black families of Tennessee, employing the "own story method" of gathering research. As she pursued this information, Mrs. Egypt came across scores of ex-slaves who were heads of households. Partially conditioned by hearing slavery reminiscences from her grandparents in Red River County, Texas, Mrs.

[32] Norman R. Yetman, "The Slave Personality: A Test of the 'Sambo' Hypothesis." Diss. Univ. of Pennsylvania (1969), 69.

[33] Ophelia Settle Egypt, J. Masuoka, and Charles S. Johnson (eds.), *Unwritten History of Slavery*, Social Science Document No. 1, Social Science Institute, Fisk Univ. (Nashville, 1945), iii. Reprinted by NCR/Microcard Press, Washington, D. C., 1968.

Egypt increasingly found herself engaging her informants in a discussion of slavery times. Eventually permission was sought and obtained from Professor Johnson to formally collect ex-slave narratives. At this point all the mechanics of a formal project were added: structuring a questionnaire and compiling the names of all known ex-slaves residing in Tennessee and Kentucky. A stenographer was also hired.[34]

The questionnaire covered such areas as residence during slavery, when and how the informant moved to his present address, and his feelings, attitudes, and experiences during slavery. In addition, he was asked about slave housing, food, clothing, work, songs, church, prayer meetings, recreation, remedies, and superstitions. Information was also included about slaves on neighboring plantations, war memories, experiences during Reconstruction, and the ex-slave's present situation and philosophy.[35]

Because of her training and special interest in slavery reminiscences, the narratives collected by Mrs. Egypt are extremely valuable. Not only were the interviews recorded verbatim, but attention was also paid to such contextual data as a description of the informant, living quarters, speech pattern, and general behavior. The problem of dialect was solved by retaining enough of the ex-slave's own language so that the reader could differentiate between lettered and unlettered persons, a difference once setting household servants apart from field hands. Unfortunately, the usefulness of this data is reduced because of the absence of informants' names and ages. The former was a deliberate omission because of legal problems concerning permission to publish private material. Final choice of selected texts for publication was made chiefly by Charles S. Johnson, who also wrote the useful, though sociologically oriented, introduction.

The most ambitious effort to collect slavery reminiscences during this decade (1929–39), however, was begun as a part of the broadly conceived work of the WPA Federal Writers Project. This project was organized to answer a three-part question: Where is

[34] Interview with Ophelia Settle Egypt, March 8, 1972.

[35] Information obtained from a paper read by Mrs. Egypt at the Black Oral History Conference, April 20–22, 1972, Fisk Univ., Nashville.

America, what is it, and how did it happen?[36] These broad questions attempted to uncover the roots of American civilization and shed more light on the divergent peoples who compose the base of American society.

By 1939 the coordinators of this project found themselves with large quantities of unpublished manuscripts in the form of more than two thousand slave narratives from seventeen states, photographs of ex-slaves, interviews with white informants concerning slavery, and other documents which were transferred to the Library of Congress for processing.[37] The work of the Writers' Unit in preparing the narratives for deposit consisted principally of arranging the manuscripts and photographs by states and alphabetically by informants within the states, listing the informants and illustrations, and collating the contents in seventeen volumes divided into thirty-three parts.[38] The criterion for selection of documents in this permanent collection was that they be historical reminiscences taken only from ex-slaves. Folklore genres such as folktales, folksongs, and superstitions were largely omitted.

Realizing the impact the project could have on Black people, leaders such as Walter White, Ralph Bunche, John P. Davis, and others, together with the organizations they represented, urged that a Black person knowledgeable in literary criticism and history be appointed at the national level to look out for Black affairs. The hand-picked choice for this position was Sterling Brown, now professor emeritus of English at Howard University. Trained at the famous Dunbar High School in Washington, D.C., and at Williams College and Harvard University, Professor Brown worked at the Federal Writers Project in an advisory position as Editor of Negro Affairs. A kind of general ombudsman, in which all things affecting the Black came to him, Brown handled editorial assignments, assisted in finding jobs for Black writers, and contributed essays to the Washington guide.

[36] *The Pathfinder*, Washington, D. C., Dec. 17, 1938.
[37] "Slave Narratives, a Folk History of Slavery in the United States from Interviews with Former Slaves" (typewritten records), Library of Congress Rare Book Room, Washington, D. C., 1941.
[38] *Ibid.*, vii.

Of these responsibilities, perhaps most important were the editorial duties in connection with the state guides, one of the best efforts of the project. During a period when Blacks were being systematically omitted from all types of historical and literary essays, as well as government reports—including the census—Brown was primarily concerned with the problems of not only getting full inclusion for the Black, but seeing that he was accurately and adequately represented in all of the official reports coming from the Writers Project.[39]

Professor Brown also worked with Benjamin Botkin, editor of folklore materials on over-all policy affecting the ex-slave narrative material. Primarily, the approach to dialect was simplified, preserving the manner of speech rather than exotic misspellings. In addition, the questionnaire was restructured to include omitted areas in the pre-Civil War period, such as the Nat Turner Rebellion in particular and slave uprisings in general; questions were added relating to post-Civil War problems, such as attitudes toward freedom, Reconstruction, voting, holding office, and the influence of secret organizations.[40]

The influence editors had at the state level contributed to a general unevenness of material in the seventeen volumes making up the slave narrative collection. Interviews from certain states, such as Virginia and Georgia, reflect a more highly trained staff at all levels, from administrative to interviewer. Perhaps the best interviews came out of a special project headed by Roscoe Lewis at Hampton Institute, Hampton, Virginia. Lewis, a Black man of considerable direction and purpose, pulled together a very enthusiastic group of Black workers who combed the state to find ex-slaves. The results of this search were interviews exhibiting great authenticity and understanding, largely because the ex-slaves were able to trust and relate to the young Black interviewers from Hampton. The over-all effort was less perfunctory than that in

---

[39] Interview with Sterling Brown, March 19, 1972. Professor Brown observed that a number of distinguished Blacks worked on various state guides, including Richard Wright, Ralph Ellison, Arna Bontemps, and Claude McKay. Zora Neale Hurston, working out of the Florida office, was given interviewing assignments.
[40] *Ibid.*

many other states. A number of these interviews have been published as *The Negro in Virginia*, edited by Lewis.

Another all-Black staff who turned in impressive results was headed by Lawrence Reddick, project director for the state of Kentucky. Reddick, then a professor at Kentucky State College, assembled his Black staff both in Kentucky and neighboring Indiana by contacting local newspapers and high schools for the names of persons with sufficient skill to work on the project. While Reddick described the training these workers received in interviewing techniques as a kind of "informal orientation that tended to the common sense approach," he felt that, on the whole, they got better results than did white interviewers. Reddick's workers were instructed to attempt to establish a friendly rapport before going into the interviewing situation. They were also to state honestly why they were asking questions and to explain what was going to happen to the material so that the informant would be less disposed to distort material based on assumed requirements of an unknown interviewer.[41]

A serious effort was also made at the national level to train workers to achieve some sort of unity of form and consistent standards of quality in these collected slave narratives. Toward this end a number of general directives were sent out from the Washington headquarters to the various state officers of the project. Such guidelines related to proper interview procedure and contained an interview guide, note-taking suggestions, and the form to be followed for submitting field material. In spite of this effort at coordination the Slave Narratives Collection has some serious defects:

1. The rewriting and editing of collected texts in the interest of telling a good story were extensive. Interviewers, who were primarily writers rather than trained historians or folklorists, in many cases were guided more by the criterion of readability than that of authenticity. Evidence of rewriting can be found in the duplicate slave narratives on file in the Folksong Archives in the Library of

---

[41] Interview with Lawrence Reddick, March 20, 1972.

Congress, where several versions of the same collected texts have been preserved along with other WPA material.

2. The majority of the documents contain excessive dialect, which seriously interrupts a smooth narrative flow. State interviewers continued their own interpretations of Black folk speech in spite of official policy recommending simplicity in recording dialect (including a guide sheet listing acceptable phonetic spellings). The serious reader is confronted with the painstaking task of translating words and expressions into conventional English before he can understand the content of a particular text.

3. The biases of both the interviewer and his informant are often reflected in the over-all pattern of answers in the slave narratives. Answers to specific questions often do not reflect the informant's private feelings as much as what he felt the interviewer expected him to say. Too often the interviewer had preconceived notions about race relations and the beliefs he wanted defended. The frequency with which ex-slaves referred to the "good old days" of slavery supports this view. The following comment is typical: "No slaves ever run away from our plantation cause marster was good to us. I never heard of him bein' 'bout to whup any of his niggers. Mother loved her white folks long as she lived an' I loved 'em too."[42] By contrast, such an attitude is minimal in Mrs. Egypt's interviews and those directed by Roscoe Lewis and Lawrence Reddick.

Slavery reminiscences collected from Black informants by white interviewers in the South during the 1930s could hardly be expected to reflect the deep, honest feelings and attitudes of the Blacks. Many of the latter, caught up in an economic depression, were trying to get on state relief rolls. It is conceivable that the unknown white WPA workers were sometimes confused with the persons in charge of relief payments. Consequently, answers were often cautious and guarded in the belief that certain answers might jeopardize chances for public assistance.

The patronizing attitude and bias of some of the interviewers

[42] WPA Files, "Slave Narratives," June Lassiter, Raleigh, N. C.

also undoubtedly affected the interview situation. Informants were described by stereotyped adjectives, such as "shiftless" and "lazy." Even the terms "aunt" and "uncle" were attached to the informants' names in keeping with long-standing, patronizing Southern practice.

Also to be considered is the role of editors in maintaining biases. It is possible that some workers submitted interviews reflecting not so much what the interviewer felt, or what the informant said, but what the editor wanted. No interviewer who hoped to maintain his job would continue to submit interviews that did not conform to his editor's standards of acceptable, "typical" responses. In most cases the only training the writers had in collecting and interviewing came from their editors, whose racial bias could be expected to show in the edited interview. Another factor to be considered was that often the editors held political positions and therefore operated under the direct influence of state political machines and bosses.[43]

4. Another shortcoming, particularly applicable to the white interviewer, was the general failure to recognize the nuances of Blacks in the form of gestures, glances, and other forms of objective behavior. "The slight, subtle movement of an informant's eyes, hands, shoulders in the form of a shrug—all with no words, but in fact communicating thought in a way no words could express," was the kind of response Sterling Brown called "inside communication."[44] This term could also include Black language. Certainly the inability to recognize and understand folk terms and expressions could seriously distort an interviewing situation.

The WPA Folk Editor B. A. Botkin selected for special treatment some of the narratives in the major WPA collection. Following a useful introduction, the texts are arranged in chronological sequence according to subject matter. Without editorial interference, the narratives are thus allowed to tell in their own way the folk history of the Black. Botkin was primarily concerned with literary

---

[43] Interview with Sterling Brown, March 19, 1972.
[44] *Ibid.*

quality, however, and consequently sacrificed the authenticity of the informant's exact words. In fact, he came to think of the narratives "not as a collection of source material for the scholar but as a finished product for the general reader."[45]

In spite of field problems of various kinds, some excellent results came from the WPA project. While the recollection of details —exact dates, names, and sequence of events—was often hazy, the WPA slave-narrative material made a major contribution in reproducing the general conditions of slavery and the post-Civil War period in terms of the relation of slaves to slaves, field hands to house workers, slaves to masters and mistresses, the type of work done by the slave, and the selling apart of families.[46]

Scholars have not yet arrived at a consensus on the validity of this material. Kenneth Stampp feels that the time lapse in collecting data renders it of little use to historians. Acknowledging the historian's failure to fully utilize Black oral tradition, Stampp nevertheless asserts that because the songs and folklore constantly change and the WPA project occurred some sixty years after slavery, the historian cannot be sure it contains true expressions of the slaves.[47] Other scholars disagree. Stanley Feldstein notes that in the nearly six thousand narratives recorded by the project, many are repetitive, describing the same conditions and the same indignities. Feldstein concludes from this "parallel thinking [that the] narratives spoke for the silent millions."[48]

Surely, however, these collections of personal history documents can be considered an important beginning in establishing a new approach to the study of Black history. What remains to be done is the analysis and interpretation of these kinds of data in order to arrive at conclusions concerning generally held social attitudes, patterns of behavior, sentiments, and aspirations. This second step, involving the effort to supplement the history of a particular people in a particular period on the basis of their oral

[45] *Lay My Burden Down* (Chicago, 1945), vii.
[46] Interview with Lawrence Reddick, March 20, 1972.
[47] *The Peculiar Institution* (New York, 1956), 367–68.
[48] *Once A Slave* (New York, 1971), p. 14.

traditions, would seem to be essential; yet only a few steps have been taken in this direction in the historiography of the Black, as, indeed, of many ethnic groups.

Where the historian has hesitated, a musicologist has charted a bold new approach in ethnohistorical study. Miles Mark Fisher's book *Negro Slave Songs in the United States* marks the first important step in attempting to understand the attitudes and thoughts of the slaves by using their songs as historical documents. A spiritual, to Professor Fisher, was a vehicle through which an individual slave commented on his social situation—be it an experience, a person, or an event. He defines a spiritual as "the utterance of an individual Negro about an experience."[49] Thus by an analysis of these spirituals he has sought to reconstruct the social concepts of the pre-Civil War Black. Furthermore, Fisher uses contemporary historical sources to reinforce his arguments.

Professor Fisher's methodology has been criticized by historians and folklorists alike, both groups decrying the tenuous nature of some of his conclusions. For example, the author describes the all-consuming desire of the Black to be sent to Africa. He also asserts that a majority of the slaves were of a dutiful, obedient nature. In contrast, he sees the spiritual as an instrument of protest, even speculating some may have been composed by militants such as Nat Turner, Denmark Vesey, and Harriet Tubman.[50] In the absence of sufficient historical evidence to support his contentions, these and other conclusions must be considered conjectural. It is the direction he points, however, rather than the arguments he presents, that is important to a full understanding of Black thought. Professor Fisher's work makes a significant contribution toward completing the historical record, not of the few articulate Blacks in the pre-Civil War period, but of the inarticulate majority relegated to obscurity in standard historical works.

[49] New York, 1963, p. 101.
[50] Vincent Harding, "Religion and Resistance Among Antebellum Negroes," *The Making of Black America*, I (The Origins of Black Americans), August Meir, gen. ed. (New York, 1969), 196. This point of view is further amplified in John Lovell's definitive study of the spiritual, *Black Song: The Forge and the Flame* (New York, 1972).

The movement toward a reconsideration of historical source materials suggested by Lawrence Reddick, John Hope Franklin, and Leo Hansberry in the thirties and forties has now been revitalized by a new generation of Afro-American historians, who see Black history as being politically oriented in its goal to totally redefine the Black experience in America.[51] It is of special interest that these "New Breeders," principally Sterling Stuckey, Vincent Harding, and John Blassingame, have turned to the Black folk tradition and culture—music, literature, and dance—as a broad base from which to evolve historical meaning. What is envisioned is an interdisciplinary approach to learning which cuts across traditional academic disciplines in an effort to re-create the human experience within a cultural context. Aside from the seminal work of DuBois on the spirituals in *Souls of Black Folk*, such a cultural approach to Black history has heretofore been unknown in historical writings. Sterling Stuckey's remarks can hardly be misunderstood:

> This growing movement among black writers and musicians, as far as young black historians are concerned, will very likely play its part in contributing to the death of that methodology whose minions either ignore slave folklore or pronounce it too ambiguous for more than passing consideration. After all, the finest Afro-American commentators on folklore, all of whom lived many of the experiences found in folklore, were not burdened by conundrums regarding the meanings set forth in the art of their fathers. If the problems of handling folklore are so great for white historians that the compelling significance of folk songs and tales is uncertain, then let them stop writing history in areas where Afro-American personality and culture are under discussion.[52]

While Vincent Harding has largely concentrated on developing the political framework of the new Black history, he also echoed Stuckey's thought concerning the need to embrace the Black folk tradition, emphasizing that the significance of folk creations to

[51] Vincent Harding, "Beyond Chaos," *Amistad 1*, John A. Williams, ed. (New York, 1970), 284.
[52] "Twilight of Our Past," 273.

27

Black history encompasses the total Black experience, including literature and music.[53]

Because of the oral quality of Black culture, it might be suggested that such an approach is long overdue. Ralph Ellison has said:

> . . . I feel that Negro American folklore is very powerful, wonderful, and universal. . . . But what we've achieved in folklore has seldom been achieved in the novel, the short story, or poetry. In the folklore we tell what Negro experience really is. We back away from the chaos of experience and from ourselves, and we depict the humor as well as the horror of our living.[54]

Further results of the interdisciplinary approach to the study of slavery can be seen in John Blassingame's book *The Slave Community*. By utilizing such folklore data as folksongs, folktales, folk beliefs, and various ethnographic and anthropological studies, Blassingame is able to illuminate the side of slavery usually untold, that of the victims. In addition, he discusses aspects of the system previously overlooked or undervalued by historians, such as the pervasiveness of African survivals, the supportive role of the slave family, and various plantation personality types.

This new historiography has sparked an interest in Black oral history projects, evidenced by the first Black oral history conference, convened on April 22, 1972, at Fisk University in Nashville, with thirty-three participants. Although the general thrust of the papers presented seemed to be that historians are willing to concede that eyewitness accounts by persons intimately involved in significant events are valid data, a blind bias to collecting oral tradition about past events in which eyewitnesses are dead was said to be still very evident in historical thinking. It is of extreme importance, however, that historians are now considering oral history and that a number of special projects have been set up to investigate these sources. Specifically, special collections focusing on Black tradition can be found at Fisk University in Nashville; Duke University in Durham, North Carolina; Mary Holmes Col-

---

[53] Harding, "Beyond Chaos," 284.
[54] P. 80.

lege in West Point, Mississippi; the Martin Luther King Project in Atlanta; and the Ralph J. Bunche Collection (formerly Civil Rights Documentation Project Collection) housed in Howard University's Moorland Spingarn Research Center. The aim of most of these projects, as is true of the Oral History Project at Columbia, is to collect personal accounts of involvement in significant historical events. Relatively little effort is being made to collect folklore in the sense of orally transmitted tradition,[55] but one hopes this will be the direction future historical research will take.

Field Work Methodology

The central idea underlying all of the folk legends in this collection is the control and intimidation of the Black during slavery and in the post-Civil War period through the use of fear of the supernatural. The narratives vary from simple episodes told in sketchy outline to full-scale narrative tales and can be divided into two main categories: (1) narratives involving the supernatural, such as ghosts and witches; and (2) narratives concerning the practice of stealing living bodies for medical experiments.

The supernatural experiences described by the informants generally occurred at a distant time and place and were related without any effort to adapt them to the informant's new community. With few exceptions, these legends rigidly retained all of the details of their original surroundings. The body-snatching traditions, on the other hand, were generally believed to have occurred in Washington, D. C. Consequently, these particular recollections abound in details which have only a local application, such as place names, street names, and public buildings.

It is especially significant that reference to control through use of fear of the supernatural is found almost exclusively in oral accounts. While some reference to psychological control is made in the body of the WPA material, it is suspected that fuller details might have been obtained under different collecting situations—

---

[55] Richard M. Dorson, *American Folklore and the Historian*, 146.

that is, if the interviewer had probed in this direction. The author's field work, on the other hand, turned up abundant information in this area. Although every effort was made to corroborate oral testimony with printed sources, the paucity of recorded information on this form of control necessitates relying almost entirely on oral testimony. Where historical corroboration could be found, however—even in secondary sources—it was used.

The important consideration concerning the accuracy of these collected testimonies is not whether they actually happened, but whether or not the people believed that they happened. Where two or more informants relate the same general information independently of one another, it can be said that a particular testimony represents a shared belief. To the extent that these shared beliefs represent ideas commonly held by Blacks as a whole, they can be said to be genuine folk history. "Though there is a strong presumption that it is untrustworthy, the general rule of historians is to accept as historical only particulars which rest upon *the independent testimony of two or more witnesses.* Where any two witnesses agree, it may well be that they agree because they are testifying independently to an observed fact."[56]

Shared beliefs occur repeatedly in the WPA material and the Congressional testimony, relating closely to the historical and folk traditions collected more recently by the author in Washington, D.C., Maryland, and Virginia. Significantly, the folklore gathered from January through May of 1964, with additional interviews in the spring of 1972, substantiates most of the earlier oral testimony, providing as the basis for this book a cohesive body of oral history.

In addition to investigating the Washington area, the writer made several short trips to Norfolk and Hampton, Virginia, and Bloomington, Indiana. The traditions collected in these areas have provided excellent comparative material, agreeing in such detail with the Washington data that it is possible to conclude that the folk history of the Black, at least concerning this subject, is not limited to the confines of any particular region, but represents

[56] Louis Gottschalk, Clyde Kluckhohn, and Robert Angell, *The Uses of Personal Documents in History, Anthropology, and Sociology* (New York, 1945), 45. Emphasis in original text.

beliefs generally held by Black folk as a body. In this sense, Washington does not represent a distinct regional collecting area, but simply a depository for Black traditions in general.

The writer interviewed approximately one hundred fifty Black informants, the majority living in the Washington area, of both sexes, representing all economic classes, age groups, and educational backgrounds. The WPA interview guide was expanded to include questions specifically relating to folk beliefs and narrative traditions, encouraging informants to reminisce freely about slavery, Reconstruction, and the era preceding the First World War. Oral interviews were recorded on a portable tape recorder and transcribed as exactly as possible, without dialect distortions but preserving stylistic and idiomatic expressions.[57]

Data collected from these informants reveal that sex differences are minimal in relating traditions, and the pattern of the narratives told by men and women is the same. However, sharp differences are apparent between the kinds of reminiscences told by different generations. The first and second generations out of slavery, those whose parents and grandparents were slaves, are by far the most active carriers of slavery traditions. The reminiscences passed on to great-grandchildren and great-great-grandchildren tend to be fragmentary.

It is both interesting and suggestive, therefore, that the most active carriers of these traditions belonged roughly to the same age group, the first generation of Blacks out of slavery, between the ages of sixty-five and eighty at the time of the interviews. Rarely were good informants interviewed who fell on either side of this range, but the sixty-five- to eighty-year-olds conversed easily about folk traditions as though they were common knowledge. The slavery experiences recalled here represent the traditions this group received from their parents and grandparents; the reminiscences dating approximately from the first decade of the twentieth century are their own experiences. In this sense, oral tradition and oral history mingle.

---

[57] Short passages of verbatim transcriptions are included in the body of the text. In three chapters, quotations too lengthy for text presentation are placed at the ends of those chapters as "Additional Narratives."

The Southern Character of Washington, D. C.

Historically, Washington, D.C., occupied a position as a border area, a role shared by certain areas of Missouri, West Virginia, Maryland, Kentucky, and Delaware. Consequently, the character of slavery and the post-Civil War racial patterns were never as pronounced in these regions as in the Deep South. Another factor which was to serve as a moderating influence on race relations in the District was its urban character. The particular brand of slavery that developed there was a distinct type, as was true in many Southern cities strongly affected by the peculiar conditions of city life.

On the other hand, these ameliorating influences were to a considerable extent offset by Washington's geographic position. Carved out of Maryland's soil, and adjacent to Virginia, the District maintained strong Southern sympathies and ties: its leading families were descendants of Maryland and Virginia stock, and their views on slavery were identical with those of the slave-holding class. Even foreign visitors were quick to recognize the essentially Southern character of Washington, as when Francis J. Grund commented on the city's Southern manners and hospitality.[58]

The Congressional controversy over the emancipation of slaves in the District of Columbia fully reflects these deeply embedded Southern sympathies. The Congressional consideration of a bill by which slaves would be freed in the District brought a wave of protest from most white residents. Clearly, the sentiment in Washington was overwhelmingly opposed to this enactment, for slavery was accepted and most people considered it an inalienable right.[59]

Most significant to the collection of folk tradition is the fact that Blacks were constantly coming into Washington from all sections of the South, a situation that early made Washington a kind of "catchall" of freed and escaped slaves. The city was both a depot for the interstate slave traffic and, after 1860, a mecca for runaway

[58] *Aristocracy in America* (London, 1839), 232.
[59] Page Milburn, "The Emancipation of Slaves in the District of Columbia," *Records of the Columbia Historical Society*, 16 (1913), 96–119.

Blacks who believed that they would be free there. Though slavery on the whole was not particularly harsh in Washington, the city earned a "tarnished" reputation because of its role in the slave traffic. During the sixty years from 1800 to 1860, both the slaves and the free Black population of the District of Columbia nearly quadrupled, with free Blacks from the South seeking a more congenial environment there.[60] Five days before the passage of the emancipation bill, a Washington newspaper reported that each week one to two hundred slaves were running away from slave owners in neighboring Prince Georges County, Maryland, and crossing into the District.[61]

Beginning as a trickle in the late 1850s, the flow of Black immigrants reached flood stage by 1863, with thousands of ex-slaves pouring into the District from all over the South. The Washington daily papers reported the presence of these immigrants—termed contraband—at first matter-of-factly and then with increasing concern, noting that in one group of approximately thirty persons most were women and young children in apparently helpless condition.[62] What was not realized in those early, anxious moments was that the city was serving as a meeting ground for those of similar skin but varying backgrounds.

This historical situation—the converging on the city of large numbers of Blacks from different cultural backgrounds—was to have special significance for the kind of Black slavery traditions existing in the District of Columbia.

Historical Materials on the District

Scholars of the Washington, D. C., area have virtually ignored the Black in their research efforts, relegating him in many general histories to an occasional mention in the index with only a brief

---

[60] E. Franklin Frazier, *Negro Youth at the Crossways* (Washington, D. C., 1940), 6.
[61] Milburn, 97.
[62] *The Evening Star* (Washington, D. C.), Feb. 13, 1862.

reference in the text. Letitia Woods Brown has partially remedied this neglect in her book *Free Negroes in the District of Columbia, 1790–1846*. Perhaps of significance, however, is the fact that Mrs. Brown's title itself focuses on the free Black, emphasizing the relative lack of treatment of slavery in this area by historians.[63]

But slavery is not the only neglected area of Washington historical studies. An equally important omission by historians is their general failure to tackle the kinds of information which Edward W. Phifer calls the "personality of the community"—that is, "the bits of local information he [the historian] has accumulated, the relevant experiences he has undergone, the wicked old tales he has been told, or his knowledge of a thousand and one happenings that go to make up the personality of a community."[64]

Insofar as legends regarding the Black are a part of this community personality, a small start has been made. Churches and houses are pointed out which served in the pre-Civil War period as waystations for the underground railroads.[65] A few native Washingtonians can remember stories concerning contraband camps in the District. Historians have even paid some attention to legends concerning such haunted houses as the Octagon House at 18th and New York Avenue, N.W., which had an infamous reputation in connection with its slave-trading activities. The slave block and the post to which slaves were chained while waiting to be sold were until very recent times visual reminders of a past age.

Travel accounts furnish one source of information about the institution of slavery in the District. The list of foreign visitors to Washington is long and distinguished and includes Ethan Allen Andrews, Jesse Torrey, Frederick Law Olmsted, Harriet Martineau, Charles Dickens, and Francis J. Grund. On the whole, however, their observations were too general and superficial to be of any real help.

[63] Typical of this practice of referring to slavery only indirectly is Edward Ingle's *The Negro in the District of Columbia* (Baltimore, 1893), 8.
[64] "Slavery in Microcosm: Burke County, North Carolina," *Journal of Southern History*, 28 (May 1962), 137–65.
[65] Hayes Johnson, *Dusk at the Mountain* (New York, 1963), 18.

Reflecting Washington's role as a "melting pot," a rich cross-section of slave-state traditions can be collected here, representing Tidewater, Deep South, border areas, lowland, and upland. As far as general Black traditions are concerned, a process has been at work to blend different types of folk narrative material, which reflects considerable borrowing and local adaptation of the Southern vein of Black traditions. But this borrowing has not produced a distinct regional type. Rather, original local patterns are still discernible within a general framework of Black folk traditions in the District of Columbia.

Found here, for instance, are reminiscences by informants who were originally from states such as North Carolina, where many small farms existed and thus the personal relationship between master and slave was often fairly close. The stories coming from this area are less bitter than those of the Deep South and are punctuated with fewer horror stories of rape, brutal beatings, and fleeing from bloodhounds. A similar lack of bitterness is reflected in oral testimonies about slavery associated with the border states of Maryland, Missouri, West Virginia, Delaware, and Kentucky. Conversely, the states of Alabama, Louisiana, and Mississippi are usually described in oral traditions as places of suffering, hardship, and maltreatment.

The problem in general terms, as one of the blights of the slave system, is readily enough discussed. But where miscegenation has been a factor, a particular informant's personal family involvement is often dismissed as something which he knew nothing about. Only through very careful questioning and an equally careful shifting of the evasive answers does the truth emerge.

In some cases it is true that the informant does not know how his ancestry became mixed. A case in point was an ex-missionary, a very fair Negro woman who told me that she realized she had a good deal of white blood in her, but when she asked her mother about it the mother would begin to cry and say that the daughter

35

was being disrespectful. All that could be learned was that her grandmother had worked as a domestic after the Civil War and had given birth to a number of children, some very light and some very brown. Apparently there was no legal grandfather. A reluctance to explain this kind of heritage within one's own family would certainly explain a refusal to divulge the information to a stranger.

Reticence in discussing slavery is motivated by still other considerations. Some Blacks were simply afraid that any discussion of slavery with younger Blacks would foster resentment and racial bitterness. Marie Bing, a domestic from South Carolina with only a third-grade education, but with surprising native perception and intuition, said that she had never told her son anything about slavery because she was afraid it would only cause resentment in him. But the collector was her idea of a neutral source to whom she could "unburden" her mind concerning slavery.

Washington's unique geographic location is further reflected in other kinds of oral tradition which could not be adapted to an urban environment. The Ku Klux Klan, including its techniques of intimidation—night parades and cross burnings—was particularly suited to a rural environment and operated with considerable difficulties within the city conditions. On the other hand, body-snatching traditions took firm root in the city. Life there fanned rather than smothered folk belief in this nefarious practice, as Blacks feared unknown urban ways and were very aware of the prevalence of hospitals in the District.

Present-day Blacks recall this folklore in all forms: legends, tales, songs, superstitions, cures, and witchcraft. One informant in twenty might relate what his grandparents said about the Civil War, but every person interviewed had something to say about witches, ghosts, and conjuring! Often these tales are dramatic and violent, the Black folk memory having retained not the details of the slave system, but the horror stories relating the cruel treatment of the Black slave by the master, mistress, patterollers, and overseer. Included in this category is a large body of rape narratives concerning the misuse of slave women by whites. One example of both the prevalence of this kind of tradition and the tenacity with

36

which it is remembered is that one informant, a Black professor at Virginia State College, remembered only one narrative about slavery—the rape of his maternal grandmother by the master's son! Of all the stories his grandmother told him about slavery this single incident remained.

One index of the present-day Black's conscious and unconscious attitude about slavery is his reluctance to admit white hereditary ties. A number of Blacks are related by blood to the white master, his son, or the overseer during slavery or to the white boss in whose home many Blacks worked as servants after the war was over. These white ties in an overwhelming number of cases are a source of apparent shame to the Black (only one informant in one hundred fifty readily admitted his white origin). He cannot hide the evidence of white heredity, his own light color, but he can refuse to talk about it—which is what happened.

Many of the Blacks approached in Washington, D.C., were unwilling to discuss slavery, often on the grounds it was "too embarrassing." It is still a very delicate subject and time has served only to intensify racial hatred and bitterness toward whites who perpetrated the system. Only now, it seems, have Blacks—especially the present generation— realized the full extent of the slavery deprivation. Any discussion of slavery, therefore, serves only to remind them of the source of discriminatory practices and segregated patterns which have been experienced.

1

THE PROBLEM OF SLAVE CONTROL

Well, one of the best controls that they had to keep slaves from straying away and having gatherings would be to scare the devil out of him. Scare them with ghost stories or tell what they saw, or actually get out in white when they knew they were going to have a meeting or something. —DARWIN SMITH

Historical Background

IN THE OLD SOUTH the slave-holding classes and their nonslave-owning neighbors lived in constant fear of uprisings. To the white population of the South, slaves posed a constant threat, a storm cloud that could erupt at any moment into a hurricane of disaster. While the news of murder, assault, poisoning, and rape caused uneasiness in the localities in which the crimes occurred, it was the report of concerted action or insurrection, or the mere mention of them, that aroused universal alarm. A white resident of Mississippi commented on this fear to Frederick Law Olmsted in the 1830s:

> Where I used to live [Alabama] I remember when I was a boy—must ha' been about twenty years ago—folks was dreadful frightened about the niggers. I remember they built pens in the woods where they could hide and Christmas time they went and got into the pens, fraid the niggers was risin'.[1]

---

[1] Frederick Law Olmsted, *A Journey in the Back Country* (New York, 1860), 203.

38

Although such slavery apologists as Ulrich Phillips, James G. Randall, and Thomas R. Dew make conservative estimates of the number of revolts, current historical thinking seems to indicate that the number was substantial. While the truth may never be known because of the successful suppression of this information by the planters, one historian estimates that at least two hundred slave insurrections were reported before the Civil War.[2] Numerous other uprisings may well have gone unrecorded. This certainly demonstrates that organized efforts to achieve freedom were neither "seldom" nor "rare," but rather a regular and recurring phenomenon in the life of the South.[3]

No section of the United States was spared these outbreaks, but Virginia and South Carolina seem to have experienced more slave rebellions than any of the other Southern states. These two states experienced three of the most important slave insurrections in American history, revolts which were to have far-reaching consequences in the area of slave control. It is ironic that the year 1800 has an important bearing on all three of them: it is the birth year of Nat Turner, the year in which Denmark Vesey bought his freedom, and the year of the great Gabriel conspiracy.[4]

Gabriel, a six-foot two-inch Black, was the acknowledged leader of the first consequential American slave insurrectionary attempt, which took place near Richmond, Virginia, in 1800. The secretly laid plans involved the seizure of an arsenal and several other strategic buildings in Richmond. It was hoped by the original conspirators that they would be joined by thousands of other Blacks once the revolt was under way.[5] In accordance with prearranged plans, about one thousand slaves, armed with clubs and swords, gathered in the fields six miles from Richmond on Saturday, August 30,[6] but the would-be rebels were forced to disperse because an unusually heavy rainstorm on the preceding day had made the

[2] Herbert Aptheker, *Negro Slave Revolts in the United States 1526–1860* (New York, 1939), 11.

[3] *Ibid.*

[4] *Ibid.*, 27–28.

[5] Harvey Wish, "American Slave Insurrections Before 1861," *Journal of Negro History*, 22 (July 1937), 299–320.

[6] Aptheker, *Negro Slave Revolts*, 28–29.

roads impassable. Word leaked out about the conspiracy, and on the following day a number of Blacks were arrested. Eventually thirty-five were tried and executed, including Gabriel.

Denmark Vesey was the guiding force behind a second abortive but significant slave uprising, which occurred in Charleston, South Carolina, in 1822. According to well-formulated plans, the city of Charleston was to be captured by six to nine thousand insurrectionists after simultaneous attacks at five points around its perimeter.[7] Before the plans could be executed, however, several Black informers exposed the conspirators and thirty-five of them were hanged. Scores of additional people were implicated and either imprisoned or transported out of the locality.

Although Gabriel's and Vesey's insurrections both aborted before any whites were harmed, the Nat Turner rebellion of 1831 in South Hampton, Virginia, resulted in the death of a number of whites before it was crushed by state militia. Apparently lacking a well-conceived plan and acting only from a desire to be free, the rebels began with the murder of Turner's master and his family. Only six slaves initiated the rebellion, but the number increased to about seventy as the conspirators moved from plantation to plantation, killing white families within a twenty-mile radius. At least one hundred slaves were murdered in retaliation by the militia before Turner and his rebels surrendered. Twelve Blacks were convicted and expatriated; Nat Turner and twenty of his accomplices were hanged.[8]

News of the rebellion spread rapidly both by word of mouth and through newspaper accounts. So distorted and exaggerated were the many accounts that *Niles' Weekly Register* tried to set the facts straight in an article, but even this well-known weekly could not maintain objectivity. The author of the article, describing the insurgents as "demons in human shape," opened his statement on a

---

[7] *Ibid.*, 42. For a more extensive study of the Vesey revolt, see Robert Starobin, *Denmark Vesey* (Englewood Cliffs, N. J., 1971), and John Lofton, *Insurrection in South Carolina: The Turbulent World of Denmark Vesey* (Yellow Springs, Ohio, 1964).
[8] H. Niles, ed., *Niles' Weekly Register*, IV, No. 26 (Baltimore, Aug. 27, 1831).

note that reflected the panic and general hysteria which had swept the white South: "I have a horrible, a heart-rending tale to relate, and lest even its worst features might be distorted by rumor and exaggeration, that has as yet reached us through the best sources of intelligence which the nature of the case will admit. . . ."[9]

When the hysteria finally subsided after 1831, the planter class began to look with a cold and discerning eye at the leaders of these revolts—Gabriel, Denmark Vesey, and Nat Turner—in an effort to find a solution to the always dangerous problem and to ascertain the cause and cure of slave insurrections. Perhaps they reasoned that the key lay in a careful analysis of these three men. What were their common characteristics, aside from their Black slave heritage? The answers the white planters found to this and similar questions were to significantly affect the pattern of slave control in the United States.

One fact was immediately clear: all three men were reputed to possess unusual intelligence and to have benefited from some type of educational training. It was said of Gabriel that he was "a fellow of courage and intellect above his rank in life."[10] Vesey spoke several languages fluently and had studied and reflected upon a wide range of subjects. His intellectual ability and cultured manner caused him to be called the "intellectual insurrectionist."[11] The last of the trio, Turner, apparently possessed a great deal of native intelligence, as a result of which he learned to read and write with little effort. He has also been described as a keen, mechanically gifted man.[12]

Another striking resemblance between Gabriel, Vesey, and Turner was their deep interest in religion. It was very significant, to the planters at least, that all three men were influenced by their religious views to the point of fanaticism and managed to use religion as a tool to foster their own ends. Gabriel studied the Old Testament assiduously and came to identify with the Biblical

[9] *Ibid.*
[10] Herbert Aptheker, *American Negro Slave Revolts* (New York, 1943), 219.
[11] Joseph C. Carroll, *Slave Insurrections in the United States, 1800–1860* (Boston, 1938), 85–86.
[12] Aptheker, *American Negro Slave Revolts*, 294.

figure of Samson, wearing his hair long in imitation of his hero.[13] Vesey was also a devoted student of the Bible and frequently quoted passages from it to support his argument that slavery was contrary to the laws of God and that slaves were obligated to attempt their emancipation, however shocking and bloody might be the consequences.[14] Nat Turner's religious fanaticism, however, made Gabriel's and Vesey's peculiar brands seem almost pale by comparison. Turner's religious attitude can be gleaned from his own words:

> My grandmother, who was very religious, and to whom I was very much attached—my master, who belonged to the Church, and other religious persons who visited the house, and whom I often saw at prayers, noticing the singularity of my manners, I suppose, and my uncommon intelligence for a child, remarked I had too much sense to be raised, and, if I was I would never be of any service to anyone as a slave. To a mind like mine, restless, inquisitive, and observant of everything that was passing, it is easy to suppose that religion was the subject to which it would be directed; and although this subject principally occupied my thoughts, there was nothing that I saw or heard of to which my attention was not directed.[15]

Dreams and heavenly revelations convinced him that he was "ordained for some great purpose in the hands of the Almighty."[16]

Thus, after 1831, the propertied classes began to suspect that education and religious training had contributed in large part to the ability of Gabriel, Vesey, and Turner to instigate revolts. It became increasingly evident that to give the Black such opportunities to develop his abilities was incompatible with the system of slavery. Education of even the most rudimentary kind made unquestioned obedience to the master difficult, if not impossible. Consequently, white Southerners began to attack the policy of

[13] Carroll, 49.
[14] *Ibid.*, 86.
[15] Herbert Aptheker, *A Documentary History of the American People* (New York, 1951), 120.
[16] *Ibid.*, 121.

educating Blacks. Men who had previously expressed themselves neither one way nor the other began to speak out against Black education when it became evident that abolitionist literature in the hands of the slaves would not only make them dissatisfied, but would cause them to take drastic measures to secure liberty.[17] The sources of slave unrest, it was believed, were the abolitionist tracts, newspapers, pamphlets, the literature of the French Revolution, and stories relating to Toussaint L'Ouverture and the political upheaval in Santo Domingo in 1793.[18]

Even religious instruction was now viewed as being detrimental to the slave system because religion served to reinforce the slave's self-assertive tendencies, made him a less docile burden-bearer, and inclined him to a revolutionary spirit.[19] The clergy, who had formerly argued that even slaves were entitled to sufficient training to enable them to understand the principles of the Christian religion, were now willing to forego Black salvation rather than see the institution of slavery destroyed.[20] Consequently, it was now thought necessary not only to prohibit the instruction of slaves in reading and writing, but also to supervise their religious exercises carefully.[21]

Although religious and educational restrictions were two important areas of slave control after 1831, each subsequent revolt tightened the legal machinery regulating slaves still further as state after state began to pass stringent laws severely restricting their freedom of movement and general privileges. Passes were more carefully regulated and penalties set for participation in unlawful assemblies, the latter being defined by state laws. Slaves were also forbidden to communicate with one another, or with free Blacks or liberal whites. Schools formerly open to Blacks were now closed, and private teaching of slaves was prohibited. State statutes

[17] Carter G. Woodson, *The Education of the Negro Prior to 1861* (New York, 1915), 158–59.
[18] *Ibid.*, 156.
[19] H. Richard Niebuhr, *The Social Sources of Denominationalism* (New York, 1957), 250.
[20] Woodson, 158.
[21] Niebuhr, 252.

either banned religious worship or brought it under the slave owners' direct supervision.[22]

Assuming that instruction of all kinds could be successfully prevented, the problem still remained of controlling the unsupervised assembly of slaves, which could be a springboard to concerted action and the breeding ground of insurrectionary activity. Development of a dangerous plot necessitated knowledge of the terrain and the availability of horses, weapons, and, obviously, the cooperation of slaves from numerous plantations. Although laws against conspiracy existed, it was far more essential to eliminate even the opportunity for such planning.[23] A way had to be found to prevent these unsupervised get-togethers, especially night gatherings, be they meetings on an adjoining plantation or simply groups of slaves assembling on their home plantation.

The patrol or "patteroller" system established by the Southern states was designed to solve this problem by providing a surveillance of slave movements, or a "night watch." By now the planter class had decided that its safety depended upon both the ignorance of the slave and a constant watch of his activities. The use of mounted patrols was not an unqualified success, however, for the local townspeople, who usually constituted the patrols, did not fully cooperate in serving. Furthermore, the districts to be covered by the town patrol were too large, the size of the patrol groups too small, and the visibility after nightfall too limited for the system to be really effective against any slave determined to ramble at night.

Harsh punishments for unauthorized absence by slaves proved only mildly successful. Severe whippings, brandings, torture, and the like, conducted in the presence of other slaves in order to inspire terror, did not serve as real deterrents against slave revolts and runaways—as attested to by slaves in frequent attempts to escape and by the sizable number of reported slave revolts. Nor were incentives—the granting of passes and privileges for good behavior—completely successful.

[22] Woodson, 164.
[23] Robert McColley, *Slavery and Jeffersonian Virginia* (Urbana, Ill., 1964), 101.

It is precisely at this point that the historical record ends and the folk history of the Black begins. It is this folk history of the Black, based on oral tradition, that sheds light on another, heretofore unexplored aspect of the continuing effort to keep the Black in bondage—the use of psychological control based on a fear of the supernatural. The system of control had one primary aim: to discourage the unauthorized movement of Blacks, especially at night. It was used during slavery to prevent insurrections by discouraging the assembly of Blacks, and it was employed in the post-Civil War period to stem the tide of Black movement from rural farming areas of the South to the cities of the North. A retired government employee elaborated on the constant pressure of fear that seemed to pervade the Black's entire life:

> In different parts of the South, they used different means to coerce and to keep the slaves frightened. One of the main things was to keep him frightened and keep the book out of his hand. My father told me many times that that was the strongest resolution that the white man had made with themselves. Keep the book out of the slave's hands, and keep him afraid of you, and keep him frightened of most everything going, and you would have a good working force.[24]

Black folk view and formal historical opinion concur on this point. Kenneth Stampp asserts in his book *The Peculiar Institution* that the predominant and overpowering emotion that whites aroused in the majority of slaves was neither love nor hate, but fear. He goes on to quote from an ex-slave: "We were always uneasy. When a white man spoke to me, I would feel frightened."[25] The identical opinion was expressed to the author by another ex-slave. When asked how she felt upon learning that she was free, she replied: "Yes, indeed, I was happy all right. Indeed I was. Because one thing when you was a slave, then you couldn't go no where.

[24] Informant William H. Henderson, March 3, 1964.
[25] Stampp, 381.

45

You wasn't like nothing. You was scared to death all the time."[26]

Fear of the supernatural in particular was a vague, indefinite kind of fear which kept slaves so constantly occupied with thoughts of impending disaster and misfortune that ideas about insurrections were stifled before they were born. Psychologists tell us that this kind of all-pervading fear becomes an important mechanism of social control, paralyzing actions and even undermining personal safety and well-being. Under such circumstances, everybody and everything become possible threats.[27] Thus the relationship even between Blacks becomes strained, and a wary, reserved attitude signals Black distrust of whites.[28] Furthermore, such an attitude can be intensified by the manipulatory devices of social control to produce a climate of "collective insecurity."

Thus, as his oral tradition records, much of the constraint and coercion employed against the Black to force him into disciplined obedience was produced by playing on his fear of and belief in the supernatural. Oral evidence further indicates that special control devices utilized by the white in this connection included intrigue, deception, and confusion. All of these devices were generally non-violent; indeed, they were hidden, for they aimed at exploitation by means of fraud.

Certainly no instrument of intrigue was more significant during slavery than the household servant. He was an important link in the chain of communication between the slave quarters and the master's house. On the one hand, he was the agent for an effective spy system, enabling the master to maintain a constant surveillance over slave activity and to acquire the information necessary for deceiving, confusing, and otherwise manipulating the Blacks. Slave tattling was encouraged and abetted. One informant observed: "They would get their house servants, certain of them who were small enough in mind to watch over the others, and in so doing

---

[26] Informant Alice Virginia Lyles, March 16, 1964.

[27] Kurt Riezler, "The Social Psychology of Fear," *American Journal of Sociology*, 49 (May 1944), 489–98.

[28] This same type of defensive insulation has been developed by Blacks in reaction to racial discrimination. Robin M. Williams, Jr., *Strangers Next Door* (Englewood Cliffs, N. J., 1964), 300.

they would find out whenever they were going out nights or anything, through the house servants, see."[29] Conversely, the house
servant was the channel for much of the information flowing the
other way—from the master's house to the field hands, who represented the bulk of the Black population. For the field hand, this
was his major source of information about the white man's world.
As noted in Austin Steward's slave autobiography:

> The field hands, and such of them as have generally been ex-
> cluded from the dwelling of their owners, look to the house ser-
> vant as a pattern of politeness and gentility. And indeed, it is often
> the only method of obtaining any knowledge of the manners of what
> is called "genteel society"; hence, they are ever regarded as a
> privileged class.[30]

Fabricated stories and distorted information designed to deceive
were passed along, too, according to Minnie Fountaine, who said
the stories were told "by other slaves who were above them. You
know there was always an element above in the slave world. . . .
There was always somebody who controlled the other."[31] As informers, house servants were the means by which intimate and
privately held ideas among the Blacks were transmitted to the slave
masters. The Reverend J. L. S. Holloman remarked that the whites
"always depended upon keeping up with the Negroes in the quarters by having Negroes in the house. They do that now [1964],
don't they, by liaisons? That is, they bring the news, what slaves
are talking about."[32]

The natural consequence of pursuing the informer's role caused
house servants to be viewed as a threat to the safety and security
of the general slave population. They were despised and feared,
an attitude reflected in both slave autobiographies and oral tradition. Especially revealing in this connection are Austin Steward's
comments:

[29] Informant Minnie Bell Fountaine, April 22, 1964.
[30] *Twenty-Two Years A Slave, and Forty Years A Freeman* (Rochester, N. Y.,
1857), 31.
[31] Interview, April 22, 1964.
[32] Interview, March 4, 1964.

hence, they are ever regarded as a privileged class; and are sometimes greatly envied, while others are bitterly hated. And too often
justly, for many of them are the most despicable tale-bearers and
mischief-makers, who will, for the sake of a favor of his master or
mistress, frequently betray fellow-slaves, and by tattling, get him
severely whipped; and for these acts of perfidy, and sometimes
downright falsehood, often rewarded by his master, who knows it
is for his interest to keep such ones about him; though he is sometimes obliged, in addition to a reward, to send away, for fear of
the vengeance of the betrayed slaves.[33]

In spite of the masters' pains to protect their informers from "the
vengeance of the betrayed slaves" they sometimes acted too late.
One informant's paternal grandmother was killed as a result of
being hit on the head by other slaves for tattling.[34]

The effectiveness of this system of tattling is evidenced by the
large number of slave insurrections that were discovered and exposed by trusted household servants. A faithful personal slave betrayed the Vesey conspiracy, even though that very danger had
been recognized by a major figure in the plot, Peter Poyas, when
he warned his lieutenant: "But take care and don't mention it [the
plot] to those waiting men who receive presents of old coats, etc.
from their masters, or they'll betray us."[35] The Denmark Vesey
rebellion was not the only one aborted in this way. Carroll's *Slave
Insurrections in the United States* records at least twelve other slave
plots exposed by Blacks. In sum, oral tradition and documented
historical sources agree that slave informers performed a valuable
service to slave owners, and that these informers were encouraged
and rewarded for their activities by white masters.

Closely allied to the intrigue used in manipulating the Blacks
was the deception practiced by the white masters, a deception made
relatively easy because it was perpetrated in an environment of
ignorance. By keeping the slave population undereducated, the
white master strengthened his own position as principal source
of information and advice. Such information might be true or

---

[33] Steward, 32.
[34] Informant Lucy Edmonds, Feb. 29, 1964.
[35] E. Franklin Frazier, *The Negro in the United States* (New York, 1949), 91.

false, the advice good or bad. According to one informant, "They couldn't read or write and didn't know any better; [they] took what the overseer said and they believed it."[36] Commenting on the same theme, Professor Floyd Wardlaw Crawford deplored especially the terrible shackles of ignorance:

> As I heard William Pickens commenting once on the ignorance of the Negro in the days of slavery, I heard him speak in Detroit in 1924 say this, that . . . "The strongest chains with which the body of a man can be bound are the chains of ignorance. You keep a man ignorant and you've got him. You don't have to stand guard over him with a shot gun. You don't have to lock him up at night. Just turn him aloose and he isn't going any place." So the Negro was kept ignorant and being ignorant he, of course, was helpless.[37]

Formal documented records and oral tradition agree that white masters, playing up slave ignorance, deliberately fabricated and falsified information passed along to the Blacks. Both sources offer abundant evidence that such practice was common, providing the masters with an important and many-sided technique of control. William B. Hesseltine discussed misinformation as a technique of control and its reinforcement through slave ignorance:

> Frequently, the master threatened to sell the recalcitrant or lazy Negro to some other master or "down the ribber" to some mystic land of harsh treatment. Thus, tobacco slaves were told of the bad conditions in the cotton fields, and cotton slaves of the terrible life on the sugar plantations. Sometimes these stories inspired the slaves to spasmodic bursts of energy. He was taught, too, that the Yankee was a "debbil wit horns," largely to inhibit any latent desire to seek freedom along the Underground Railroad. The ignorant credulity of the slaves was as potent a factor as the overseer's whip in maintaining discipline and productivity on the plantation. It is not surprising that southern laws forbade teaching Negroes to read.[38]

People and places—indeed, anything that in any way threatened the slave system—were described in such distasteful terms that

---

[36] Informant William H. Henderson, March 3, 1964.
[37] Interview, Feb. 8, 1964.
[38] *The South in American History* (New York, 1943), 267.

slaves would be influenced to avoid them out of fear. Particularly subject to misinformation were those items most likely to be stolen, such as food. The following informant's statement about this technique is interesting not only for its content, but for the degree of sophistication she reveals in being able to recognize this practice despite her obvious educational deficiencies:

> Dey used to skeer us out 'bout red 'taters. Dey was fine 'taters, red on de outside and pretty and white on de inside, but white folks called 'em "nigger-killers." Dat was one of der tricks to keep us from stealin' dem 'taters. Der warn't nothin' wrong wid dem 'taters; dey was jus' as good and healthy as any other 'taters.[39]

Part of the mechanism for inducing fear in the slaves was the use of the Indian as a devil figure. The technique was especially important in the Eastern colonies during the earliest plantation days, arising mainly from the problem of troublesome communities of runaway slaves who had settled in uninhabited areas of Southern states and the fear of possible conspiracies between Indians and Blacks against the whites. To forestall such cooperative efforts between these two groups, the whites adopted a policy of divide and conquer, in which Indians and Blacks were played off against each other in an atmosphere of contrived hostility and suspicion. In the Black community this climate of distrust was created by spreading rumors of bizarre, painful, and slow deaths suffered by victims of Indian capture. Details of atrocities were spelled out, dwelled upon, and endlessly recited in the presence of slaves. The Indians, on the other hand, were encouraged in their superstitious fears of Blacks. Some Indians, for example, believed that they had been created by the Great Spirit, but Blacks by the Evil Spirit.[40] Reinforcement of the rumors was provided not only by encouraging Indians and Blacks to murder each other, but also by using Black soldiers to fight in Indian wars and encouraging Indians to catch runaway slaves.[41]

---

[39] WPA Files, "Slave Narratives" (Rachel Adams, Athens, Ga.).

[40] J. Norman Heard, *The Black Frontiersmen* (New York, 1969), 71.

[41] William S. Willis, Jr., "Anthropology and Negroes on the Southern Colonial Frontier," *The Black Experience in America*, James C. Curtis and Lewis L. Gould, eds. (Austin, 1970), 43.

Abolitionists and Yankees, however, bore the full brunt of distortion and exaggeration in the planters' efforts to keep slaves from running away. Concerning the Yankee, an ex-slave commented, "Oh, they tried to scare us; said they [Yankees] had horns but when we saw them with their blue clothes, brass spurs on their feet and their guns just shining, they looked just pretty to us."[42] Bell I. Wiley elaborated on this subject:

> Southerners were not unaware of the wholesome influence which a fear of the "Yankees" would have on the loyalty of their Negroes. This coupled with the amusement which they derived from working on the imaginations of their servants, led to the origination and circulation of many stories of the diabolical appearance and cruel practices of the Federals. Some of these were exaggerated as they were retold by the Negroes. A slave who escaped to the South Atlantic blockading fleet from Georgia in April, 1863, said that his mistress had "told him that as soon as he came to the 'Yankees,' so soon would they put a harness, prepared for the purpose, on him and compel him to drag cannons and wagons about like horses." An old colored woman in Shelby County, Tennessee, said that when she asked her mistress what the "Yankees" looked like, she was told, "They got long horns on their head and tushes in their mouth and eyes sticking out like a cow. They're mean old things." Georgia owners told their slaves that the Federals threw women and children into the Chattahoochee River, and that when the buildings were burned in Atlanta they filled them with Negroes to be roasted by the flames.[43]

Still other slaves were under the impression that the Yankees would seize them and send them to Cuba.[44]

Abolitionists were said to be slave dealers who conducted a profitable business by enticing slaves to run away, only to resell them in the Deep South.[45] But this was a relatively mild falsification when compared to more elaborate stories that "abolitionists would

---

[42] Egypt, Masuoka, Johnson, 16.

[43] *Southern Negroes, 1861–1865* (New Haven, Conn., 1938), 13.

[44] *Ibid.*, 12.

[45] Margaret Jackson, "An Investigation of Biographies and Autobiographies of American Slaves Published Between 1840 and 1860" (Diss. Cornell Univ., 1954), 85.

eat him, sell him, or put him, blinded, in an underground mine to pass the remainder of his days."[46]

Planters took great pains to inculcate false ideas in the slaves about possible destinations for a Black inclined to run away. Canada, for example, was a special subject of terrifying descriptions during the slavery period. It already was characterized by the strangeness of a far-off place, which lent some credence to the stories circulated by the slaveholders:

> I could not forget all the horrid stories slaveholders tell about Canada. They assure the slave that, when they get hold of slaves in Canada, they make various uses of them. Sometimes they *skin* the *head*, and wear the wool on their coat collars—put them into the lead-mines, with both eyes out—the young slaves they eat; and as for the red coats, they are sure death to the slave. However ridiculous to a well-informed person such stories may appear, they work powerfully upon the excited imagination of an ignorant slave.[47]

In the post-Civil War years, this same pattern of deliberately falsifying information was used to describe the Northern cities that lured the Black laboring forces with promises of higher wages and better living conditions. Widely circulated stories concerning body-snatchers who trafficked in "living" victims were an integral part of this white effort to keep the Black on Southern farms in the late nineteenth and early twentieth centuries.

Belief in the appearance of supernatural creatures, such as witches and ghosts (in reality, whites masquerading as such), was another form of deception and often was the basis for rumors which spread swiftly through the Black community. The emotional excitement of this kind of news led to its rapid transmission, as each individual felt strongly motivated to pass exclusive news along to someone else. Opportunities for verification were minimal, and each repetition of the rumor only strengthened the general atmosphere of fear and terror from which it originated.[48]

[46] *Ibid.*, 315–16.
[47] *Ibid.*, 85.
[48] J. Prasad, "The Psychology of Rumour: A Study Relating to the Great

The System of Psychological Control

Although it may be assumed that the whites hit upon the device of circulating false rumors about the supernatural through accident, present-day authorities on rumor have perceived its potential as a method of control. J. Prasad, a recognized student of the problem, has stated that the strongest and most persistent rumors are those arising from powerful traditions, such as legend, socially important beliefs, and superstitions which have not passed away entirely and have been more fully believed than the rumors themselves. Prasad finds rumor, when based on traditions which have been both popular and powerful, can be particularly effective, because rumor temporarily strengthens the traditions, apparently increasing suggestibility.[49]

Confusion through emotion (a conscious attempt to confuse the emotional responses of the Black) was another hidden control procedure designed to mold the Black into an obedient member of the laboring force. Two closely allied techniques were involved here: the calculated inflaming of hatred and the promotion of suspicion. With plantation rivalries between house and field servants firmly implanted, resourceful planters used this control device—confusion through emotion—to separate the field hands from each other and all of their chattel from those of the neighboring plantations. James Tolbert observed:

> I used to hear my father talk about his father, saying how they would teach the colored people to hate each other. For example, say you owned a group of slaves, and this gentleman a group, and I had a group. I would tell my slaves that you are bad Negroes, and he would do likewise, and that kept them always, you might say, at dagger's point, always at one another's throat, mad with one another. Didn't have to do anything to each other. Just mad before they even saw you.[50]

Such a climate of fear promoted automatic suspicion between all slaves, and deep-seated enmity in cases of suspected treachery. The

Indian Earthquake of 1934," *British Journal of Psychology*, 26 (July 1935), Part I, 1–15.
[49] *Ibid.*
[50] Interview, April 9, 1964.

deliberate inflaming of emotions in effect created a community of personal enemies in which the whole atmosphere was charged with anger and terror.[51]

The Black's fear of conjuring was, of course, a ready-made tool for the whites to use in fostering suspicion and hatred among the slaves. The comment of Mary Howard Neeley, a retired school teacher, is typical: "And they [whites] would beat up brick and pepper and put down at the Negroes' gates, you know, hoodooism . . . to scare them, you know. 'You better stay home. So and so put that down for you.' They taught them that. Took them [Blacks] a long time to grow out of it. Some are not out of it yet."[52]

The climate was such that white masters needed only to reinforce existing beliefs, for in the superstitious world of the slaves no one knew who his enemy was, from which direction he would strike, or what form his spell would take. Slaves tell of burying frogs, snakes, or lizards at the doorsteps of persons they disliked. According to Mrs. Charles Reed: "If the enemy walked over it, it would be painful. They could also fix something to separate husband and wife."[53] One ex-slave, recalling "I was a great believer in tricks, conjuring and witchcraft,"[54] said that conjure bags and cloths were planted at the door and within the house. Another informant stated that salt and pepper would be sprinkled in those places to kill such "conjure."[55] "Spreading dusting powder for his enemy"[56] is the phrase one Black used to describe this practice. Other testimony indicates "they never tried it on whites, because they were afraid."[57]

Many ex-slaves believed that all Southern plantations had voodoo advisers who concocted charms for various uses.[58] Matilda Marshall, an ex-slave, recalled:

[51] Bruce, 119.
[52] Informant Mary Howard Neeley, Feb. 8, 1964.
[53] "Texas Slave Narratives," Mrs. Charles Reed folder.
[54] Ibid., Henry Ellis Forder folder.
[55] Ibid., I. B. R. Roberts folder.
[56] Ibid., James Williams folder.
[57] Ibid., Bill Murphy folder.
[58] Ibid., Reverend Reuben Anderson folder.

> The slaves were superstitious. They would sometimes throw away good hats and dresses that they thought someone had hoodooed. They wore a silver dime in their shoes to keep them from being conjured. Nearly everybody that had a severe pain or was sick for a long time was hoodooed. They were very careful not to let anyone get any of their combings. They thought that if they got a piece of your hair they could make you do as they wished.[59]

Sudden death in a Black community meant to many, if not all, witchcraft by a secret foe. Evil charms even entered into disputes between Blacks, at least one of whom would be convinced he had been victimized either by a trick doctor or his opponent. Women were particularly acrimonious, author Philip A. Bruce noted, and always suspicious that their enemies were using the same black art against them that they themselves sought to use.[60]

Indeed, every conceivable misfortune—including sickness, death, and alleged disloyalty of one's spouse—was attributed to the work of conjurers. Each new evidence of ill fortune served to reinforce the existing belief in witchcraft, and the greater that belief the more susceptible the Blacks became to harboring ill feelings toward other Blacks. The white man capitalized on the opportunity to promote such rancor and fear, as illustrated by William Henderson's statement: "Well he [father] told me that there were certain people after the war, and that the white folks got them to perform as witches. And they would tell your fortunes, and they would tell you if you were sick, somebody had fixed your business."[61] Another informant, Evelyn McKinney, described how stories about the supernatural served as an effective means of controlling the Blacks' movement at night:

> These stories were about things that happened at night. And these were the things that kept you from going out. You see, now they knew that on a dark night, a dark man could get away and he could not be seen. So they'd tell you these various stories about these night things, I mean these things that kept you in fear not

[59] *Ibid.*, Matilda Marshall folder.
[60] Bruce, 121.
[61] Interview, March 3, 1964.

55

of the master himself, but of the supernatural. You knew that you may be able to avoid the master because perhaps he was sleeping. But you couldn't avoid the supernatural. So that he, that way, he left controls on you.[62]

In view of the persistent references in oral testimony to personal enemies during slavery, developed most often from misinformation, and the recurring testimony about the widespread fear of the supernatural, there appears to be no doubt that white masters knowingly utilized these methods of psychological control. Whether the scientific basis of the techniques was recognized or not, the control measures were effective. Emotions of hatred and revenge were nourished on the belief in witchcraft and conjuring, pitting slave against slave and fostering a continuing state of anxiety and fear. Group cooperation, especially in the direction of insurrectionary activities, was thus discouraged; furthermore, the master class hoped that the Black's intense preoccupation with his own safety would leave little time or desire to plan for a better life by means of rebellion. Significantly, the pervading fear of the supernatural suited the planter's interest as well, for it resulted in a reluctance by slaves to ramble unsupervised at night. As long as this general fear was maintained and promoted, the Black was inclined to stay at home rather than face the unknown "out there," and the planter was thereby relieved of the necessity of repeated instructions to the slave and constant surveillance of his activities.

Aspects of this system of nonviolent control have a counterpart in primitive societies. Luther Lee Bernard asserts that man's practice of falling back on the supernatural when other controls fail was common in very early times, even before spirits supposedly determined men's destinies, and has continued to the present day.[63] Bernard also states that supernaturalism has been resorted to in nonliterate societies because it requires more than codes, convictions, mores, conventions, and the like to keep members of society in line.[64]

Certainly one can easily find parallels in nonliterate society to

---

[62] Interview, April 8, 1964.
[63] *Social Control* (New York, 1939), 451.
[64] *Ibid.*

the bogeyman idea. Elsie Clews Parsons stated, "In savagery, as in civilization, the supernatural sanction has a nursery role."[65] In the South the bogeyman took the form of ghosts, witches, and night doctors. In nonliterate societies he parades under a number of forms, but the aim is essentially the same—the deliberate effort to keep children or adults from straying away from home, especially at night, because of the fear of encountering supernatural monsters. As Parsons further observed:

> Aside from the problems of forcing small children to conform to group standards of good social behavior, specific traditions are inculcated in the young concerning the consequences of straying away from home at night. A "good" child does not cry. Nor, for the peace of his elders, must he be adventurous. It is troublesome to look for children who run away. And so would-be explorers are threatened with supernatural mishap. A Koita child who strayed in the bush at night would encounter a *vadavada*, a man who traveled by night and who brings sickness and death to those he meets. The Euahlayi tribe of New South Wales have a bogey called from his cry Gineet Gineet. He goes about with a net across his shoulders into which he pops any children he can see. Chemosit is a Nandi devil, half man, half bird, with one leg, nine buttocks, and a red mouth which shines at night like a lamp. He catches children who are foolish enough to be lured away from home by his night song. 'Nenaunir of the Masai is a kindred monster; he is an invulnerable, stony-bodied creature with a head of a beast of prey, and feet with claws. "Don't go too far," a mother says to her children, "or 'Nenaunir will get you!"[66]

Formal historians, with their obvious preference for documented sources, have largely omitted any mention of psychological control. The one possible exception is Kenneth Stampp, who asserts in *The Peculiar Institution* that "the successful master was often a keen student of human psychology."[67] He goes on to at least hint of more subtle techniques than have been documented. "The techniques of control were many and varied, some subtle, some inge-

[65] "Lines Between Religion And Morality In Early Culture," *American Anthropologist*, N.S. 17 (Jan.–March 1915), 51–57.

[66] *Ibid.*

[67] Stampp, 143.

nious, some brutal. Slaveholders generally relied upon more than one."[68] But Professor Stampp barely touches the periphery of the whole area of control that is common knowledge among the Blacks. Their story of the various phases of manipulation is found primarily in a source that only lately has come under scholarly scrutiny—the oral testimony related to the Black's folk history.

ADDITIONAL NARRATIVE

"What You See, You Don't See"

Aunt Berdie used to tell a very pitiful one. And we were children and we used to cry because we loved her so dearly. . . . But she said that they were not ever given any real . . . they always felt that the good food was not for the slaves. There were certain things that they were to have. But in order to have a feast every now and then, some of the slaves, who could trust the others, would steal a sheep and kill it, and they would have something good to eat, and they would have their big day. So Aunt Berdie said she was a little girl, but she did not know what, why they did it, but she knew that the table was laid out with all of this good food, and that she was going to get some of it. So she said she passed by the table, and childlike she smoothed her hand along as she went. But due to the fact that she was raised in the house with the mistress' children, they didn't trust her. So she said this old man took her out. I don't know who . . . she never called his name. She may have called his name but I don't recall it.

And he said, "I'm going to teach you how to see and not see, and hear and not hear."

So she said he took her out back of the quarter house where all of these oyster shells were, and he whipped her terribly. And she said in prancing around on these oyster shells she cut her little bare feet. Oh, she said, and I know this to be a fact, she said she could never stand to see blood on anything because she said her poor little feet were just bleeding terribly all over. But they whipped her.

And when he finished whipping her, he told her, he said, "Now what you see, you don't see, and what you hear, you don't hear."

She didn't know the meaning of it until she got grown; and she did not know the meaning of the whipping, but she realized that they were afraid she would tell in the house that she had seen all of this lamb on the table, because they weren't given lamb, and that they had to steal it and kill it and cook it among themselves. . . . It was a very pitiful thing. And many is the time that Aunt Berdie would take off her shoe and hold up her foot and show us the marks. Her feet were, you know, like that all under it and she said that that was what it was for.

—Informant MINNIE BELL FOUNTAINE, April 22, 1964. [Story learned from an aunt, a former slave in Caroline County, Virginia.]

[68] *Ibid.*

58

THE ROLE OF THE MASTER AND OF THE OVERSEER IN THE USE OF SUPERNATURAL SUBTERFUGE

*My grandfather was a slave and he said
that they [masters] used to tell them frightening, well tales, I might say, to keep them from
going out. And of course they believed it and
they wouldn't go out.* —DANIEL MIXSON

FROM THE POINT OF VIEW of the slave, the master and overseer represented mortal men whose power and authority could be successfully challenged and defied in any number of ways. Even escape, though difficult, was not impossible, given the proper set of circumstances—a head start, careful planning, and the ability to remain hidden from those who sought the runaway. Written historical records indicate clearly that violent, even inhumane punishments failed to deter runaways or night ramblers.

If slaves could not be sufficiently frightened with things of this earth, one other recourse was open to the masters and overseers— fear of the supernatural, primarily ghosts. The master or his guards could be in only one place at any given time, but a ghost could appear any place at any time in a kind of all-seeing capacity. The master, for all of his power, was only flesh and blood and bones; the ghost was not subject to such limitations.

The white stereotype of the fearful, fleeing Black, running at full speed from ghostly apparitions, has been visually depicted in movies, plays, and early television, as well as in the general body of Southern literature. But the point that has been too long overlooked is that what was simply "funny" to whites was often utilized by Blacks to counteract the fear that was an essential ingredient of the slave system. Roger Abrahams is one of the few scholars to understand Black humor in the context of a defense mechanism developed for survival.[1] Abrahams suggests that, historically, Blacks have converted traits such as laziness and childishness into mechanisms of defense. These conversions are expressed in Black oral tradition in the cycle of tales commonly designated as Master and John; the white man, Negro, and Mexican; the Negro and white man; and the Negro and animal. In all these narratives one theme dominates—an aggressive superiority of Blacks pitted in competition with men of any hue or ethnic origin and with animals, natural or supernatural.

If the master could develop this existing fear by carefully channeling certain selective information into the Black community, slaves would be afraid to wander out at night lest they accidentally run into unearthly creatures. Julia Brown stated, "They were afraid that if they ran away, that they would become entangled with witches and ghosties or what not."[2] Such a definite fear would keep the slaves bound to their quarters better than any number of armed guards. Henry Lewis Brown was told by his grandfather that some of the slaves "would be afraid to go from one plantation to the other on account of they [the masters] would tell these ghost stories, you know, about the graveyard."[3]

This is the folk view of the kind of control fostered by white planters in an effort to maintain slave discipline. Although the image of the superstitious, ghost-fearing Black is common, it is little known that Southern whites deliberately encouraged Black superstitions. "They got all this stuff like ghost tales and bad religion, they got it from the master. And if you can get a man believing in ghosties and such a thing that ain't or don't exist, then you'll know he's thinking small."[4] The Reverend E. C. Smith,

1 *Positively Black* (Englewood Cliffs, N. J., 1970), 60–82.
2 Interview, April 10, 1964.
3 Interview, April 11, 1964.
4 Informant William Willis, Feb. 28, 1964.

former pastor of one of the largest Baptist churches in Washington, D.C., sums up this point of view:

> That was one of the controls that the people, that the master used to control the slaves. He would tell him that there was something out there at night that would catch him, say if he goes out, and that thing got in the thinking of the slaves and was a great system of control. Now my grandfather was so afraid of ghosts until you couldn't shove him off on the porch at night. He was just afraid of the dark. Well, the white people knew that that was a great system of control and so they used it to tell the slaves that if they attempted to go anywhere at night that something was going to get them. . . . In preference of guards, they used that and the Negroes really believed that there was something in the dark. And that's the reason this ghost business is so prominent among Negroes now. Psychologically it got into their makeup.[5]

Sufficient historical evidence supporting this Black view of antebellum psychological slave controls by masters simply does not exist. Indeed, the matter of the control of slaves through fear of the supernatural is a blind spot in most published scholarly works on slavery. While the institution of slavery has been covered from many angles, the almost total neglect of this aspect is disappointing.

The one notable exception to this void is the comment of J. Reuben Sheeler. He stated in part:

> Superstition and fear of ghosts were promoted among the slaves so that they would be more fearful in their movements, especially at night. In the spring of the year patrols were organized with crew and captain to patrol and visit all Negro quarters and other places suspected of unlawful assembly of slaves . . . and any other straying from one plantation to another without a pass. The slave found guilty was to be whipped. These patrols were infamous for their night activity and were known to the slaves as "paterollers." That their duty might be effective even when they were not present, these patrollers were assisted by masters who found ghost stories effective in scaring the Negroes. Negroes in Jefferson County, Virginia, circulated numerous stories of ghosts chasing them home

[5] Interview, March 3, 1964.

at night. "Uncle Rube," a Negro in Clarksburg, tells of meeting the devil in the courthouse yard. Without a doubt "Uncle Rube's devil was a white citizen or the result from overindulgence in the intoxicating beverages."[6]

Professor Sheeler's suggestive reference to the misadventures of "Uncle Rube" in his confrontation with the devil is completely described in Henry Haymond's *History of Harrison County of West Virginia*:

> "Uncle Rube," a slave of the Stealey family, had many amusing and mysterious tales to tell of his adventures. One was that one night when returning home from a corn shucking, he was confronted by the Devil in the Court House yard, who handed him a brass jug and ordered him to take a drink. Just as Uncle Rube lifted it to his lips, the devil, jug and all vanished in a sheet of fire, leaving Old Rube senseless on the ground. He did not recover consciousness until daylight and said he then could detect a strong odor of brimstone in the air and that his head ached for two days after. "Uncle Rube" always regretted that he lost that drink of liquor.
>
> It was strongly suspected that the old man had freely imbibed at the corn shucking before he thought he met the Devil.[7]

"Old Rube" actually existed. According to Harrison County Court House records, the will of a white man, Jacob Stealey, was probated in October 1841. By the terms of the will:

> I give and bequest to my son, John Stealey a tract of land containing about 24 acres being south of where I now live being the same that I purchased from Benjamin Wilson, Jr. and a moity of a tract of land that I purchased from John and Thomas Haymond lying northeast of Clarksburg about 3 miles, also one Negro man slave named Reuben.[8]

Whether "Uncle Rube's" devil resulted from intoxication or a white man's masquerade, the encounter illustrates the Black's ex-

[6] "The Control of the Negro, Body, Mind, and Soul," *Negro History Bulletin*, 12 (Dec. 1957), 67–69.

[7] Morgantown, W. Va., 1910, p. 304.

[8] Work Projects Administration, West Virginia Historical Records Survey Harrison County, Calendar of Wills Form, Data of Probate, October Term, 1841.

perience with the supernatural. The master's technique of utilizing the supernatural for slave control employed three associated methods, the individual planter using any one or all three of them. The basic, and simplest, technique was the systematic use of simple narrative statements concerning the appearance of supernatural figures, such as ghosts and witches. To implement this imaginative base, the planter often designated as haunted places usually located strategically along heavily traveled roads. Of course, the final step in the methodology was to actually masquerade as ghosts in order to reinforce the belief in the supernatural.

Circulation of Ghost Tales

According to Black belief, the most important part of this technique of exploiting fear of the supernatural "rested on telling the story itself."[9] These so-called stories were not fully developed narratives, but simple statements concerning the appearance of supernatural figures. As one ex-slave recalled: "We were very superstitious as our masters would tell us tales to scare us and make us do nothing but what he told us to do."[10]

Rumor was the method used not only to circulate the falsified story as legitimate news throughout the Black quarters, but to expand and exaggerate the account as it was verbally transmitted from one excited person to another. By definition, rumors collectively form as they evolve from a corroborating process, with each individual hearing the information, responding, and transmitting it in his own words.[11] Therefore, in states of heightened tension, as in a rumor-producing situation, suggestibility increases as credibility decreases. In this case, vagueness assumed additional value because the unbridled imagination of the slave simply filled in the details.

Ghosts and witches, haunted places, and supernatural animals generally constituted the subjects of these narrative statements

[9] Informant, J. L. S. Holloman, March 4, 1964.
[10] "Texas Slave Narratives," Richard Gober folder.
[11] Tamotsu Shibutani, *Improvised News* (Indianapolis, 1966), 13.

that were injected by white masters into the stream of Black oral tradition. Ghosts were unquestionably the most frequently used subject for this form of control. They were discussed in order "to spell terror in the hearts of slaves so they wouldn't go out at night."[12] One ex-slave said, "Marse used to try to scare us by telling us dar was spooks."[13] All that was needed to keep the slave population indoors at night, according to the Black's own testimony, was to circulate the story that ghosts had recently been seen in the neighborhood. This is the meaning behind William Henderson's succinct remark, "The ghost story took care of the slaves at night."[14]

The terror of nameless, unknown ghosts was real enough, but the dread of the return of dead people the slaves were acquainted with held a special kind of fear. When told the dead would come back for them, many Blacks were afraid to go outside after dark.[15]

The masters also planted narrative statements concerning witches, which were equally as effective as ghosts in keeping slaves close to their quarters after curfew hours. Mary Howard Neeley stated, "The white people taught them about witches and ghosts and such stuff as that. That was to make them to have fear."[16] The psychological conditioning that resulted from this kind of indoctrination caused Samuel Chappell to remark, "They carried a fear of a witch and a ghost."[17] That Blacks remained terrified of witches as night-riding creatures during and after slavery is expressed in Jessie Brown's testimony:

> They said that the witch will get you. They were led to believe that these things existed, and they tried to put it on their children, because my mother even tried to frighten me with it. That's right. And I will never forget how one night I went to see a young lady,

12 Informant J. L. S. Holloman, March 4, 1964.
13 WPA Files, "Slave Narratives" (Fred James, Newberry, S. C., Jan. 10, 1938).
14 Interview, March 3, 1964.
15 *Ibid.*
16 Interview, Feb. 8, 1964.
17 Interview, March 7, 1964.

and her father was one of these who believed in it, so I got ready to leave. You see, I had to walk about three miles back to my house. So he said, "Man, you sure must have loved this girl. You come all the way over here. Man, I'm telling you, witches or anything is liable to get you before you get home." Of course, I did have to go pass a cemetery, but I never did believe too much in that stuff. I never did. [18]

Finally, mysterious supernatural animals were often described to the slaves as marauding night creatures. Generally the animal to be feared was not named but only partially described, which added to the slave's fear by leaving his imagination free to explore all kinds of terrible possibilities. Masters told slaves about "something coming in and they saw it when it came in, and it had big eyes and black paws and all like that, you know." [19] Headless animals were described fairly frequently. One informant, Lucille Murdock, testified that her grandmother said that one of the stories told by her master was "about a mule coming in the kitchen with no head on." [20] The following text taken from the WPA collection seems to fit this pattern of deliberate falsehoods by the masters about supernatural sights: "De master once saw ghosts. He come from his sisters and passed de graveyard and saw 9 cows with no heads. His horse jest flew home. Most white folks didn't believe in ghosts, but dat is one time de master believed he saw some." [21]

Usually accompanying stories about supernatural animals was an effort on the part of the masters to produce evidence of their existence. Consequently, "They would have a puddle of blood and claim that something came and killed someone. . . . Well, they would make as though there was probably some ferocious animal, or some spirit coming back. I mean, they used all types of tactics to keep the people afraid down there." [22]

[18] Interview, April 23, 1964.
[19] Informant Mary Elizabeth Jones, March 23, 1964.
[20] Interview, April 11, 1964.
[21] WPA Files, "Slave Narratives" (Madison Griffin, Whitmire, S. C., June 18, 1937).
[22] Informant Jessie W. Brown, April 23, 1964.

Haunted Places

Strategic areas along heavily traveled routes—main roads, cemeteries, woods, houses—were labeled as being haunted. J.L.S. Holloman said: "They would even point out places that were haunted, like certain places, certain houses, certain graveyards. You see a man come riding on a horse with no head on."[23] The major reason for declaring an area haunted was that it was a place that normally would have to be passed if a slave planned any type of illicit meeting or escape. If a real fear of enough such spots could be established, it would be virtually impossible for a slave to travel too far in any direction without being forced to pass a supposedly haunted location. The feeling of being effectively hemmed in was described by Matthew Hurley:

> Nearly anyway you turn, you lived in the country, you try to go home or go away from home at night, you had to go by a spooky place. It's either an old house that someone has seen ghosties there, and the reason why the ghosties be hanging round, or either it was a cemetery where some wicked person been buried, and you will see a spook around his grave.[24]

A slave might or might not encounter a ghost on any given night, since there were many more slaves than there were slave owners and overseers. But by deliberately designating certain areas as haunted (with occasional visits by people in ghostly garb to reinforce the belief), the system of psychological control through fear of the supernatural was maintained with a minimum of personnel. A second reason for the masters staking out haunted areas was that certain places, such as fields adjoining the slave quarters, cemeteries, and abandoned plantations, made exceptionally good hiding places for runaway slaves. It took a long time to locate a slave hidden in the woods, for example. If the use of good hiding places could be discouraged, the planter's problem of searching out miss-

23 Interview, March 4, 1964.
24 Interview, March 12, 1964.

66

ing slaves was greatly simplified. The effectiveness of the white masters' system of designating ghost areas is indicated in part by the following observation on the extent to which slaves would avoid haunted places:

> The more superstitious blacks of Edisto Island frighten themselves with stories about "sumpen" in a certain woods that pursues women and children, and makes strong men take to their heels. At the start the creature is described as a wild man, but soon it becomes noised about that this man has supernatural powers, and by common consent all of the Negroes in the neighborhood avoid the haunted woods even though they are obliged to go miles out of their way to reach their respective destinations.[25]

Occasionally natural events, such as an unusual number of deaths due to exposure, played directly into the hands of the masters. "They believed strickly in ghosts, because on this plantation one cold winter many slaves died from exposure. After this everyone told some tale about ghosts and many became afraid to steal out after dark. There was a certain tree at the crossroads where the horses would refuse to pass, day or night."[26] Sometimes areas believed to be haunted were associated with sensational local murders or tragedies of one kind or another. Excited news of such occurrences spread rapidly throughout the Black community. Haunted areas of this type were coincidental to the planters' system of control, but they served the same purpose of restricting slave movements. Further, it is safe to assume that the planters were quick to encourage belief in these "legitimate" ghosts. These areas usually became identified with the ghost of the murdered victim or the central figure in a tragic episode. William Willis related an incident in which the spirit of a person reincarnated in animal form was believed to appear regularly at a particular place: "It was certain areas when I was a boy was marked out as ghost areas. Dogs with no heads had been seen and he was old

[25] Project No. 1655, C. S. Murray, District Director, Charleston, S. C. IV South Carolina (folder), Federal Writers Project, Folklore Material, June 7, 1937.
[26] "Texas Slave Narratives," Tobe Garrett folder.

mister so and so. . . . And another dog was seen on a given hill with a red hot chain, you know. He had a chain, dragging a red hot chain, see. He represented somebody that had been killed in back times."[27] In another case, he told about the ghost of a slave woman who searched in vain for her lost children. Her search was always conducted in a certain locality. "And there was a woman who was often seen in another area with a shawl. She was looking for her children. That was a ghost tale of some Negro slave whose children were sold away, and she was always back looking for them."[28]

In slave autobiographies one finds many instances recorded of haunted areas associated with slave murders. Charles Ball reported the death of two Black men accused of dragging a white woman from her horse and brutally murdering her in an area known as Murderer's Swamp. After this tragic episode a series of unexplained events was believed to have occurred there which Ball described in vivid detail:

> Within a few weeks after the death of the two malefactors, to whose horrible crimes were awarded equally horrible punishments, the forest that had been the scene of these bloody deeds was reported, and believed to be visited at night, by beings of unearthly make, whose groans and death struggles were heard in the darkest recesses of the woods, amidst the flapping of the wings of vultures, the fluttering of carrion crows, and the dismal croaking of ravens. In the midst of this nocturnal din, the noise caused by the tearing of the flesh from the bones was heard, and the panting breath of the agonized sufferer, quivering under the beaks of his tormentors, as they consumed his vitals, floated audibly upon the evening breeze.
>
> The murdered lady was also seen walking by moonlight, near the spot where she had been dragged from her horse, wrapped in a blood-stained mantle, overhung with gory and dishevelled locks.
>
> The little island in the swamp was said to present spectacles too horrible for human eyes to look upon, and sounds were heard to issue from it which no human ear could bear. Terrific and ghostly fires were seen to burst up at midnight, amongst the evergreens that

[27] Interview, Feb. 28, 1964.
[28] Ibid.

clad this lonely spot, emitting scents too suffocating and sickly to be endured; while demoniac yells, shouts of despair, and groans of agony mingled their echos in the solitude of the woods.[29]

He further stated that as long as he lived in this area, no Black person ever traveled this road alone after dark.

Masquerading as Ghosts

Some masters undoubtedly did no more than circulate rumors to frighten their slaves, but a hard core of slave resistance to accepting only verbal statements prompted other masters to initiate a second step in this control process—masquerading as ghosts. A few critically minded slaves required evidence of the kind of "scary things" that were supposed to come out at night.[30] Grace Lyles spoke of efforts her grandfather made to obtain verification:

My grandfather said they'd peep out through the cracks to see if they would see what they told them they would see if they'd come out. . . . They didn't have no windows, he said. They just had a door to go in, and he said they were made out of, they called them planks. And the cracks would be like that [informant indicated size], they'd say. And they would peep out through the cracks. And it would be so dark that they wouldn't see anything.[31]

Julia Henry's grandmother also peeped out at these sheeted figures from the vantage point of a house or a tree. "She said when she saw these ghosts, she would go and hide behind the tree or hide behind the house, where she used to be peeping at the ghosts, you know."[32]

---

[29] *Slavery in the United States; A Narrative of the Life and Adventures of Charles Ball, a Black Man, Who Lived Forty Years in Maryland, South Carolina and Georgia as a Slave* (Lewiston, Pa., 1836), 224–25.

[30] Deliberate staging of events for the purposes of control has been historically recorded. Cromwell is known to have crushed Irish resistance in 1649 by ordering massacres in two towns in which some 4,000 people were slain. Rumors of atrocities and mass murder were enough to crush any remaining Irish resistance. Shibutani, 198.

[31] Interview, April 7, 1964.

[32] Interview, March 3, 1964.

To the white planters, those who listened to fabricated narratives of the supernatural were of three types: Blacks who believed the tales unequivocally; those who were uncertain; and those who simply did not believe. For the benefit of the last two groups, verbal statements were reinforced by the sight of men disguised as ghosts. It was the touch of realism that the fabrication needed:

> Back in those days they had little log cabins built around in a circle, around for the slaves. And the log cabins, they dabbed between two logs, they dabbed it with some mortar. And of course when that fall out, you could look out and see. But every, most every night along about eight or nine o'clock, this overseer would get on his white horse and put a sheet over him, and put tin cans to a rope and drag it around. And they told all the slaves, "Now if you poke your head out doors after a certain time, monster of a ghost will get you." They peeped through and see that and never go out. They didn't have to have any guards.[33]

The disguise affected for this purpose was simple. Since the orthodox apparition of a ghost was that of a tall, white figure, a sheet was all that was needed to transform the master or overseer into a "haunt." There is no indication in the folk record of more elaborate costuming attempted at this point, but the sheet itself caught the folk imagination and is frequently referred to in Black oral tradition. In fact, according to Henry Lewis Brown, the sheet was one means of identifying a ghost: "And they had all the time talked that when the ghost come you see them in a white sheet."[34] White-sheeted figures were also a central part of the ghost stories told Francis White Chisholm by her grandfather: "And he would tell us about he would walk in the middle of the road, see, dark night, and he figured he saw something with a white sheet over him. Those kind of stories. That's the kind he would tell. And, see, it would frighten us to death."[35]

Stage "props" were generally limited at this time to the use of tin cans used as noisemakers,[36] stilts to give the appearance of

[33] Informant William H. Henderson, March 3, 1964.
[34] Interview, April 11, 1964.
[35] Interview, Dec. 16, 1964.
[36] Informant William H. Henderson, March 3, 1964.

ghosts walking up off the ground,[37] and a headless disguise. Concerning simulated headlessness, William Henderson stated: "They used to formulate that kind, go 'round that kind of a way [headless] to frighten the people. . . . But the slaves believed that it was ghosts. But they got up that program to hold them down."[38] Headless disguises continued in popularity even after the Civil War and were later adopted with embellishments by the Ku Klux Klan.

According to Black oral tradition, masters often resorted to masquerading as ghosts in order to solve special problems that arose, in addition to generally trying to discourage night travel. Since planters feared the assembly of slaves for any reason, even religious meetings were often broken up by "ghost visits." Jessie Brown recalled, "They would, according to some of the tales of my grandfather, and my great-grandfather whom I remembered vaguely, was that they would at times come in the settlements where the Negroes were even at their church, in order to keep them afraid of ghosts."[39]

Another continually annoying problem was the theft of small articles, especially food stores, from the plantation. Even brutal punishments, often far exceeding the magnitude of the crime, failed to have much of an effect in halting the thievery. One owner was having difficulty trying to save his watermelon patch from thieves. He adopted a quota system, which failed to work, whereby so many watermelons were given to the slaves. Finally, as a kind of last resort, "Every once in a while he would march through the watermelon patch dressed in white in order to frighten them away."[40] In this particular incident, Jessie Brown was certain that it was the master and not the overseer doing the masquerading. "Well, they eventually found out it was the owner, because of . . . the way the story broke, one . . . they had a maid living in the house, and she saw him dress and go out one night, and that's how it got out that he was performing these acts."[41]

[37] Laura Randolph, "Uncle Si'ah and the Ghosts," *Southern Workman*, 32 (Oct. 1903), 506.
[38] Interview, March 3, 1964.
[39] Interview, April 23, 1964.
[40] *Ibid.*
[41] *Ibid.*

Interestingly enough, old mistress was also said to have patrolled slave quarters at night dressed as a ghost. Jim Goff remembered such an incident when questioned concerning his superstitious beliefs: "Wasn't scared or superstitious. One night old mistress hid in a corner of the fence to scare me. She put a sheet over her head and when I came by she jumped up to scare me. I didn't run. I just began throwing rocks and she ran out from there and didn't try to scare me again."[42] A reliable substitute for acting out a ghostly role was used by the owners of the Melrose Plantation in Louisiana. From the 1780s to 1880 this plantation was owned by free men of color who held slaves. In order to keep unruly slaves in their cabins at night, a small black coffin was placed in front of their doors.[43]

Actually impersonating the supernatural proved most popular, however, and "the chase" was the dominant device when masquerading ghosts performed their "night watch." It was believed they were accustomed to chase back home any stray Black who happened to be away from his quarters. Narratives concerning this kind of chase by sheeted masters and overseers were forerunners of the harrowing tales about similar experiences with the antebellum patrol system, the post-Civil War Ku Klux Klan, and the night doctors of the late nineteenth and early twentieth centuries. As each group succeeded the other, the pattern of the chase remained the same: a Black saw something unnatural which chased him to the point of exhaustion. Elizabeth Reed's father recalled an experience told by his parents concerning an overseer who, dressed as a ghost, gave chase to the slaves under his authority:

> They would call them the boss [overseer]. They would go down there, he said [the father repeating his parents], with something like a sheet to the pasture. And if you just want to go anyway, and you're passing by, he'd jump out and chase you, you know. And you'd think it was something, and it wouldn't be nothing but just your own boss.[44]

Mary Elizabeth Jones commented further about slaves being chased by masters and overseers:

[42] "Texas Slave Narratives," Jim Goff folder.
[43] Letter dated Aug. 13, 1970, from Robert DeBlieux, Natchitoches, La.
[44] Interview, April 3, 1964.

72

Well, they said that they used to put sheets over them, and try to frighten them you know, at night, and make them stay home, and all the things like that. And they would get out and dress different and when they'd pass by, they'd jump up, you know, and do all that kind of stuff, they say. Because if you didn't get home in time, and you, just like you stayed quarter of an hour over time, they would try to scare you, you know. Make you think that there was something after you. I heard Grandpa say that. He said he run a many a night. Say he almost run himself to death one night, running from something he thought he saw. But it could have been someone trying to scare him, you know. [45]

"They believed in ghosts which were among the night riders, things to be feared at night." [46] The fraudulent ghost, then, was the first in a gradually developed system of night-riding creatures, the fear of which was fostered by whites for the purpose of slave control.

Influence of Psychological Control on Black Narrative Tradition

In Black oral tradition the borderline between human beings and ghosts is often very thin. Black folklore is frequently characterized by vacillations between the natural and the supernatural, and the distinction becomes even more blurred when natural men disguise themselves as supernatural agents. One body of tradition concerns revenants who were not pictured as eerie shadowy forms —silent, serious specters—but as ghosts who enjoyed playing pranks and who displayed strikingly human behavior as they chased, spied on, and talked to their intended prey. One informant stated that ghosts "would come up to your house at night and peep in your windows, or peep in your doors, and such as that." [47] Another one observed: "And [grandmother] said sometimes they would talk to you, them ghosties." [48] The very human nature of the

45 Interview, March 30, 1964.
46 Informant James Daniel Tymes, March 25, 1964.
47 Informant Ella Davenport, April 2, 1964.
48 Informant Lucille Murdock, April 11, 1964.

ghosts' actions lends some credence to the Black folk assertion that these were, after all, real men. The following narrative illustrates this type of "human haunt." Though several different ghostly encounters are described, the comic tone is maintained throughout. The revenants described by Richard Johnson sing in the graveyard; use racial terms of derision, such as "nigger"; demand the use of proper social forms when being addressed (Johnson refers to each of them as "Mr. Ghost"); and above all, engage him in amicable conversation:

> I has seen plenty of ghos's. Dey had eyes like balls of fire, and dey chased me. I shore did run. One time one jump behind me on my horse, and put his hands on me, and dey wuz cold. I says, "Mr. Ghos', what you after me for? I ain't never done nothin' to you." He says, "I want to ride." And so we rid, and finally dat ghos' jes' went. One time I wuz up in de top of a house, and it wuz dark, and I started down de stairs, and de ghos's got after me. I heard 'em, and I shore did run away from dere. One time I wuz passin' a graveyard, and some ghos's wuz in dere singin'. I started runnin', and one of 'em run after me, and he ketched up wid me, and he says, "Where you think you are goin', nigger?" An' I says, "Don' know, Mr. Ghos'. I is jes' goin' 'way from here fas' as I can." He says, "Nex' time you come 'round we'll run a race." I says, "Yes, sir," but I thought dey ain't goin' to be no nex' time. Lots of people don't think dere is any ghos's, but I know dere is 'cause I seen 'em. Dey's lots of 'em. Dey wuzn't people fixed up to look like ghos's. Dey wuz real ghos's cause no people would look like dey did. De ghos's look white as cotton. Dere wuzn't none look black like niggers.[49]

The Black's tendency to laugh off fears is particularly evident in these stories of "spirit visitants, generally taking the form of reflections upon white men, the picturization of abject terror of meeting ghosts, or the skill of the Negro in avoiding them."[50]

Humor, then, is the dominant tone of this type of narrative. Supernatural legends are mixed with certain elements of the tall tale

[49] WPA Files, "Slave Narratives" (Richard Johnson, Waco, Tex.). (J–K. Texas. Supplementary Slave Interviews.)
[50] Newbell Niles Puckett, *Folk Beliefs of the Southern Negro* (Chapel Hill, 1926), 131.

because the ingenious escapes and hair-raising experiences are "told for true." This is often the Black folk's way of laughing at themselves and at the white man. If the ghosts who chased Black folk were not real, neither were the stylized, highly exaggerated narratives about the Black's experiences with fraudulent "haunts" altogether true. But truth and fiction, legend and folktale do intertwine in a type of narrative still current in Black oral tradition.

The Black is never caught (at least by the ghosts, and seldom by the patterollers—or any other night rider, for that matter—according to his account of these experiences), but the story of his chase leaves the listener with the impression that escape was by a hair's breadth. He bumbles and fumbles in flight, mostly out of the sheer fright associated with a supernatural encounter, but he always manages to escape. The narrator is clearly the defenseless underdog who, faced with overwhelming odds (a supernatural competitor), wins the race. But the listening audience is forced never to forget that he has just barely won. This is the essential realism on which these stories are based.

The effectiveness of these tales stems in part from the use of colorful folk expressions that are direct, vivid, and forceful. They abound in ludicrous imagery and similes based on humorous, unlikely comparisons, achieving their comic effect through the use of exaggeration of detail, but exaggeration within the bounds of realistic possibilities.[51] Two elements are especially exaggerated: the degree of fright at the initial encounter of a supernatural agent (or night rider) and the swiftness of the victim's flight.

The kind of fear the Black describes in his encounter with supernatural or other night riders is overwhelming terror. He is so thoroughly frightened that it is humorous. The following description is an example: "De very last time I went to a dance, somepin got atter me and skeered me so my hair riz up 'til I couldn't git my hat on my haid, and dat cyored [cured] me of gwine to dances. I ain't never been to no more sich."[52] Another Black, describing a

[51] Mody C. Boatright, *Folk Laughter on the American Frontier* (New York, 1942), 97–98.

[52] WPA Files, "Slave Narratives" (Georgia Baker, Athens, Ga., Aug. 4, 1938).

75

supernatural encounter, said, "an' all de time I helt my bref so hard an' tight, I couldn't see which way I wuz goin' much less no ha'nt!"[53]

Thus the teller is busy convincing the listener of the extreme "humanness" of his reactions under especially trying circumstances. He pretends no cool self-possession or clear-headed actions—in fact, the reverse. One is carefully led to believe that the narrator was almost paralyzed with fear. Only at the end of the breathless narration does the listener realize that he has been "took" with a description of an escape that reaches herculean proportions under impossible circumstances. Samuel Chappell's narrative at the end of this chapter is a classic example.

Another highly exaggerated element in this type of tale is the description of the speed of flight. Obvious embroidery and high coloring come into full play here. Solomon Jackson, for example, said, "Sometimes I got so scairt an' run so fas' hit look lack my shadder wuz go'ner overtake me. Hit de Gawd's trufe! Dem ha'nts kep' right up wid me, no matter how fas' I run."[54]

Often the Black is pitted against an animal with a known reputation for speed, such as a dog. But the animal always fails to run faster than the man. In an unusual daylight encounter an ex-slave recalled:

> One mornin' my uncle was passin' a church an' a ghost appear' on the porch. My uncle had a dog wud 'im. He start to run an' the dog start to run too, an' down the road dey went. He didn't hab on anything but his shirt an' he say he run so fas' 'till the wind had his shirt-tail stiff as a board. He couldn' outrun the dog, nor could the dog outrun 'im.[55]

Sometimes comic effect in the description of the escape is achieved through understatement. When Solomon Jackson in the following narrative finally feels the ghost tap him on the shoulder, full comic impact is achieved through his simple statement, "I wuz *gwine home!*":

[53] *Ibid.* (Solomon Jackson, Evergreen, Ala.). (Alabama: Slave Narratives, Duplicates 2.)
[54] *Ibid.*
[55] *Ibid.* (Thomas Goodwater, Charleston, S. C.).

Whenever I got back to de house an' saw dat de ha'nts had done away wid my water, I know'd hit wuz all to do over again. Lawd! Lawd! Goin' back in dem woods wid dem ha'nts took all de grace of Gawd, an' sump'n besides. I kep' my han' on my rabbit foot whut had done hopped over Marse Jim Knight's grave, an' I made sho my hog's toof wuz fastened good aroun' my neck, 'cause ha'nts ain't got no time fer no hog's toof. On de string wid de hog's toof, I had my mole's foot tied hard an' fas'! Dat kep' de snakes offen me, an' all de time I helt my bref so hard an' tight, I couldn't see which a way I wuz goin' much less no ha'nt! An' dat way I made out pretty tolerable, till somethin' frum behind would sorter tap, tap, on my shoulder, an' breathe hot like down de back of my neck— then I wuz *gwine home*! Yes ma'am! De Good Book says, "Solomon in all er his glory wa'nt 'rayed lack one er dese here!" But I wants ter tell yer dat when hit come ter gittin' home fas'—dis here Solomon sho wuz 'rayed![56]

The following folktale combines all of the elements discussed in this section: whites masquerading as ghosts; the chase, with the master instead of the slave running; and the prevailing tone of humor that characterizes this type of narrative. This tale was told to the writer as a slavery ghost story, but it is frankly comic in its tone. Attitudes toward the white man implied in other narratives are clearly revealed here. He is regarded by the Black folk as being very superstitious, keenly afraid of the supernatural, and unintelligent enough to be easily duped (by even an imitating monkey). The would-be trickster is himself tricked, and the lowly Black again emerges as the dominant, superior figure.

Now, about the slavery stories. One is about this man and the monkey. And he had these children that he would let go bring in the cows every afternoon. And he would always want them to be back before it gets dark. But they wouldn't never get back until after dark. They would play and play. And on the way back home they had to come pass this church and this cemetery. And so he decided that if something would frighten them enough, maybe they would hurry back home afterwards because they had to come by the cemetery. So, he decided to make himself a ghost. He gets him

[56] *Ibid.* (Solomon Jackson, Evergreen, Ala.). (Alabama: Slave Narratives, Duplicates 2.)

a big bed sheet, and he makes this hole, and wraps himself up in it, and he goes and sits up in the cemetery.

And his little monkey always like to do everything that he saw him do. So he, the monkey, gets the pillow slip and he puts it over his head, and he goes up in the cemetery, and he sits there too, waiting for the children to come by. And so, when the children got near the cemetery, the man stands up and holds up his arms and says "wooo wooo," and the children stopped. And the monkey, he stood up and he held up, too. He was standing behind the man, to the side. So the children stopped. They was, some of them, the smaller ones was afraid cause "Oh, there's a ghost! There's a ghost out there. Now how are we going to get home?" And another one say, "Yes, but look. There's a little ghost behind the big one." And so when the man looked back and saw this little ghost, he knows what he was, but he didn't know what that was, and so he left. The ghost chased away . . . the little ghost chased the big ghost away. And then the children went happily home. But that was one of the ghost stories.[57]

Black folk believed there was a multitude of ghosts in the period before and immediately following the Civil War. The verbal expression of this phenomenon depended on the imagination of the teller, but the central point was always present—the profusion of ghosts. "Back in them days it was ha'nty."[58] "They said there was ghosties along then, and so much so until I used to believe it."[59]

---

[57] Informant Marie Bing, March 6, 1964. See also Puckett, 31, for a similar text. In some versions a second episode is included in which the monkey is tricked into committing suicide by imitating his owner (or in some cases a slave) in the act of shaving. See Arthur Fauset, "Negro Folk Tales From the South," *Journal of American Folklore*, 40 (July–Sept. 1927), 269–70.

Also see WPA files, "Slave Narratives," Nap McQueen, Beaumont, Tex. (Texas Duplicates 2), and Botkin, 23. Richard M. Dorson in his *Negro Folktales in Michigan* (Cambridge, Mass., 1956), 187–88, has recorded an interesting version of this tale which contains a third episode about the monkey taking a train ride. It is apparently the only published text of this particular version.

This folktale has had wide circulation. Newbell Puckett reports versions recorded in Alabama, North Carolina, and Florida. Ernest W. Baugham lists 17 versions in *Type and Motif Index of the Folktales of England and North America* (Bloomington, Ind., 1966). The author collected one text in Washington, D. C. Other texts can be found in the WPA "Slave Narratives" collection and the Indiana University Folklore Archives.

[58] Informant Rufer Smith, Jan. 3, 1964.

[59] Informant Lillian Bradley, Feb. 11, 1964.

"Long about den, too, seem lack ha'nts an' spirits was ridin' ever'-thing! Dey raided mostly 'round de grabeyard."[60] "They was more ghosts and ha'nts them days than now. It look like when I's comin' up they was common as pig tracks."[61] These comments were from the unsophisticated who noted and observed a strange phenomenon but who failed to adopt a critical attitude toward it. Other Blacks explain the great number of strange supernatural phenomena during this period on the basis of fraud. They believed that the ranks of "regular" ghosts were swelled with masters and overseers (and later the patterollers and the Ku Klux Klansmen), who attempted to reinforce belief in the supernatural by disguising themselves as ghosts.

There is definitely a consensus of opinion among Blacks that whites dressed as ghosts. Texts of both the WPA Slave Narratives Collection, made in 1937, and the writer's own interviewing project, conducted in 1964 and 1972, agree completely on this point. An ex-slave told a Federal Writers Project worker: "Ha! ha! dey jest talked 'bout ghosts till I could hardly sleep at nite, but the biggest thing in ghosts is somebody 'guised up tryin' to skeer you. Ain't no sich thing as ghosts."[62] Another former slave reported, "Dey's ghost dere—we seed 'em. Dey's w'ite people wid a sheet on 'em to scare de slaves offen de plantation."[63] Julia Henry stated, "It was peoples made to pretend like they was ghosts. But they wasn't regular ghosts sure 'nough."[64]

The use of ghost stories and supernatural disguises by masters and overseers helped restrain the nocturnal ramblings of their slaves between visits of the county patrols. Fear on the part of the Blacks was the key emotion produced, but it was not so much fear of unknown ghosts as it was of known whites. For the whites had achieved their goal—indeed, the goal of all such manipulators—

[60] WPA files, "Slave Narratives" (Aunt Cheney Cross, Evergreen, Ala.). (Alabama Slave Narratives, Duplicates I.)
[61] *Ibid.* (Jordan Smith, Marshall, Tex.). (Texas Duplicates 2.)
[62] *Ibid.* (Jane Lassiter, Raleigh, N. C.). (J–O. North Carolina: Slave Narratives. Duplicates.)
[63] *Ibid.* (William Watkins, Beaumont, Tex.). (T–Y. Texas: Slave Interviews. Duplicates.)
[64] Interview, March 3, 1964.

in creating a climate of terror in which rumors of the omniscience and vengefulness of those in authority can flourish.[65] Reacting more to this condition than to any innate superstitious fears, the Blacks played the game according to the rules of the supernatural phenomena designed to control them.

ADDITIONAL NARRATIVE

Ghost Chases Uncle Daniel Home

My Uncle was born, my mother's brother, named Daniel Wheeler. And he tells a story about a ghost and himself. Uncle Daniel said that he was terrible to run around at night. . . . He said the other hands said to him, said, "You are always gone somewhere at night." Said, "Something is going to scare you to death some of these nights." Uncle Daniel said, "Hey boy, why don't you go on about your business?"

He didn't believe in such things like that. So he went on. And said it wasn't long before he was coming in one night, here at home, to get on the plantation before the hands got up, and on the road a path led up the side of a big road, and a body of woods was on one side. And said he walked up where a little pig was grunting, rooting in the leaves, about 3 o'clock in the morning.

Said he said, "What is this pig doing out here this time of the morning?" Said when he said that the pig turned from a pig to a calf. Said he said to it—now, I would sit and listen at Uncle Daniel tell this tale. Said the pig changed from a pig to a calf and he said he said to it, said he wasn't afraid, not then. Said, "What is this? I rekon this is something or other what the boys were talking about." Said he said to it—now I don't know whether there was any truth to this. I'm not responsible for . . . They say, I've always heard it being said by older people that if you say to a spirit, "What in the name of the Lord and Christ and the Holy Ghost do you want?" Say if you use that word Holy Ghost, you are going to get scared to death.

Now whether that's true or not, I don't know. But Uncle Daniel said he stood right over that calf like and looked down on him, when he was a pig. Said, "What are you doing out here this time of night?" "What in the name of the Father, the Holy Ghost and the Son do you want?" He said that thing tore out, down through the woods. Said when it took to stomp, like a stomp you ever heard in your life . . . and disappeared. He said, "Well." So he started for home. He done got scared now. He's been brave all of the time. . . . Said he could feel like there was something behind him, but he wouldn't look back.

So he got to the plantation fence and he went to crawl up on the fence, and just as he went to throw one leg over and get down on the inside of the fence, said something like a hand started at the back of his neck. Started at the back of his neck on down to his bottom—scraped down. . . . He didn't have time to ask any questions. He'd been game before. Said he started out running. He got to the other side of the fence that led up to the lot. Said he didn't take time to crawl up

---

[65] Shibutani, 198.

on the fence. Men used to do what they called wheel barrel, you know. You put your hand up, and then swing your body around. He didn't have time to crawl up on the fence. He put his hand up to wheel barrel. Said that thing, said whatever it was, that thing scrapped him down. Said he commenced to hollering then. Said, "Open the door."

Uncle Daniel sat in our house in Lawrence County and declared it was the truth. Said when he got to the house and he went to make for the door, said that thing told him, "Good night, Daniel." Said he didn't take time to knock on the door. Said he just broadside hit that door and landed in the middle of the floor. Lord, and you couldn't get that old man, you couldn't get him to go nowhere at night unless he had company. Uncle Daniel said he had been hard to believe, but nobody didn't have to tell him after that.

—Informant SAMUEL CHAPPELL, March 7, 1964. [This text was related as the slavery experience of Samuel Chappell's uncle, who was a houseboy on a plantation.]

3

THE PATROL SYSTEM

*My father was in slavery about six or seven
years just as a lad. His father was a white man
whose mother was half Negro and half Indian.
His father was vulgarly or typically referred
to as a patroller, which was like a foreman
during the slave days, to keep the slaves under
control—discipline them. I would say that I
don't suppose I would be very proud of him
neither because he's a white man, and certainly I wouldn't be proud because he's a
patroller.* —SAMUEL FRANCES COPPAGE

Conditions Making a Patrol Necessary

MASTERS AND OVERSEERS who disguised themselves as ghosts were
the first group of night riders in Black oral tradition; ante-bellum
patrollers were the second. Several historians have already suggested that the patrol system was based on the Black's fear of
ghosts. Indeed, Ivan McDougle asserts that "such an institution
was based on good Negro psychology, for his fear of the spirits of
night was well known."[1] However, the historical record as it now
stands fails to explain how the patrol system was related to the
control of slaves through their fear of the supernatural.

An indoctrinated fear of the supernatural was a device used by
the planters to keep slaves on their owner's plantation at night,
and as far as possible behind the locked doors of their assigned

[1] *Slavery in Kentucky, 1792–1865* (Lancaster, Pa., 1918), 41; also J. Winston
Coleman, *Slavery Times in Kentucky* (Chapel Hill, 1940), 96.

82

quarters. Nocturnal visiting, even between cabins, was discouraged because of the opportunity it afforded for slaves to concoct mischief, especially insurrections. This effort, important as it was, represents only one aspect in a complex problem of slave control. The free movement of slaves while outside the boundary of the master's estate, and hence beyond the range of plantation authority and control, was another potentially dangerous problem.

A certain amount of authorized but unchaperoned travel from one place to another was necessary for the smooth operation of the plantation. In the days before modern communications, many errands were assigned to individual slaves which took them to other plantations or to nearby towns. In addition, the services of skilled slaves, such as carpenters, bricklayers, and nurses, were often hired out to other slave owners, making it necessary for these slaves to be able to travel freely to their places of employment.

In addition to legitimate business reasons for unsupervised travel, slaves undertook private errands away from home, often without permission. Sometimes this illegal travel involved attending parties and dances on adjoining plantations, or unauthorized religious meetings in the brush harbor,[2] or simply visiting friends or the slave's spouse owned by a neighboring planter. Legitimate business pursuits were one thing, but unauthorized trips created a situation fraught with dangerous possibilities for the masters. Especially feared were the gatherings of slaves in large numbers after dark. Such group meetings afforded an opportunity for slaves to discuss their mutual grievances and thus further the general dissatisfaction with their lot. Even more important, these meetings exposed slaves to the influence of troublemakers who might encourage escape at best, or insurrection at worst.

Other practical considerations led to the demand for more stringent legislation regulating interplantation and intercountry slave movement. Unsupervised slave excursions from one plantation to another might also result in unnecessary fights and brawls

[2] Brush harbors were improvised Black churches held without either the master's knowledge or consent and were so-titled because they were held deep in the woods—hence "brush"—or they were constructed of a few tree limbs and branches.

among slaves, thus endangering the life and limb of valuable property. Further, the efficiency of the slave would be greatly reduced because of the loss of sleep and energy from his aimless carousing.[3] Finally, as one author observed, the unhampered movement of slaves "afforded opportunity for stealing, the colored person's inherent weakness."[4]

Consequently, both state and local governments passed laws to control the slave when off the plantation. To insure the effectiveness of these laws, most Southern states established police patrols detailed to enforce the slave code in the cities and off the plantation ground in rural sections.[5] These patrols were really a part of the police system of the state. Their origins go back to the pre-Revolutionary period. In South Carolina, for example, as early as 1636, an act was passed which allowed any person to "apprehend, properly chastise, and send home" any slave found outside his master's plantation. In 1690, a penalty of forty shillings was imposed on any person who failed to carry out the above order. An act passed in 1704 allowed setting up a military force of about ten men in each district to patrol the streets in times of emergencies. By 1721, the patrol system in the state was meshed with the militia, and this would remain the situation until 1860. Similar actions were taken by North Carolina in 1741 and by Tennessee as early as 1753. The patrol system was thus a fundamental part of the evolving systems of control designed to institutionalize effective control of the Blacks socially and economically.[6]

[3] Howell M. Henry, *The Police Control of the Slave in South Carolina* (Emory, Va., 1914), 28.
[4] *Ibid.*, 30. In connection with slave thefts, Clement Richardson in "Some Slave Superstitions," *Southern Workman*, (April 1912), 246–48, uncovered an interesting superstition which probably had its origin during this period. It was believed by the slaves that if a turkey buzzard lighted on your chimney or housetop it was a sign that the occupant was a thief, and that stolen goods were at that moment being concealed. Richardson asserts that this belief was probably based on the fact that it was very difficult for slaves to steal any articles except food, under the watchful eye of the overseer or master. Thus, when taken by surprise, slaves would throw half-eaten pig or lamb or chicken into the loft, where it would remain for an indefinite length of time. In warm weather the meat quickly spoiled, and its odor attracted the attention of turkey buzzards.
[5] *The Negro in Virginia* (Compiled by Workers of the Writers Program of the WPA in Virginia), 140.
[6] John Hope Franklin, *From Slavery to Freedom* (New York, 1967), 188–89,

Policy concerning the composition of the patrols differed from state to state. In those Louisiana counties where the slaves outnumbered the whites, community patrols, made up of volunteers, were formed.[7] In Tennessee, patrol service was obligatory for all citizens.[8] The patrols in Mississippi were composed of all slave owners and all other persons subject to militia duty below the rank of captain.[9] The general pattern in most of the Southern states, however, was that membership in the patrols was mandatory for males of a certain age group. In spite of state statutes which made service in the patrols obligatory and stiff legal penalties which were imposed for noncompliance with the law (in Tennessee five dollars had to be paid for each refusal to serve),[10] available records indicate that efforts to evade patrol service were common.

Except in those communities where patrolling was considered a civic duty, the patterollers were compensated for their service either directly by the slaveholders, who paid a share proportionate to the number of slaves they owned,[11] or from the county treasury, with funds obtained from a special tax levied on taxable slaves for this purpose. In the latter case, patrollers were often paid one dollar per day or night for their service. Masters or mistresses who served received nothing.[12]

The varying number of men who constituted the county patrols

---

describes the evolution of the system in rather general terms. The system as it developed in South Carolina is well documented in Howell M. Henry, *The Police Control of the Slave in South Carolina* (Emory, Va., 1914), 28–52. For the situation in Tennesee, see Caleb Perry Patterson, *The Negro in Tennessee, 1790–1865* (Austin, Tex., 1922; rpt. Westport, Conn., 1968), 38–41.

[7] Vernie Alton Moody, *Slavery on Louisiana Sugar Plantations* (rpt. from the *Louisiana Historical Quarterly*, April 1924), 24.

[8] Caleb Perry Patterson, *The Negro in Tennessee, 1790–1865* (Univ. of Texas *Bulletin* No. 2205, Feb. 1, 1922), 39.

[9] Sydnor, 78.

[10] Patterson, 39.

[11] Joe Gray Taylor, *Negro Slavery in Louisiana* (Baton Rouge, Louisiana Historical Association, 1963), 204.

[12] Patterson, 39.

had fairly extensive powers and duties. They were authorized to search all places suspected of harboring unlawful slave assemblies and to seize any slaves found away from their owners' plantations without written permission—a pass—from the master or overseer. This "pass and repass" order permitted the slave to be away for a specified time period.[13] The power to enforce passes was designed to curb all unnecessary slave rambling and prowling. Further, patrols were required to search the Black quarters at regular intervals (usually once a month) for guns or other weapons which, if found, were turned over to the county court or returned to the offending slave's owner.[14] Finally, patrols were empowered to enter any house which a slave had been seen to enter. Any fowls or provisions found on the person of a slave caught away from home without written permission might be taken for the patrolman's own use.[15]

Three types of Black offenders could be apprehended by these patrols:

> If the Negro were free but in an illegal assembly, he should be delivered to a justice of the peace. If he were a runaway slave, the same procedure was followed, and the patrol received six dollars. Finally, if the slave were away from home and without a pass, but was apparently not a runaway, the law required the patrol to administer fifteen lashes. A distinction was thus made between the slave caught visiting on the next plantation without a pass and the bonafide runaway.[16]

Techniques of Surveillance

Evoking fear in the slaves was the object of the patterollers and the element of surprise their best ally. Only Black oral tradition records the details of the patrollers' methods. The slaves never knew when or where their gatherings would be disrupted by the sudden arrival of the patrollers, and this anxiety kept them fearful.

[13] Henry, 29.
[14] Patterson, 39.
[15] Henry, 33.
[16] Sydnor, 79.

One ex-slave described slave reaction to such an unexpected arrival (note the use of the term night rider):

> Onct I slipped off wid another gal an' went to a party dout asking Old Mis'. When dem Night Riders come that night, de Niggers was a-runnin' and a-dodgin' and a-jumpin' out-a winders lak dey was scairt to death. I runs too, me an' dat other gal. I fell down an' tore my dress, but I warnt studyin' dat dress. I knows dat dem white folks had dat strap an' I's gettin' 'way fas' as I could.[17]

A certain type of dress was affected by patrollers in some sections in order to be able to take slaves unaware. Ex-slaves reported that some patterollers wore black caps and put black rags over their faces.[18] A variation of this outfit was the wearing of white boots, black shirts, broad-brimmed white hats, and black breeches.[19] In the latter version only the hat and boots were visible at night, which suggested an apparition. Most patrollers used horses, preferring dark-colored ones because they were less visible from a distance. As one writer observed, "To be pursued by such an individual mounted on a black horse at a late hour of a dark night would create a sense of fear in the heart of the best of us."[20]

With the intent to play on what J. Winston Coleman termed the slaves' "superstitious fear of the 'sperits' of the night,"[21] the patrollers sometimes wore white robes, or sheets, and masks. One Black commented that "De white folks were the 'Paddle-Rollers' and had masks on dere faces. They looked like niggers wid de devil in dere eyes."[22] When this type of costume was worn, the technique of frightening the slaves was the same as that used by masters and overseers. The patteroller would hide in a strategic spot and suddenly spring out upon some slave passing by: "Sometimes they would disguise themselves, you know, or get maybe in a pasture or in a bend of a road, you know. And when they would see colored

---

[17] WPA Files, "Slave Narratives" (Jane Sutton, Gulfport, Miss.).
[18] Botkin, 87.
[19] Indiana Univ. Folklore Archives. Indiana Negro Material Folder.
[20] *Ibid.*
[21] Coleman, 96.
[22] WPA Files, "Slave Narratives" (Marshall Butler, Dist. No. 1, May 8, 1937).

people coming along, they would be frightened. I think that must have been these patrollers. . . ." [23]

Several stage props were introduced by some patrollers to enable them to achieve their supernatural disguises. One of these devices was a rotating false head, which gave the appearance of all-around vision. An ex-slave described it:

> What wuz de Patty Rollers? Well dey wuz tall an most usually wore white robes, sometimes dar head would jes turn roun and roun an be lookin at you fust from de front and den frum his back. Dey wuz somethin like de ghosts but dey sometimes had paddles an effen dey caught you den you had a paddlin. Dey mostly wuz after de niggers dat would run off to de udder plantashuns. [24]

Another stage prop introduced by patrollers was a collapsible rubber bag concealed under their costume. When gallons of water, demanded from frightened Blacks by a so-called "thirsty ha'nt" were secretly poured into it, the bag inflated with results described by Leonard Franklin:

> A paterole come in one night before freedom and asked for a drink of water. He said he was thirsty. He had a rubber thing on and drank two or three buckets of water. His rubber bag swelled up and made his head or the thing that looked like his head under the hood grow taller. Instead of gettin' 'fraid, mother threw a shovelful of hot ashes on him and I'll tell you he lit out from there and never did come back no more. [25]

Patrol disguises depended very much upon the whim of individual patrollers. While disguises were frequently worn and commonly reported by former slaves in their oral testimonies, costuming did not become a standard practice until the Ku Klux Klan was organized in 1865. In the earlier patrol days, frightening Blacks by dressing in ghostly garb was an effective and important technique of control, but there was always an element of fun attached to the practice, as reflected in the following text:

[23] Informant Mary Howard Neeley, Feb. 8, 1964.
[24] WPA Files, "Slave Narratives" (Henry Freeman, Falls St., Mart, Tex.). (F–G. Texas: Supplementary Slave Interviews.)
[25] *Ibid.* (Leonard Franklin, Little Rock, Ark.). (E–G. Arkansas: Slave Interviews, Duplicates.)

And 'bout de time Marse Ike slip up on a heap of niggers at a frolic 'twixt Sumterville and Livingston and put a end to de frolic. De niggers having a big dance, and Marse Ike and de patterollers having a big run, said dey wanted to have some fun, and dey did. Said he eased up on 'em wid a white sheet 'round him and a big bresh in he hand, and somehow or 'nother, dey didn't see him tell he spoke. Den he holler "By God, I'm bird-blinding," and he say dem niggers tore down dem dirt chimleys and run through dat house. He say he ain't never heerd sich a fuss in a corn field in his born days. What he mean 'bout bird-blindin'? When you goes in de cane-brake is so thick, you takes a light to shine de bird's eyes and blind 'em, den you kin ketch 'em. Dat what he call bird-blindin'. Yassum, Marse Ike in dat too. He couldn't stand for 'em to have no fun 'thout he in it.[26]

Fun was not intended, however, as the whites enforced the slaves' fear of the patroller as a kind of night-riding "bogeyman." As one ex-slave commented, "Our Master use tuh tell us if we left de house de patarollers would catch us."[27] The dread of meeting a patrol group while on a nocturnal escapade was quite genuine. Some slaves feared the patrol even more than the Klan, whose techniques were far more brutal. "I don't think the Ku Klux ever got after any us but I seen em, I recken. I don't know but mighty little. The paddyrollers is what I dreaded. Sometimes the overseer was a paddyroller."[28] Another Black observed, "Us wuz mo' skeered er patter-rollers den any thing else."[29]

Evolution of the Patrol System in Washington, D.C.

The type of patrol system established in Washington was fairly typical of most slave-holding cities of the ante-bellum South. Police constables were responsible for controlling the movements of free Blacks and slaves as a part of their over-all policing duties. For the

[26] *Ibid.* (Josh Horn, Livingston, Ala.).
[27] *Ibid.* (Charity Morris, Camden, Ark.).
[28] *Ibid.* (Ambus Gray, R.F.D. 1, Biscoe, Ark.). (E–G. Arkansas: Slave Interviews, Duplicates.)
[29] *Ibid.* (Lucy McCullough, Athens, Ga., May 8, 1937).

purpose of policing and other public services, Washington was divided into wards, one constable being appointed yearly from each ward. There were originally four wards, but in 1820 two more were added.[30] It was the duty of these appointed constables to enforce District curfew laws and regulations against slave and free-Black assembly. The Ordinance of 1836 declared illegal all assemblages of free Blacks, mulattoes, or slaves after ten o'clock at night.[31]

All places of suspected slave assembly were to be visited once a month by these constables, and any slave apprehended without a pass from his master or overseer was to be whipped on his bare back, not exceeding thirty-nine lashes. All Blacks and slaves belonging to the owners of the place where the assembly took place, if required, were directed to aid and assist the constables in carrying out the punishment or be liable for the same punishment themselves.[32] If the slave being chastised struck back at the officer (or any other white person, for that matter) his ear was to be cropped upon order of a justice of the peace. It is said that the latter provision of this law was never enforced in Washington, but the law existed and was probably used to terrorize the slave population.[33]

Apparently the laws pertaining to the assembly of Blacks, free and slave, were enforced. Frederick Law Olmsted during his Washington sojourn commented about the arrest of twenty-four "genteel colored men" who were assembled in a private home for apparent "benevolent reasons": upon apprehension, one, a slave, was ordered to be flogged, four free Blacks were sent to the workhouse, and the remainder, on paying court costs and fines amounting to $111.00, were permitted to leave.[34]

To supplement the meager number of police constables pro-

---

[30] Constance McLaughlin Green, *Washington Village and Capital, 1800–1878* (2 vols., Princeton, 1962), I, 91.

[31] *Ordinances of the Corporation of Washington*, Washington, D. C., Oct. 29, 1836, sect. 5.

[32] *Ibid.*

[33] Walter C. Clephane, "The Local Aspects of Slavery in the District of Columbia," *Records of the Columbia Historical Society*, 3 (1900), 224–56.

[34] *A Journey in the Seaboard Slave States* (New York, 1859), 14.

vided for by city ordinances, the mayor was authorized to call up volunteer patrols in times of local crisis. This power was exercised at least twice before the Civil War because of matters pertaining to the control of the Black population. During the War of 1812, while the city was preparing itself against British attack, local citizens were especially fearful that District slaves might make use of this opportunity to stage an insurrection. To at least partially alleviate these fears, Mayor James Blake appointed a night watch to patrol the streets after dark.[35] A local citizen wrote regarding this patrol:

> In the city and Georgetown the gentlemen who by their age or other circumstances are exempted from service, have formed volunteer companies both of horse and foot, who nightly patrol the streets. The members of congress have determined to join the citizens, in case of an attack and there are many old experienced officers amongst them.[36]

In 1835 a week-long hunt for persons accused of handing out incendiary abolitionist literature to the Black people of the District[37] finally culminated in the calling up of a volunteer patrol composed of some three hundred male citizens.[38] Before it was organized, mobs of boys and unemployed white men destroyed several Black tenements and schoolhouses, broke out the windows in a Black church, heavily damaged a restaurant and bar belonging to a free Black—Beverly Snow (who was reputed to have made some insulting remarks about the wives and daughters of local mechanics)—and completely demolished "a hut, in which lived an old negro woman, the *regular* conjurer of the blacks in this city."[39]

There is some evidence that citizen patrols were sometimes composed of lawless elements. One author reported that "White

[35] Green, 58.

[36] Gaillard Hunt, *The First Forty Years of Washington Society* (New York, 1906), 90.

[37] Green, 141.

[38] *Washington Mirror*, Saturday, Aug. 15, 1835.

[39] *United States Telegraph*, Thursday, Aug. 13, 1835.

men, acting as vigilantes, patrolled the streets at night, often warmed in their mission by alcohol."[40] This view was supported by Ethan Allen Andrews, a foreign visitor, who observed "great cruelty . . . often practised by the patrols." Andrews commented:

> Often have I known a company of licentious and inebriated young men sally forth after an evening's carousal, and in the stillness of the night commence their round of domiciliary visits to the quarters of the negroes while their inmates were buried in sleep. The principal object of such visits is to terrify the slaves, and thus secure their good behavior, and especially to prevent their wandering around at night.[41]

Not only were slaves brutally beaten until the patrollers were exhausted by fatigue, but the women were sometimes raped and generally molested by the patrollers.

It may well have been dissatisfaction with the conduct of volunteer patrols that caused the city council to be petitioned in 1837 for a legally established night-patrol force. The council failed to act on the petition,[42] and it was not until a salaried police department was established in 1851 that the city's pressing problems concerning adequate policing were partially solved. At this time the daytime staff of constables was increased to seventeen and an emergency night watch of forty men was created to supplement a thirty-man federal auxiliary guard formed in 1842 primarily to protect government property.[43]

In Washington, as in most incorporated towns, a written pass was not required of slaves during the daytime; such a regulation would have interfered with legitimate industrial operations within the city. Slaves were allowed to move about freely on errands of their masters since many of them were known to the local police force.[44] After the ten o'clock curfew, however, they were required to have a pass.

[40] Johnson, 20.
[41] *Slavery and the Domestic Slave-Trade in the United States* (Boston, 1836), 101–2.
[42] Wilhelmus Bogart Bryan, *A History of the National Capital 1815–1878* (2 vols., New York, 1914), I, 148.
[43] Green, 217.
[44] Henry, 42.

General Ineffectiveness of the System

Historical material strongly suggests that the patrol system functioned poorly, particularly in the ante-bellum South. However, the few patrol records that exist do little more than indicate general planter dissatisfaction with the system without going into any great detail concerning specific grievances against it. Once more, folk sources supply the missing information that fairly well determines why the patrol system was not effective in the pre-Civil War South. What historians conjecture, the folk specify—in surprising detail.

A major reason for the over-all failure of the patrol system was that the slaves learned to circumvent successfully the techniques of surveillance employed by the patrollers and the regulations regarding the use of passes. Patrollers found it increasingly difficult to surprise slaves in secret assembly because of an elaborate communications system devised by the slaves. Such a system was used to warn each other of the imminent approach of a patrol party during illicit meetings, of patrol presence in a particular neighborhood on a scouting mission, or of the plans of patrollers to ride on a given night.

The system was based on the maintenance of a systematic watch. During meetings one person usually served as a lookout, and he might use one of several methods to determine the approach of the patterollers. Sometimes he would lie down with his ear to the ground and listen for them,[45] or he might use another device described by Mamie Ardella Robinson as "the first telephone in existence":

> I know they used to break up their meetings and that they had the first telephone that was in existence. They . . . tied a rope running it up across the mountain, or through the valley, and somebody up there to watch the road while the rest of them was down there having service. Well, when he saw someone coming and knew that they were in danger, he would just pull this. They might be a mile away but they'd know to scatter. They used a rope, across a woodland,

[45] WPA Files, "Slave Narratives" (Andy Williams, Waco, Tex.). (T–W Texas: Supplementary Slave Interviews.)

93

maybe across a field. It had to be something there to support the rope, so it had to be up off the ground in order to make a sound over where it was supposed to be. . . . And then they would have their meeting around there and that tree began to shake, they'd know that there was a danger and they would run. I've heard of that.[46]

If the patrollers took the lookout by surprise, his duty was to serve as a "raid fox" by leading the patrollers along false trails and at the same time yelling a warning to the assembled slaves.[47]

If patrollers were sighted on a routine mission, slaves sounded a general warning of their presence in the neighborhood by starting a kind of murmuring chant. Millie Williams explains: "When we's in de fields and sees de padder roller ride by, we starts murmurin' out loud, 'Patter de pat, patter de pat.' One after 'nother took it up and purty soon everybody murmurin'. We allus do dat to let everybody know de padder roller 'round."[48] The well-known folk song "Run, Nigger, Run" was also originally sung as a warning, but later it came to be a very popular piece sung and played at dances and parties.[49]

Finally, slaves working in patrollers' homes would sometimes learn which plantations were scheduled for visiting and pass the information along to house servants and field hands. The very innocent-sounding question, "Did you know dey was bugs in de wheat?," often asked by one slave of another under the nose of the master, was really an alert that the patrollers would be riding that evening.[50]

There can be little doubt that the slave's secret system of communication played an important role in undermining the patrol system. J. Winston Coleman commented on this point:

It was known for many years before the Negroes were emancipated that, notwithstanding the patrol system kept up in Kentucky,

---

[46] Interview, April 2, 1964.
[47] *The Negro in Virginia*, 144.
[48] WPA Files, "Slave Narratives" (Millie Williams, Fort Worth, Tex.). (Texas, Duplicates 2.)
[49] *Ibid.*
[50] *The Negro in Virginia*, 148.

94

slaves would secretly travel over a large scope of country at night and manage to be back in their quarters before morning. They had a grapevine telegraph or secret system of communication never known or comprehended by their masters.[51]

An ex-slave's terse observation summarizes the Black view of their efforts to outwit the patrollers: "Yes, suh, Cap'n, dy wuz a lot happen in dem times dat de mahsters didn't know nuthin' about."[52]

Slaves also found a way to circumvent the regulation regarding the use of passes. The system of requiring written permission for slaves to travel freely rested on certain assumptions. Basically, it was assumed that those in authority—the patrollers—would be able to read the information written on the passes. But in the pre-Civil War South general education was extremely limited as far as middle- and lower-class whites were concerned, and these were the people who constituted the majority of patrollers. (Indeed, free public education was a postwar development.) According to Black oral testimony, the slaves knew this and capitalized on it many times. One informant stated:

Well, that's the joke about it. That's one of the jokes about it. Now I've heard that not only was it true that the patrollers couldn't read, but most of the policemen in the little towns couldn't read, and consequently, sometimes, the Negroes would take a pass a year old and put it in his pocket and when he met a policeman or met a patroller, hand it to him. And the policeman or the patroller did not want the Negro to know that he couldn't read, so he would pass him on. . . . The Negroes were smart enough themselves to know that most of the police and most of the patrollers couldn't read, and they knew the ones who couldn't read. But the patrollers and the police didn't know the Negroes knew they couldn't read. So the Negroes could hand him a pass a year old, and he would pass him right on. Yes, that many times did happen.[53]

A second fundamental assumption was that Blacks would be successfully prevented from learning to read and write. Again, the folk record indicates that such was not the case. Blacks who could

[51] Pp. 98–99.
[52] WPA Files, "Slave Narratives" (Preston Kyles, Texarkana, Ark.).
[53] Informant Floyd Warlaw Crawford, Feb. 8, 1964.

read and write frequently forged passes for their less accomplished fellows.[54] An ex-slave commented: "Ol' Miss taught de niggers how to read an' write, an' some ob dem got to be too 'ficient wid de writin', 'case dey larn how tuh write too many passes so de pattyrollers wudn't git dem. Dat was de onliest time I ebber knowed Ol' Miss tuh hab de slaves punished."[55]

In most cases, however, slaves simply went about their business at night—visiting friends or relatives on nearby plantations, attending frolics and brush harbor meetings—in total disregard of the pass requirement. This relative ease of movement was facilitated by the many clever tricks the slaves used to outwit the patrollers. Among them was the practice of tying cowbells around their necks so that the patrollers would think that they were cows moving around at night.[56]

Many planters gradually became opposed to the patrol system. Doubtless they were aware of the degree of success on the part of slaves who sabotaged the operations of the patrollers, but many slave owners realized the existence of additional problems, principally that the patrol system instituted in the ante-bellum South was inefficient on the whole. One author observed, "In spite of legal penalties both for its leaders and members for non-performance of duty, the patrol seems to have been no more efficient than the medieval town watch."[57] It simply failed to do the job for which it was often paid and which was detailed in various state laws.

In addition to the general neglect of their duties, there were often "irregularities" in performance when they did ride patrol. Excessive drinking while on duty is one charge made by folk narrators, which historical evidence supports. "Often these patrols would rush half-drunk into the parties being held by slaves and begin thrashing around with their sticks, without even asking for passes."[58] The South Carolina Patrol Act of 1740 made a flat

[54] *The Negro in Virginia,* 148.
[55] WPA Files, "Slave Narratives" (Joseph Holmes, Prichard, Ala.).
[56] Texas "Slave Narratives," Mrs. E. Gilmore folder.
[57] Sydnor, 79.
[58] Jackson, "Investigation of Biographies," 130.

statement regarding this problem: "Many irregularities have been committed by former patrols arising chiefly from their drinking too much liquor before or during the time of their riding on duty."[59]

Planter opposition to patrol authority may have sprung from the excessively cruel treatment some slaves received from patrols. Slaves complained of being "whipped unmercifully," lashed "til' you was black and blue," and beaten "mos nigh to death." Sometimes deliberate cruelty was inflicted upon slaves who allegedly had too many privileges. Lorenza Ezell said on this point: "Old Ned Lipscomb was one de best massa in de whole country. You know dem old patterollers, dey call us 'Old Ned's free niggers,' and sho' hate us. Dey cruel to us, 'cause dey think us have too good a massa. One time dey cotch my uncle and beat him most to death."[60]

Another charge levied against the patrollers was that a lawless and irresponsible element among them began to abuse the patrol privilege by molesting the slaves as a kind of sport. As J. B. Cade stated, "Negro hunting, Negro catching, Negro watching and Negro whipping constituted the favorite sport of many youthful whites."[61] Often patrollers were accused of beating Blacks whether or not they had passes.[62] Alice Duvall stated, "The master's young boys used to get together, see, and at night time with their horses . . . catch the slaves and beat them. That was their recreation— having fun."[63] In other instances, such persons were believed to be guilty of deliberately chasing Blacks just to see them run. "These young men," said William Mason Cooper, ". . . didn't have anything else to do and thought it would be very entertaining to see these Negroes run."[64] Samuel Chappell added, "That was their fun . . . the white man's fun, running Negroes."[65]

Added to the charges of beating and chasing Blacks for fun were

---

[59] Henry, 34.
[60] WPA Files, "Slave Narratives" (Lorenza Ezell, Beaumont, Tex.). (C–F. Texas: Slave Interviews, Duplicates.)
[61] "Out of the Mouths of Ex-Slaves," 294–337.
[62] Henry, 34.
[63] Interview, April 12, 1964.
[64] Interview, Feb. 10, 1964.
[65] Interview, March 7, 1964.

other forms of "mischievousness." Henry Lewis Brown described an incident in which his grandfather was forced to perform for the patrollers:

> In his traveling, you know, like if he leaves his plantation, he was gone from his plantation over to another plantation, and on the way over there he was challenged with these patrollers on the way, and they made him one time buck dance, and they blew the mouth harp and made him buck dance until he buck danced a hole right down about a foot, about a foot in the ground. . . . So he said he buck danced and kicked dirt and buck danced and kicked dirt until he kicked a hole about a foot and a half deep in the ground. So he said they told him, "Say Nigger, you can't go no further and can't go no deeper?" He said, "I've got to go home. . . ." So they let him go because they knew that, they knew where he come from, and what plantation, and they knew where he was going. But just like, more or less mischievous you know.[66]

The patrols, often made up of nonslaveholders, may have resented planter wealth and social position, of which the slave was a visible symbol. The "haves" and the "have nots," though theoretically working toward a common goal—the safety of the community from slave insurrection—in practice often found themselves on opposing sides, with the slave caught in the middle.

It is clear from an examination of slave testimony that many planters distrusted the patrollers and were strongly opposed to their slaves' falling into the hands of these men.[67] Even more, many masters refused to allow patrollers to punish their slaves or even to trespass on their property—another indication of the growing antagonism between slaveholders and nonslaveholders. Planter hostility toward patrollers is revealed in the following text:

> Massa ain't 'lowed no patterollers on his place, but one time when he wuzn't ter home my mammy sent me an' Caroline ter de nex' door house fer something an' de patterollers got us. Dey carried us home an' 'bout de time dat dey wuz axin' questions young Massa Knox rid up.

[66] Interview, April 11, 1964.
[67] Henry, 39.

He look dem over an' he sez, "Git off dese premises dis minute, yo' dad-limb sorry rascals, if us needs yo' we'll call yo'. My pappy patterolls dis place hisself." Dey left den, an' we ain't been bothered wid 'em no more.[68]

Some planters were said to have actually killed patrollers while protecting their slaves. G. W. Pattillo recalled:

Master Ingram placed signs at different points on his plantation which read thus: "Patterollers, Fishing and Hunting Prohibited on this Plantation." It soon became known by all that the Ingram slaves were not given passes by their owner to go any place, consequently they were known as "Old Ingram's Free Niggers."

Master Ingram could not write, but would tell his slaves to inform anyone who wished to know, that they belonged to J. D. Ingram. "Once," said Pattillo, "my brother Willis, who was known for his gambling and drinking, left our plantation and no one knew where he had gone. As he sat around a big open fire cracking walnuts, Willis came up, jumped off his horse and fell to the ground. Directly behind him rode a 'Paterroller.' The master jumped up and commanded him to turn around and leave his premises. The 'Paterroller' ignored his warning and advanced still further. The master then took his rifle and shot him. He fell to the ground dead and Master Ingram said to his wife, 'Well, Lucy, I guess the next time I speak to that scoundrel he will take heed.' " The master then saddled his horse and rode into town. Very soon a wagon came back and moved the body.[69]

Ex-slaves repeatedly referred to a regulation prohibiting patrollers from molesting slaves on their owner's property. The slaves believed that they could be pursued only off the limits of their masters' plantations. Once its safety was reached, any slave apprehended without a pass was safe from punishment by the patrollers. Floyd Wardlaw Crawford explained this practice:

You know the practice was that if a slave was caught off the plantation by the patrollers without a pass, the patrollers were

[68] WPA Files, "Slave Narratives" (Elbert Hunter, Method, N. C.). (D–H. North Carolina: Slave Interviews, Duplicates.)
[69] WPA Files, "Slave Narratives" (G. W. Pattillo, District 5, Ga., Jan. 22, 1937).

free to whip him. But if a slave who didn't have a pass got back to the plantation, without being caught, the patrollers were not permitted to come on to the plantation and whip him. Most masters would not permit that.[70]

The slaves further believed that there were consequences for patrollers who violated this code. An ex-slave stated, "The rule was not to whip you on your master's plantation, or they would have to pay for it."[71]

Published accounts of patrol regulations in the various Southern states do not support this folk interpretation, almost universally held among the slaves. One can only conjecture that this particular limitation on patrol authority had the force of an unwritten law in the ante-bellum South. Whatever the legal status of this regulation, the whole pattern of black resistance to the patrol system was based on "beating the patroller back home."

Slaves were also known to retaliate against patrol abuses. A commonly practiced trick was to tie grapevines or ropes across dark country roads at night "about as high as a horse, so as to strike a man about his waist."[72] Serious injuries often resulted from this practice. An ex-slave stated that "sometimes they would be knocked off their horses and crippled up so that they had to be carried off from there."[73] Frequently, broken bones were suffered by horses and men (necessitating shooting the horses), and patrollers were said to have lost their lives from injuries so incurred. Mandy Cooper recalled such an incident:

> Paddy-Rollers were a constant dread to the Negroes. They would whip the poor darkeys unmercifully without any cause. One night while the Negroes were gathering for a big party and dance they got wind of the approaching Paddy-Rollers in large numbers on horseback. The Negro men did not know what to do for protection, they became desperate and decided to gather a quantity of grapevines and tied them fast at a dark place in the road. When the Paddy-Rollers came thundering down the road bent on deviltry and

[70] Interview, Feb. 8, 1964.
[71] Egypt, Masuoka, and Johnson, 145.
[72] Coleman, 98.
[73] WPA Files, "Slave Narratives" (Charles Green Dortch, Little Rock, Ark.). (C–D. Arkansas: Slave Interviews, Duplicates.)

unaware of the trap set for them, they plunged head-on into these strong grapevines and three of their number were killed and a score was badly injured. Several horses had to be shot following injuries.

When the news of this happening spread it was many months before the Paddy-Rollers were again heard of.[74]

One patroller was reported to have been killed when he got tangled up in the vines and accidentally choked to death. "Dem vines wuz wind aroun' his neck so many times they had choked him. Dey said he [was] totely dead. Serve him right 'cause dem ol' white folks treated us so mean."[75] One variation of this trick was to tie a rope across a bridge, causing patrollers who ran into it to be thrown into the water.[76] While they struggled in the water the slaves escaped. J. Winston Coleman stated that the grapevine trick was practiced so much that travel on foot came to be considered the only safe method for the scouting patrollers.[77]

Slaves used another form of retaliation when they were surprised by patrol parties while holding illegal meetings indoors. Hot coals, ashes, or pieces of burning wood were shoveled in the patrollers' faces as they entered the door. While the startled patrol party attended to their burns, the cornered slaves escaped. One Black, relating an incident of this type, said, "All of the slaves escaped unharmed, while all of the patrollers were badly injured."[78] If coals were unavailable, a handful of hot pepper served the same purpose.[79]

The following narrative, though told for true, could well belong to the Master-John cycle of tales in which John, the protagonist, usually outwits the master:

Dere am big woods 'round de plantation, an weuns sees lots ob runawayers. Dere am old cullud fellow name John, dat have been

[74] *Ibid.* (Mandy Cooper, Franklin, Ind., July 29, 1937). (Indiana: Slave Interviews, Duplicates.) See *The Negro in Virginia*, 146, 148, for other slave reminiscences concerning the use of this trick.

[75] *Ibid.* (Minnie Fulkes, Petersburg, Va., March 5, 1937).

[76] *Ibid.* (Berry Smith, Forest, Miss.).

[77] P. 98.

[78] WPA Files, "Slave Narratives" (Samuel Simeon Andrews, Jacksonville, Fla.).

[79] *Ibid.* (James Morgan, Little Rock, Ark.). (M. Arkansas: Slave Interviews, Duplicates.)

de runawayer nigger fo' 'bout fouah yeahs. De Marsters an' de Patterollers tries all deys tricks, but dey can't catch him. Dey wants to catch him bad, 'cause dey thinks 'twill 'spire tudder niggers to run if he keeps loose. He have been 'way so long dat his shoes am wore out, an' his feet am solid callus. Finally de Patterollers 'ranges de trap fo' him. Dey knows all niggers laks good eats, so dey 'ranges fo' de quiltin', an' gives chittlin's an' lye hom'ney fo' 'freshments.

Well, John falls fo' de trap, an' comes to de quiltin'. Me am inside an' eatin' 'way w'en de Patterollers rides up to de dooah. Ever'-body gits quiet, an' John stands neah de dooah, 'taint no windahs, wid his arms folded. De Patterollers says, "Yous might's well come out, John 'cause yous am right whar weuns wants yous."

W'en he don't move, dey stahts to come in. W'en dey fills de dooah, John darts to de ash pan, grabs de old time flat shovel, digs into de hot ashes, an' th'ows dem into de Patterollers faces. Dat cleahs de dooah, an' John gits through. As him am leavin', he hollers, "Bird in de air!"[80]

Black Folk View of the System

The historical picture of the patrol system as it functioned in the towns and rural areas of the pre-Civil War South is incomplete. Volunteer patrols probably kept no record of their operations,[81] and legally constituted patrols were not required by law to make a report of their activities. As Joe Gray Taylor has suggested, "It is only by chance or because of some unusual circumstance that any records of patrol activities have survived."[82] Historical sources provide some idea of the legal basis for the patrol system in the various Southern states—the method of selecting patrols, the manner of payment, if any, and their prescribed duties in the eyes of the law. But the actual operation of the system, the extent of its use, and its general success still constitute an almost complete historical void.

[80] *Ibid.* (Walter Rimm, Ft. Worth, Tex.). (Unmarked.) This same narrative appears in Botkin, *Lay My Burden Down*, 189; also see *The Negro in Virginia*, 144, 146–47, for additional texts reporting the use of the "live-coal trick."
[81] Moody, 24.
[82] Pp. 210–11.

It is in exactly these areas that history preserved in Black oral tradition can fill the gaps. There are certain broad lines of agreement between oral and historical records, namely the organization and purpose of the patrol system and the regulations regarding the use of passes. But the folk tradition provides, in addition, invaluable information and insights about the behavior of patrollers, their techniques of surveillance, the ineffectiveness of the system, and the abuses it fostered.

It is significant that oral accounts agree with the organization and purpose of the patrol system as presented in historical sources. Patrols were, to the folk, legally constituted bodies. One ex-slave said, "The pateroles were for Niggers just like police and sheriffs were for white folks."[83] Another said, "De Paterollers was de law, kind of like de policeman now."[84]

Ex-slaves referred to them as "patterollers" (the most commonly used expression), "patter-roses," "paddle rollers" (because of their use of paddles to whip slaves), and "patter-rolls." Such usage suggests the possibility of word-play by subtly changing the form of the word, though leaving it recognizable. Thus a powerful word became even more powerful by enabling the speaker to play upon its multiple meanings. This versatility of expression also permitted the slaves a form of word disguise by which they were able to talk freely about patrol activities in the presence of whites. Another example of this type of word disguise was the murmured phrase "patter de pat, patter de pat," which was used to warn fellow slaves of the presence of patrols in the neighborhood.[85]

The duty of the patrollers was also clearly understood by the Black folk. The patrollers' "business was to see that niggers would not rove around at night without the master's knowing about it."[86] The comment from another Black was, "It was to see that the

---

[83] WPA Files, "Slave Narratives" (H. B. Holloway, Little Rock, Ark.).

[84] *Ibid.* (Polly Colbert, Colbert, Okla.). (A–L. Oklahoma: Slave Interviews, Duplicates.)

[85] For the functioning of multimeaning words in Afro-American speech, see Karl Reisman, "Cultural and Linguistic Ambiguity in a West Indian Village," *Afro-American Anthropology*, Norman E. Whitten, Jr., and John Szwed, eds. (New York, 1970), 138–39.

[86] Egypt, Masuoka, and Johnson, 32.

Negroes went to bed on time and didn't steal nothing."[87] "De patrollers would go about in de quarters at nights to see if any of de slaves was out or slipped off."[88]

It is a matter of historical record that the patrollers were often paid a fixed fee for their services. The folk seemed to understand this point, too. As one observed, "When we had the patrollers it was just like the white man would have another white man working for him."[89] Another Black said, "De patterollers am rough with niggers, but dey gits paid for dat."[90] The comment of Hammett Dell was, "The way that Patty Rollers was. The masters paid somebody. Always somebody round wantin' a job like that."[91]

Written permission of the master or overseer to travel from the plantation was known by the folk as a pass, ticket, permit, or leave paper. "You had to have passes to go from one plantation to 'nother."[92] Another slave comment was, "My father said that the patrollers would run you and ketch you and whip you if you didn't have a pass. . . ."[93] The pithiest comment concerning the patterollers and the pass system came from William McWhorter.

> Show me a slavery-time Nigger dat ain't heared 'bout paterollers! Mistess, I 'clar to goodness, paterollers was de devil's own hosses. If dey cotched a Nigger out and his Marster hadn't fixed him up wid a pass, it was jus' too bad; dey most kilt him. You couldn't even go to de Lord's house on Sunday 'less you had a ticket sayin': "Dis Nigger is de propity of Marse Joe McWhorter. Let him go."[94]

Some informants even understood the manner in which county patrols operated:

[87] WPA Files, "Slave Narratives" (Dicey Thomas, Little Rock, Ark.). (S–T. Arkansas: Slave Interviews, Duplicates.)
[88] Ibid. (Sallie Carder, Burwin, Okla.). (A–L. Oklahoma: Slave Interviews, Duplicates.)
[89] Ibid. (Dicey Thomas, Little Rock, Ark.). (S–T. Arkansas: Slave Interviews, Duplicates.)
[90] Ibid. (Willie Blackwell, Fort Worth, Tex.). (A–B. Texas: Supplementary Slave Interviews.)
[91] Ibid. (Hammett Dell, Brasfield, Ark.). (C–D. Arkansas: Slave Interviews, Duplicates.)
[92] Ibid. (Ferebe Rogers, Baldwin County, Milledgeville, Ga.).
[93] Ibid. (Ida Blackshear Hutchinson, Little Rock, Ark.). (H. Arkansas: Slave Interviews, Duplicates.)
[94] Ibid. (William McWhorter, Athens, Ga., Sept. 30, 1938).

You see de City policemen walkin' his beat? Well, dats de way
de patty-rollin' was only each county had dere patty-rollers, an'
dey had to serve three months at a time, den dey was turned loose.
And if dey cotch you out without a pass, dey would gib you thirty-
nine lashes, 'ca'se dat was de law. De patty-rollers knowed nearly all
de slaves, an' it wurn't very often dey ever beat 'em.[95]

While Frank Gill remembered the number of lashes inflicted
upon slaves to be thirty-nine, in the testimony of other ex-slaves
the number was variously set at fifteen, twenty-five, and thirty,
depending on the state in which a particular slave resided. Punishment, slave narrators recall, was inflicted by tying a slave to a tree
or a post and whipping him with any one of a variety of instruments
—paddles, straps with belt buckles attached, rawhide, and black-
snake and buggy whips.

But the portrait of the ante-bellum patroller in Black oral tradition is quite different from his portrayal in published historical
accounts. Though written records concerning the patrol system in
general, and patrollers in particular, are admittedly scarce, the
pieces that are presented in published form generally picture patrollers as "discreet and sober men"[96] who, for the most part, served
on the patrols out of a sense of civic duty and responsibility. They
were, perhaps, sometimes overzealous and occasionally lax, but
mostly they cooperated to maintain the peace and safety of the
community against slave insurrections.

The patrollers ex-slaves talked about, however—and their descendants still refer to—are viewed in an entirely different light.
To the Black folk, the patrollers were a mean and sadistic lot who
reveled in the abuses they heaped on the shoulders of the slaves.
Marie Bing's testimony reflects the Black's bitterness toward the
pre-Civil War patrollers and shows how this feeling has even
affected her present-day relations with whites:

My father did tell some of the stories about how they had to get
permission to go from one plantation to the other, and if they was
out after a certain hour the patrols . . . would catch them. And if

[95] *Ibid.* (Frank Gill, Mobile, Ala.).
[96] Coleman, 95.

they'd catch them, sometimes they wouldn't take them in but they would whip them every step of the way from there as far as they had to go to get back to their plantation. . . . they'd be whipped from there all of the way in. Or then sometimes they would take them back in and whip them as a punishment. And they, how they would have to run and dart and dodge like some kind of animal. They would be chased around at night. And so it was, that was one of the things that when I was growing up was in me against the white man.[97]

Patrollers were almost always considered "poor white folks," with all the derision and scorn this label connoted. They stand accused by the Black folk of murder, rape, brutal whippings, chasing slaves for sport, and general "meanness." While white historical records essentially paint a picture of civic virtue, Black oral tradition portrays a picture of ruthlessness, cruelty, and inhumanity. There is no "gray" on either side, but the folk view serves at least to balance the record by presenting the other side.

The planters, however, growing increasingly disenchanted with the patrol system even before the Civil War, recognized and resented irregular and abusive patrol practices. The war itself and the end of the formal institution of slavery made the necessity of changing the control procedures even more urgent, a sentiment that was to have a very practical result for the Black.

After the Blacks were freed the problem of Southern landowners was how to maintain their Black laboring force on the farms of their former masters. Viewing the system of prewar slave control as a whole, two defects were clear to former slaveholders: the technique of masters and overseers disguising themselves as ghosts now had only limited effectiveness because ex-slaves were beginning to "catch on" to this practice, and the patrol system was largely ineffective. Some changes in control procedure had to be instituted. The next phase in the system of the supernatural control of the Black reflected planters' efforts to find new solutions to old problems. The most effective features of the old systems, the ghost garb and the mounted horsemen, were combined into a new organization—the Ku Klux Klan.

[97] Interview, March 6, 1964.

ADDITIONAL NARRATIVES

Patroller Taylor Burned with Hot Coals

In one of their steal-away meetings, this time they were to come to my father's grandmother's house, Grandma Courtney. His mother died when he was, my father's mother died when he was eight hours old, so Grandmother Courtney raised him, and he knew no other mother but her. And everywhere that they would go to hold their meetings at night here was an old, what did you call him, patteroller? Well, that's what he was referred to and his name was Taylor. And everywhere they would go Taylor and his gang would break them up.

So, as I said, the Virginia people were liberal. They let them have much freedom. And this particular night they, the women had got together and said they were going to stop him. So Grandma Courtney had a big fire in her fireplace. Have you ever seen the fire, the instruments that they used like a pork iron and a shovel with a handle about that long, and a small fork?

So Grandma Courtney decided that night that they were going to break him up. So they had the windows open as usual, and when they began their meeting, they were all shouting and singing. As he came in, Grandma pushed more and more to the fireplace where the live coals were. And they were singing, "We're going to stomp the devil down, bright mansions above." And everyone shouting and singing, and he was right in the midst of them. "Mr. Taylor gonna beat you, bright mansions above," right in the midst of them, up and down. So, as he got near enough they inched him up because the others knew what was going to happen. Grandma Courtney, this is evidently true, took the shovel and got the thing full of coals and threw it in his chest like that. His shirt was open. The coals went down.

His gang who was around the window didn't know what happened. He ran out screaming to the first, because have you ever heard that most of their plantations were surrounded by swamps. That was to keep them from escaping. He ran to the swamp, and they didn't know, the helpers didn't know what was wrong with him, but they followed him. And he was crawling up and down the swamp on his stomach because he was being burned, badly burned. But they broke him up. . . . He never bothered them anymore. That was Mr. Taylor.

—Informant MINNIE BELL FOUNTAINE, April 22, 1964. [This story was told to her by her parents, both of whom were slaves in Carolina County, Virginia]

Lucy Cotton Outruns the Patrollers

I was telling you about the matter of the different forms of amusement that the colored people had in the days of slavery, and one of the forms of amusement was of course the frolic, the Saturday night frolic. When I was a youngster about 15 years old, I remember hearing a man in my community, in the community in which my grandfather lived, named Flem Bowden. That was his name Flem Bowden. I don't know how to spell the word F-l-e-m, but that was the name by which he was called. I remember that he was the old man with a long beard, and he was a grown man in the days of slavery before the Civil War.

And he used to come to my grandfather's and tell lots of stories. And on one occasion he told the story about a frolic that he and some of the other slaves went to one Saturday night.

This frolic was held in a little log cabin down in the woods, you see, and the young people gathered there, the young men and the young women. It was pretty late in the fall. It was pretty cool and a good fire was built in the fireplace and the embers were hot. And this man went ahead to tell about how the banjo picker came in and he began to pick the banjo, and then the couples began to dance.

And he said that he was a very good dancer himself, and he said, "Brother Jim," that's what he called my grandfather. My grandfather's name was Jim. "Brother Jim," he said, "I danced with a girl named Lucy Cotton. Lucy Cotton is the finest dancer in the world. She was such a good dancer," he said, "till she could dance with a tumbler of water on her head and not spill a drop." And then he just burst out in a big laugh, you see. And he said they were dancing and the banjo was going and they were just having a good time, and the fellows were clapping their hands and all that sort of thing. He said that all of a sudden the patrollers, they were called patterollers by the slaves, the slaves called them patterollers, but they were really patrollers. All of a sudden the paterollers rode up into the front of the cabin. They dismounted, and they rushed into the door which was open. And those men were dressed, those men were wearing coats and they had on shirts with the collars open. And they rushed into the door and they said, "All right, all right, let me have your passes, let me have your passes, let me have your passes." They started popping their whips you know.

And he said that there was a big fellow sitting by the fireplace that hadn't danced at all. He was just sitting looking at the others dancing and when he looked up and saw the patrollers, he reached back and grabbed a shovel and shoveled up a scoop full of, a shovel full of those red hot embers and threw them right into the faces of those men, those patrollers, you know. Those embers went right down their shirts and they, they started jerking their shirts out and fighting fire. Of course, the hot coals lodged around their waist, you see, and they fell back out of the door.

And they were fighting fire, and the people, the slaves, ran out over them and started running for home, you see. You know the practice was that if a slave was caught off the plantation by the patrollers without a pass, the patrollers were free to whip him. But if a slave got back to the plantation, the slave who didn't have a pass got back to the plantation, without being caught or without getting caught, the patrollers were not permitted to come on the plantation and whip. Most masters would not permit that, you see. They would permit the patrollers to whip them as much as they wanted to if they were caught without passes off the plantation, but not on the plantation. So, of course, most of the people there didn't have passes, and they started running for their plantation.

And this man, Flem Bowden, told my grandfather that he went down the road toward his plantation as fast as he could go. It was several miles away. My grandfather asked him what about Lucy Cotton. He said, "Oh Brother Jim," he said, "Lucy Cotton just passed me." He said, "The last time I saw that gal she had her dress up around her knees and she was running like a deer." That was the way he put it, you see. He said, "That Lucy Cotton could run." He said, "That gal just outran me, you know." And so he said he was running and he said he had on some new shoes that his master had bought him, and the old shoes hurt his feet somewhat, and he couldn't run any more than just so fast. And while he was going down the road trying to get to the cabin, he looked back and saw the banjo picker coming. And this banjo picker had his banjo under his arm with the stem sticking out in the back, you see. So he said when the banjo picker passed him he grabbed the stem of the banjo, and then this man was pulling him along, you see, faster than he could really run. And he said he ran so fast that he burst his shoes on both sides, and the shoes turned around on his feet, and his heels came out on one side and his toes on the other.

Of course, that must have been exaggeration, but this is the story he told, and he just had everyone laughing. There is a grain of truth in it though. You see something about the tribulations of the slaves, you know, how they had to sneak out to go to the frolics; how when they got caught at the frolics without passes, they had to run to keep from getting a whipping, and all that sort of thing. So he said he and the banjo picker were going down the road, the banjo picker was pulling him along. That was the only way he was able to run so fast. The banjo picker was pulling him along, you know. So he said they ran and they ran until they got to a curve in the road, and there was a big chestnut rail fence on both sides of the road, and instead of them making the curve they just went straight, and over the fence, you see and into the woods. And they escaped from the patrollers, you know. So that was the story he told, you see. Said the last time he saw Lucy Cotton, she had her dress up around her knees and she was out-running everybody. He said, "That gal not only was the best dancer in the world, she's the best runner too!"

—Informant FLOYD WARDLAW CRAWFORD, Feb. 8, 1964. [Crawford, carefully maintaining the flavor of the story, related it exactly as told by him by his grandfather, an ex-slave.]

4

THE RECONSTRUCTION KU KLUX KLAN

*The Ku Klux Klan was based on stamping
fear in the ex-slave's heart. And you see, the
Ku Klux uniform was suggestive from ghost
stories. . . . They wore these uniforms with
the faces covered up, nothing open but the
eyes and the nose. Make them look like hants.*
—J. L. S. HOLLOMAN

Origin of the Klan

REPEATED REFERENCES have been made to the amusement some
whites purportedly enjoyed in chasing, frightening, and whipping
slaves. Before 1865 these diversions had been a sideline of the
patrollers, who were supposed to have been engaged in the more
serious business of preventing slave assemblies. But in the fall of
1865, six war-weary, restless, bored youths of Pulaski, Tennessee,
organized a social club, expressly to have fun at the Black's expense. The avowed purpose of this new club was to "have fun,
make mischief, and play pranks on the public."[1] To these youths
the Black population constituted "the public," and the pranks they
organized consisted of dressing in ghostly garb and frightening ex-
slaves. The Klans that resulted found that "terrorizing of the Blacks
successfully provided the amusement which the founders desired
and there were many applications for admission to the society."[2]

[1] Walter L. Fleming, "Prescript of the Ku Klux Klan," *Publications of the
Southern History Association,* 7 (Sept. 1903), 327.
[2] Walter L. Fleming, *The Sequel of Appomattox* (New Haven, 1919), 246.

The element of fun is a recurring theme in Southern historiography and oral tradition. "Playing ghosts at the graveyard" was apparently a pastime engaged in by young boys of both races, though Blacks were the more frequent victims. A white Alabaman recalled this traditional prank when he appeared before a Joint Select Commitee created by Congress in 1871 to gather testimony concerning the Klan's operation. "The only other case I can think of," the witness said, "was a boy who went to a graveyard one night to scare some negroes. . . . He went with a mask, and I told him to be cautious."[3]

Ingenuity in Southern fun apparently knew no bounds. A white man who extended a Sunday-school class into a two-day school for poor children was called on by irate Klan members. He was taken out, blindfolded, and forced to kiss the private parts of several assembled Blacks:

> Well, they made me kiss the negro man's posterior, and held it open and made me kiss it, and as well as I remember a negro woman's too, and also her private parts, and then told me to have sexual connection with her. I told them they knew, of course, I could not do that. They struck me, and some of them begged for me. They asked me how I liked that for nigger equality. I told them it was pretty tough.[4]

According to a white eyewitness, "I think that was the cause, or one cause, of his being whipped. That was what they professed, that he was equalizing himself too much, and that was the reason they made him take that kissing negro equality."[5]

Perhaps one explanation for such excessive interest in "fun" is that many of the Klansmen were relatively young. According to a contemporary account: "Generally, they are young men. In one or two cases I have found amongst them older men—say forty-five years of age. Occasionally they are married men, but they are, principally, unmarried men. These bands are made up of a class of

---

[3] *Report of the Joint Select Committee to Inquire into the Condition of Affairs in the Late Insurrectionary States.* House Report, 42nd Congress, 2nd Session, No. 22 (13 vols., Washington, D. C., 1872), Alabama, 253. This report is subsequently referred to as KKK Report.

[4] *Ibid.*, South Carolina, 366.

[5] *Ibid.*, 382.

men, generally, ranging from eighteen to thirty-five years of age."[6]

The decision to formalize an old Southern custom of Black-hunting, Black-chasing, and Black-whipping into a social organization marked the beginning of the Reconstruction Ku Klux Klan. Perhaps out of a need to "whitewash" the motivations of the founders, defenders have perpetuated an interesting myth concerning the group's origin. General historians, limiting themselves to threadbare written source material and blind to the value of oral tradition, have unwittingly kept the tale alive. William Peirce Randel tells of the first parade through the streets of Pulaski, Tennessee, the six original Klan members arrayed in sheets stolen for themselves and their horses:

> One unexpected result, reported by various observers, was that the superstitious Negroes had not been amused by the spectacle, but instead, had taken the riders for ghosts of the Confederate dead. What had been conceived as a lark to relieve the general tedium took on a sudden new dimension: if idle Negroes could be frightened so easily, perhaps they could be persuaded to resume work, and something like the prewar balance could be restored—the plantation system that kept the Negroes subservient and at work, producing the income that white men had been accustomed to. (The Romaines recorded [*A Story of the Original Ku Klux Klan*, 1924; see footnote 10 below] that parading was not begun quite so early as the second meeting, and followed, instead of preceding, the decision to try to frighten Negroes back to work.)[7]

In point of fact, it was not the beginning, as Randel states and as students of Southern history generally believe, but one of the final stages of a contrived system of supposedly supernatural control of the Black. This is the tone of John Hope Franklin's remarks:

> The Young Tennesseans who organized late in 1865 the frolicking secret lodge that was to be known as the order of the Ku Klux Klan, or the Invisible Empire, could hardly have been unaware of what they were doing. Even if they were bored and impatient with life, as has been claimed in their defense, this was nothing new for young bloods in the village of Pulaski, Tennessee. Nor were wanton

---

[6] *Ibid.*, Mississippi, 1159.
[7] *The Ku Klux Klan*, (Philadelphia, 1965), 8–9.

attacks on helpless Negroes new. If the young men were looking for fun, they did not have to go beyond the nearest Negro settlement, and furthermore, they would be performing a service to the white community if they whipped Negroes to keep them in line.[8]

While historians have stumbled around the truth without being fully aware of the origin of the Reconstruction Klan, Black folk have recognized that Klan techniques were simply a continuation of earlier forms of psychological control. Minnie Bell Fountaine explained her ideas concerning this continuing tradition:

> They [overseers] would dress as ghosts, and I think, I shouldn't say that because it's being recorded, but I think that's where the Ku Klux Klan got their point of dressing as ghosts to scare the Negroes, to scare the slaves. . . . I've often thought that; I've often thought that because in seeing their pictures they always represented in my mind what ghost stories were. You know they wore the white sheet all over them with their eyes showing. Well, that was the way that the ghosts always was presented to us as children. That you see something coming with a white sheet. You see it moving, but it didn't move, and then it would disappear. That was supposed to be a ghost, see. And I firmly believe that that is where the Ku Klux Klan got that idea from because they were considered night riders. They were called night riders as much as Klan. They would leave off the Ku Klux and call it Klan or the night riders.[9]

The Reconstruction Ku Klux Klan passed through two distinct periods of development. In the first phase, from 1865 to 1867, the Klan relied almost exclusively on the Blacks' fear of ghosts, intimidating them by capitalizing on their known superstitions.[10] Folklore was at the center of this technique of supernatural control. What Blacks thought they saw was not in their imagination, as Javan Bryan stated in the report of the Committee on Investigations in the Third Congressional District:

> No one can fail to be struck, upon reading the evidence taken by the committee, with the many vague, incoherent, and ludicrous accounts given by these poor colored people, many of whom were

---

[8] *Reconstruction: After the Civil War* (Chicago, 1961), 154.
[9] Interview, April 22, 1964.
[10] William Bethel Romaine, *A Story of the Original Ku Klux Klan* (Pulaski, Tenn., 1924), 13.

so ignorant as not even to know their own names, of the herculean size, hideous proportions, and diabolical features of what they called the Ku-Klux. And it affords me great pleasure to be able to report, that, after having "thoroughly investigated" the matter, I am of opinion that the ghosts, hobgoblins, jack-o'-the lanterns, and Ku-Klux of the third congressional district are but allotropic conditions of the witches of New England, whose larvae, having long lain dormant until imported hither in the carpet-bags of some pious political priests, germinated in the too credulous minds of their poor proselytes, and loomed into luxuriance in the fertile fields of their own imaginations.[11]

Although, as Bryant's report indicates, psychological intimidation can remain invisible, not so the harsher methods characterizing the Klan's second phase, from 1867 until it was officially dissolved in 1869. Efforts to psychologically frighten Blacks gave way to more violent forms, such as beating, shooting, and lynching offenders. During this time the Klan relentlessly pursued its stated purpose: to prevent the enforcement of the Thirteenth, Fourteenth, and Fifteenth amendments; to punish troublesome Blacks; and to defeat the Republican party.[12] Indeed, almost immediately after forming, the frolicking, fun-loving social club was transformed into a band of regulators, for as postwar Southern problems continued unabated the fear of a Black insurrection was still a pressing concern in the reconstructed South. An ex-Confederate general is said to have told his neighbors: "I advise you to get ready for what may come. We are standing over a sleeping volcano."[13]

Aside from the constant fear of Black uprisings, other problems demanded immediate solutions. How to fill the vacuum created by the freeing of its slave-labor force was a major postwar concern. Many planters, their domains dependent on labor, could not believe the Black would work voluntarily. Even when he did, nocturnal perambulations to attend political meetings or social affairs made the freedmen less effective daytime workers. In addition, they often abandoned crops to attend these meetings. Many al-

---

[11] KKK Report, South Carolina, 929.
[12] Elizabeth M. Howe, *A Ku Klux Uniform* (Buffalo Historical Society *Publications* 25 [1921]), 25.
[13] Fleming, *Sequel of Appomattox*, 244.

leged insults to former masters arose from freedmen's refusals to complete their labor contracts.

Southern whites believed this unreliability, and a sizable amount of petty larceny, as well as the Black's participation in the Loyal or Union League of vocal Blacks, necessitated an organization to resume the activities of the ante-bellum patrols. Whatever the rationale, a close reading of available literature suggests that the word "Ku Klux" was widely circulated among Blacks and whites, becoming a kind of byword: "I will tell you that the Ku Klux has got to be such a common word, by-word, that the children and all call their mammies Ku Klux and daddies Ku Klux, and everything is called Ku Klux."[14]

In the absence of news media—except for some city newspapers —information concerning unusual events was circulated by word of mouth. In a climate of rumor, exaggerations, distortions, and embellishments were bound to occur. Congressional testimony is dotted with references to "dark and painful rumors," "statements based on rumor," "it was rumored around," and "country rumors."

According to popular imagination, the Klan was everywhere in everything. Evidence of this kind of mania was the widely circulated rumor of a monstrous child born in October 1870 in Blount County, Alabama, to the Benjamin Horton family. The child was reported as being a perfect representation and facsimile of a disguised Ku Klux:

> The head of the child was about three times the size of an ordinary child's head, with a soft, spongy fungous growth over the skull. . . . The forehead was flat and square, and about perpendicular, about three times the height of the forehead of an ordinary child. In a straight line from the crown of the head to the front of the forehead, commencing at each cheek bone, there was a sort of fringe flaring very little to near the top, and then full around the top. It was about an inch wide and about half an inch thick at the base; a gristly fringe, of a dark purple color. At two points near the temples were two gristly horns of the same consistency, about an inch and a half or an inch and three-quarters long, projecting out from the forehead. . . . The eyes and mouth were about one-third smaller

[14] KKK Report, South Carolina, 655.

than those of an ordinary child. The face was nearly flat, with but little nose. The eyes and mouth were of a scarlet red. The chin sloped off on a plane with its body. Around the neck was a scarlet red band; and from the point of each shoulder, extending down each side to about the center of the abdomen, was all a scarlet red.[15]

This child was reported as having been born dead, about two miles from a religious camp meeting at Gum Grove, Alabama. After some seventy-five people viewed the child at the family home, the body was taken to the camp grounds and shown to from a thousand to fifteen hundred people, none of them Black.[16] Born on a Sunday morning, it was buried that same night. A local Methodist preacher advised the family to have a doctor "fix up the child," so it could be published in the papers that the child was all right.[17]

Testimony indicated that the Klan had paraded past the parents' home twice a week for months. In the mother's fourth or fifth month of pregnancy, some Klan members had come up to the house and pushed the door in. According to gossip, it was this later series of events that had caused the peculiar markings of the child.[18] It had also been reported that the mother had recurring dreams about the Klan in which she found herself at her father's house, desperately trying to keep the Klan members away from him. "They had been some half a dozen times to his house of nights while she was there, and scarcely a night passed, after they were there the first time, but whenever she got to sleep all through the night she was screaming and scuffling to keep them off of him, and thinking she was in the house of her father, and the Ku-Klux were after him."[19] Apparently disturbed by the birth of a child with Klan markings, the local Klan went to the parents' home, called out the father-in-law, and whipped him. The child's father was also whipped, apparently because he said that the "child had on a false face."[20] The witness ended his testimony by stating: "I don't know

[15] *Ibid.*, Alabama, 118.
[16] *Ibid.*
[17] *Ibid.*, 759.
[18] *Ibid.*, 118.
[19] *Ibid.*, 759.
[20] *Ibid.*, 732.

Intimidation, as well as force, was a weapon of the mounted patrols (known to the Blacks as "patterollers" or "night riders"), shown here checking a slave's pass—his authority to be absent from the owner's plantation. Wood engraving from *Frank Leslie's Illustrated History of the Civil War*, courtesy of the Library of Congress.

Although relatively safe within their own quarters, slaves were never beyond surveillance. The slave quarters depicted here are typical of those found on the large plantations, which offered Blacks some opportunity for community life. Courtesy of the Library of Congress.

The recording of oral testimony of Blacks—some born free—began long before the Civil War, as shown in this 1822 engraving (by Alex. Lawson after a sketch by Alex. Rider). Popular in their day as antislavery literature, the narratives must be checked carefully for authenticity but provide an important historical source. Courtesy of the Library of Congress.

The underground railroad, depicted here, led often to Washington, D.C., which was a mecca for runaway Blacks, the traffic beginning in the late 1850s and reaching a peak in 1863. From the painting by Charles T. Webber, Cincinnati Art Museum, print courtesy of the Library of Congress.

Horror stories about kidnapping and other atrocities abound in Black folk memory. Whites are accused of spreading rumors that abolitionists would eat the victims or sell them for medical experiments. Engraving by Goodman and Piggot after a sketch by Alex. Rider, courtesy of the Library of Congress.

One slave recalled from Ku Klux days that "Dey would come around wid 'dough faces' on and peer in de winders and open de do'. Iffen you didn't look out, dey would skeer you half to death." This "visit," drawn by Frank Bellew, is reproduced from *Harper's Weekly* (1872), courtesy of the Library of Congress.

The "night doctors" of Black folk tradition were body-snatchers who sold their victims for medical dissecting, supposedly following the example of the infamous Scottish night doctor William Burke. Burke's execution in 1829 is depicted above, courtesy of the National Library of Medicine, Bethesda, Maryland.

The Black community in Washington staged a joyous celebration of the Emancipation Proclamation, as shown in this sketch by F. Dielman, but oral tradition records that white control by fear and intimidation was to continue for many years. From *Harper's Weekly* (1866), courtesy of the Library of Congress.

The Ku Klux Klan provided the most dramatic evidence of psychological control of Blacks in the postwar era. Klansmen dressed as grotesquely as possible to capitalize on the Blacks' fear of ghosts. Wood engraving from *Harper's Weekly* (1868), courtesy of the Library of Congress.

Control of the Blacks by fear and other means continued long after they were emancipated, as indicated in this wood engraving by Thomas Nast in *Harper's Weekly* (1874). Courtesy of the Library of Congress.

which looked the worst, a Ku Klux fifty yards off by moonshine, or that child in the coffin in the fix it was in."[21]

At least six or seven other such monstrous births were reported in Alabama. "They were nearly all living, but not marked to the extent of this one. This was the most marked of any that had been born."[22] One informant recalled: "I saw one child, a negro child, that had a fierce, wild look, with a head somewhat in the form of the Ku-Klux caps, and a very unnatural chin. . . . [It was] thick and heavy underneath, as though something had been thrown over it."[23]

Abnormalities, such as these monstrous births, illustrate but one application of the word Ku Klux. In its broadest connotations, the term signified the violation of law by men in disguise. In this sense, it was used as a reproach:

> I think it consists of disguised men who are somewhat organized, who have banded together for the purpose of horse-thieving, stealing, and thieving generally, and whenever they have any private or malicious purpose to carry out, for assisting one another in that; that they are men who do not labor, and are disposed to make their living by preying upon the country. I think the main man, Mr. Gibson, has been engaged in a clan of that kind for some time, and I think they have taken the disguise of what was once called the old Ku-Klux organization, to palm themselves off as Ku-Klux, and do their devilment in disguise, so that they may not be known.[24]

The origin of the name Ku Klux Klan has been the subject of much theorizing, complicated by absurd and misleading stories deliberately circulated by the Klan members themselves for the purpose of throwing inquisitive people off the track. One writer proposed that the term Ku Klux Klan was suggested by the sound made in the act of cocking and discharging the rifles and shotguns carried by them: the first two syllables—Ku Klux, which represented the cocking of the piece—being repeated in a subdued tone

[21] *Ibid.*, 759.
[22] *Ibid.*, 120.
[23] *Ibid.*
[24] *Ibid.*, 649.

of voice and the last syllable—Klan—being repeated with emphasis, suggesting its discharge.[25] Other writers presented the view that the Klan had derived its name from ancient Scottish clans, who summoned their men to war by sending a messenger around bearing a blazing cross. From this, writers surmised the origin of the Klan's fiery cross.[26]

Newspaper reporters seemed particularly inventive, the *Memphis Appeal* quite seriously suggesting that Ku Klux Klan is a Hebrew term, "Cu-Clux Clan," found in a very old Jewish work entitled "A True and Authentic History of the Great Rebellion of the Hebrew Against the Ancient Egyptian King Pharoah, B.C. 2000."[27] The *Richmond Whig* in 1868 earnestly stated that the term originated in China among the merchants engaged in smuggling opium into that empire.[28] Yet the *Pulaski Citizen* developed one of the most absurd theories. Recalling the large number of volunteer troops from Tennessee who went to the Mexican War, the editor felt it was not unreasonable to assume that some may have become familiar with Mexican mythology, learning of the god of light called Cukulcan. He points out that "members of the Ku Klux occasionally referred to themselves as 'sons of light.' "[29]

The most commonly accepted origin of the term is that Ku Klux was coined from the Greek word *kuklos*, meaning a circle. To carry out the alliteration Klan was added, and hence the name Ku Klux Klan. According to the *Kourier Magazine*, the official Klan journal, in an article published in 1925: "It can readily be seen how the word '*Kuklos*' can phonetically be transformed into the word Ku Klux. Such was the case, and such is the meaning generically of the words 'Ku Klux'—a circle of friends."[30] The official Klan endorsement of this theory may be motivated by the fact that the use of the Greek word *kuklos* projects an image of the six

[25] John P. Green, *Recollections of the Inhabitants, Localities, Superstitions, and Ku Klux Outrages of the Carolinas* (Cleveland, 1880), 136.
[26] Winfield Jones, *Knights of the Ku Klux Klan* (New York, 1941), 23.
[27] Stanley F. Horn, *Invisible Empire* (Boston, 1939), 8.
[28] *Ibid.*
[29] Romaine, 4–5.
[30] "Letters to the Editor," *The Kourier Magazine*, 1 (Dec. 1924–Nov 1925), 7.

charter members of the Reconstruction Klan as men of education, culture, and refined tastes, who would have been familiar with classical languages.

A final theory too long overlooked by historians is one found in W. B. Romaine's book *A Story of the Original Ku Klux Klan*, published in 1924. According to this source, the first name suggested at the organizational meeting of the Pulaski Social Club was *kuklos*. At this point a Georgia soldier proposed the word *Clocletz*, the name of a phantom Indian chieftain whom the Georgia Blacks believed led his skeleton followers over the swamps and savannas of Georgia. Another ex-Confederate soldier suggested combining the sounds of the words and evolved the name Ku Klux, seemingly fraught with meaning and yet really meaning nothing whatever, but in its very sound suggesting mystery and the rattling together of dry bones.[31]

Though this is all that Romaine reports, a much greater elaboration of the Cocletz Indian legend can be found in N. J. Floyd's pro-Klan novel *Thorns in the Flesh*, published in 1884. Deriving the spelling *Cocletz* from the tribal name, Floyd traces in considerable detail the history, migration, intermingling with neighboring tribes, and final settlement in Limestone County, Alabama, of this legendary Indian tribe, originally belonging to the Catawbas, a South Carolina tribe. What is of special significance to this discussion is Floyd's account of the eventual downfall of the small Cocletz clan, which had found a permanent and apparently prosperous home in Alabama. The group, led by Clopton Cocletz, a great-grandson of the original and once powerful Co-Cletz, became known for their drunken excesses and abandoned living habits. According to legendary accounts, the appearance of Clopton himself served to intensify local gossip. The disfigurement of an eye lost in some earlier misadventure, together with his general irascibility, supposedly evoked great fear in the neighborhood Blacks. It was even rumored that Clopton had murdered several of his slaves during his drunken brawls, and all were threatened with massacre if the news leaked out.

[31] Romaine, 5.

Quite unexplainable, and shrouded in mystery, was the sudden disappearance of the Cocletz Clan. It was said that "the devil had claimed them at last, though their ghosts continued to ride through forests and barrens." This quotation was written by John Knox, who published an article explaining his own doubts about the authenticity of the Cocletz legend and describing in a fascinating account his efforts to historically verify the oral tradition. He discusses his search of gravestones and the sites of mansions in Limestone County, relating as well his conversations with local citizens. Aside from the general factual accuracy of Floyd's novel, Knox found no hard corroborative data, but a powerful superstition among the Blacks concerning the legend.[32] N. J. Floyd himself writes:

> According to veracious negro authority there is not a night, from the first to the third quarter of the moon, that the sound of the horn and the yelp of the hounds of old Cyclops and the boys, may not be heard in some dark and dismal forest; while occasionally one or more of them may be seen to flit across an open field, with their phantom steeds at full speed, in mad chase after the shadow of a passing cloud.[33]

While Floyd undoubtedly used literary license to embroider the legend of the Cocletz Indians, much of the material he reports can be corroborated in historical sources. The Catawbas were, in fact, a major Indian tribe in South Carolina, having moved to that state in 1762 on a tract of fifteen acres of land that had been reserved for them. Ultimately, their reservation was increased to eight hundred acres, and the main body of the Catawbas continued to live in South Carolina.

Isolated families intermarried with the Cherokees in Georgia, a few others went to the Choctaw Nation in what is now Oklahoma, and still other families settled in Arkansas, Colorado, and Utah.[34] At least one source documents the presence of a small band

[32] "Mystery Shrouds Lost Clan of Cocletz," *The Decatur Daily*, Feb. 14, 1965.
[33] *Thorns in the Flesh* (Lynchburg, Va., 1884), 167.
[34] John R. Swanton, *Indian Tribes of North America*. Smithsonian Institution, Bureau of American Ethnology, Bulletin 145 (Washington, D. C., 1969), 90.

of Catawbas in Alabama.[35] Historically verifiable is the fact that in 1816 ten thousand acres of land in Limestone County, Alabama, were granted to a mixed Indian-white family named Colbert, possibly an Americanized version of Cocletz.[36]

Also a matter of historical record is the strong antipathy between the Blacks and Catawbas. Not now, or at any time in the past, has there been social intermingling between them. One source, an aged Indian, reported that, so far as he knows, not one drop of Black blood has ever flowed in the veins of a Catawba Indian. When asked how the Catawbas and Blacks got along, the Indian replied: "Fine. We have nothing to do with them, and they have nothing to do with us. There hasn't been a Negro on the Reservation in five years."[37] During slavery, runaway slaves who escaped to swamps were often known to return to their masters only when a party of Catawbas was sent to locate them.[38]

Admittedly, data concerning the pre-Civil War existence of the Cocletz Indians are not conclusive. However, oral tradition clearly indicates that the term Ku Klux existed before 1865. One finds this statement repeatedly made in dozens of WPA narratives and in oral testimony. While the following testimony can be construed as illustrating similar techniques, it also says quite plainly that this ex-slave recognized a clear distinction between the patrols and the Klan: "It was before the war that I knew 'bout the Ku Klux. There wasn't no difference between the patroles and the Ku Klux that I knows of. If th'd ketch you, they all would whip you. I don't know nothin' about the Ku Klux Klan after the War."[39]

Oral testimony, then, offers convincing evidence both of the prewar existence of the term Ku Klux and of the fact that the Klan relied heavily on traditional methods of supernatural control. In view of this, it is extremely likely that the charter members of the

[35] Douglas Summers Brown, *The Catawba Indians* (Columbia, S. C., 1966), 329.

[36] Knox, "Mystery Shrouds Lost Clan of Cocletz."

[37] W. R Bradford, *The Catawba Indians of South Carolina* (Columbia, S. C., 1946), 14.

[38] *Ibid.*, 14–15.

[39] WPA Files, "Slave Narratives" (J. T. Tims, Little Rock, Ark.). (S–T. Arkansas: Slave Interviews, Duplicates.)

Klan would have chosen a name for their organization already in oral circulation and both familiar to and feared by Blacks. The name Cocletz fits this description. Surely this Indian legend should not be so lightly banished by students of Southern history as being "fishy and woefully unclassical."[40] More thorough research into the problem is certainly in order.

Costume of the Klan

It was easy to settle on a club uniform once the purpose of the new society had been established. White sheets—worn over the head, with apertures for eyes, nose, and mouth, and belted around the waist—were by now traditional ghost attire. The original founders of the Klan did not stumble on this disguise, as many Klan apologists would have us believe, but they simply made use of a pattern early established in Southern life and based on the Black's belief in the supernatural.

As Klan members realized that one of the most effective instruments of social control through intimidation was its costume, the tendency was to depart from the early simplicity of dress. Color, style, and ornamentation were often left to the individual whims of Klansmen. The sole criterion was that one's dress should be as grotesque as possible. The early Klan costume served two functions: to feed upon the presumed superstitions of Blacks by creating garb that gave a supernatural appearance, and to hide the identity of the wearer in order to avoid identification and prosecution.

In terms of color, white, black, and red robes became favorites in many Southern states. White was chosen because it naturally helped to create an unearthly, ghostly image. Black robes and masks, earlier worn by patrollers, were a common choice of Klansmen because they could thus sneak up on their victims unaware. Apparently, black costumes became increasingly popular by 1868, even when white had initially been worn. A Georgia informant testified: "That same night they rode in black, though they were

[40] Randel, 6.

going in white before that night, and they have been in black ever since that."[41] Red was also frequently worn, probably because this color helped to dramatize the claim that Klansmen were Confederate dead returning from hell. Gray, yellow, and blue were also used, often in combination with the basic black, white, and red robes. For example: "Dr. Avery had on a red gown with a blue face, with red about his mouth, and he had two horns on his cap about a foot long."[42]

Not all Klansmen wore costumes for every occasion. Strangers who would be unknown by sight to a particular community often went undisguised.[43] This was especially true when Klansmen rode in squads of from forty to a hundred men. According to a Congressional witness: "The two that came to my house in the first place were strangers, because they did not have their face-pieces. It was pretty warm. They were strangers."[44]

In general, Klan disguises fell into two categories: prepared uniforms, carefully made and identically worn by members of the same Klan unit; and unplanned disguises, quickly improvised for a particular occasion. Two types of prepared disguises were fairly widely used. The first style was the long, loose-fitting robe or gown that extended to the knee, described by one ex-slave as "near like these singing robes the church choirs have. But they were long— come way down to the shoe tops."[45] Big, loose sleeves and slits or buttoned openings provided the flexibility of movement that Klansmen needed for their various activities. This type of garment was variously described in the Congressional testimony as an overcoat, apron, sheet, wrapper, gown, or frock. A very observant witness described this uniform:

> The gown they had on came just about half way down below the knee; it was cut rather like a tight night-gown, and was close fitting over their coats, and slashed up on each side, so as to allow them to step well. There was a band around the waist, and all up and

[41] KKK Report, Georgia, 649.
[42] *Ibid.*, South Carolina, 1951.
[43] *Ibid.*, Alabama, 753; South Carolina, 369.
[44] *Ibid.*, Alabama, 919.
[45] WPA Files, "Slave Narratives" (Ida Blackshear Hutchinson, Little Rock, Ark.). (H. Arkansas: Slave Interviews, Duplicates.)

down, in front of their gowns, were the same sort of buttons that struck me as another singular thing; they were all pearl buttons. Their head-piece, the front part of it, was a piece of cloth rounded to a point, and came down to about the pit of the stomach, long enough to cover the beards of most of them; but I saw the beards of several of them, even under that, those who had long beards. In these face-pieces were large round holes for the eyes, two inches across; they were very large, and, in fact, in one instance, the face-piece moved, and I saw and recognized the man through the eye-holes; the hole for the mouth in the face-piece was a very large hole. Around those mouth-holes and eye-holes were rings of red, to make them look like blood; I do not know what they were stained with. The back part of the head-piece, when placed around in front, came down just over the eye-brows; when riding, or not at their work, they always put their head-pieces on with the long piece back, and the back-piece in front, in order to give them an unobstructed view.[46]

A second style of prepared disguise involved the use of pants and jackets made from a variety of material, such as calico, oil-cloth, or homespun cotton fabric. The top portion was sometimes a regular shirt, one described in the South as an old-fashioned hunting shirt. Both styles were worn with an ordinary belt or one to which a black leather cross had been attached.[47] A jacket or sack was sometimes worn instead of the shirt.[48] The bottom portion of this costume, the pants, was often black, either trimmed or un-trimmed, depending on the whim of the Klansman. A Congressional informant testified:

> I will say further, before the committee, as to that, the man who was killed. I took his mask off of him, including the mask over his face, a pair of pants made out of black calico, and what we called in the army a blouse. We took them off of him. They were all of them black; and the blouse had white ribbons of some kind—very common. His pants had a white ribbon here, and they were over a brown jeans suit.[49]

[46] KKK Report, Mississippi, 274.
[47] *Ibid.*, Georgia, 568.
[48] *Ibid.*, Mississippi, 854.
[49] *Ibid.*, 1102.

124

Sometimes the outer covering was made of oilcloth; at other times the entire outfit—pants, coats, caps, and veils—was made from this material. Homespun, calico, and cambric were also used.[50]

Headpieces for prepared disguises often consisted of veils or cloth sacks with openings for the eyes and mouth. They hung down around the shoulders and could be attached to a hat, or made by combining several pieces of cloth. A captured uniform displayed at the Congressional hearings in Mississippi had this type of head covering:

> Here are various face disguises—one red, two of them white, with holes cut in them for the eyes and mouth. This one, which is a terrible-looking one, is an officer's disguise, and has a flap over the mouth so contrived that upon his blowing it makes a vibrating noise.[51]

Klan masks were usually referred to by slave narrators as false faces, dough faces, or scare faces. The headgear worn by Klan members was variously described by the folk as "big high hats,"[52] "three cornered white hats with de eyes way up high,"[53] or "some kind of hat that went over the man's head and shoulders and had great big red eyes in it."[54]

Frequently attached to a head mask were horns, usually made of cloth and stuffed with cotton[55] or whalebone.[56] Some were as long as two feet, curled like sheep's horns and tied on.[57] Horns seem to have been a particular favorite of Klansmen because they could be shaken in the victim's face. As one eyewitness described it, "Some had one horn; some had two horns; some had one horn hanging down and another sticking up."[58] Another informant commented:

[50] *Ibid.*, Georgia, 645.
[51] *Ibid.*, Mississippi, 1160.
[52] WPA Files, "Slave Narratives" (Ann Matthews, Nashville). (Tennessee.)
[53] *Ibid.* (Jim Allen, West Point, Miss.).
[54] *Ibid.* (H. B. Holloway, Little Rock, Ark.).
[55] KKK Report, South Carolina, 617.
[56] *Ibid.*, Alabama, 546.
[57] *Ibid.*, Mississippi, 667.
[58] *Ibid.*, South Carolina, 403.

They had cloths banded around their faces. I think the first band was around the forehead, and there was one around the chin and one under the chin, tied on top of the head. I was deliberate enough to take my finger and touch the horn of one who had a horn. It was of cotton sewed together. He was walking up in front of me and pushed it in my face, and said, "Did you ever see the Ku-Klux?" I touched his horn; I had heard that they could hook. They had some other disguises; some had no horns at all.[59]

Tremendous, high-crowned hats made of paper were frequently reported. Although tassles and horns often adorned the hats, sometimes the trimmings were more flashy, featuring spangles and stars. "One had a paper hat on, painted red, and it looked like there were square stars tacked about on it; they appeared to be crossed on it."[60] A false sheep's head was also worn: "Some had on something that stuck away out in front like a sheep's head, and some stuck way up high."[61] Another head disguise was achieved by imitating terrible head wounds. "They had things fitted on their heads, scooped out, that came down just like a hat, but had no brim . . . that part was painted red, as I could see in the night, but whether the balance of it was green or red I could not tell, for it came down to the neck."[62]

Elaborate Klan costuming often included the use of other frills and accessories which varied from region to region. False facial attachments were either sewn to the headpiece or worn alone. Examples included huge teeth, either painted on the mask or made from quills or bone[63] and false animal ears, usually resembling a horse's or mule's ears, which hung down like tassels.[64] Also reported were excessively long noses[65] and a long tongue, which stuck out about six inches and was manipulated by the wearer's tongue.[66] Fake beards and mustaches were also worn by Klansmen,

[59] *Ibid.*, 394.
[60] *Ibid.*, Alabama, 668.
[61] *Ibid.*, 574.
[62] *Ibid.*, South Carolina, 296.
[63] *Ibid.*, Alabama, 528.
[64] *Ibid.*, South Carolina, 409.
[65] *Ibid.*, Georgia, 690.
[66] Walter L. Fleming, *Documentary History of Reconstruction* (2 vols., Cleveland, 1907), II, 364.

usually of an exaggerated length of twelve to eighteen inches. This long facial hair was described as being black, white, or gray, and was sometimes the only facial disguise worn.[67]

The individual Klansman had full opportunity to express his creativity by the choice of ornamentation, ranging from the Arkansas horses and riders disguised in black calico trimmed with metallic, cabalistic signs, to a Tennessee headdress ornamented with gold braid and black lace over the eyes and nose.[68] Tin buttons, an inch and a half in diameter, sometimes covered the entire robe, appearing as miniature moons in the starlight.[69] Red, white, or blue plumes (depending on rank) on the headpiece and silk scarves around the waist often completed the costume.[70]

Although oral sources add little to the documented picture of the Klan costume, Black folk seem to remember with some detail this impressive ornamentation, frequently mentioning such accessories as cow horns and long, mulelike ears. According to some slave narrators, wings were also worn as a part of the Klan costume. Nicey Pugh described an encounter with winged Klansmen:

> I 'members one evenin' Margaret Shaver an' I wuz goin' atter de cows down in de fiel' an' us seed whut I reckon wuz de Ku Klux Klan mens. Us wuz so skeered us didn't know what it wuz, us told Marse Jim dat we seen sumthin' whut had long ears, a' wings, an' dey axed us who libed on dis place? An' us tole dem dat us didn't know, us wuz jes' going atter water, but dey didn't bodder us. Marse Jim jes smiled an' said dat dey wouldn't bodder us so long as us behaves.[71]

The folk easily distinguished between the crude, improvised outfits, thrown together for a particular occasion, and the well-constructed garb of established Klan units:

> what I suppose are our homemade Ku-Klux, have rather a cheap rig on by the side of our ordinary Ku-Klux. This gown I found was just

---

[67] KKK Report, Mississippi, 663; Georgia, 360; Alabama, 723.
[68] Horn, 64.
[69] *Ibid.*, 62.
[70] *Ibid.*
[71] WPA Files, "Slave Narratives" (Nicey Pugh, Prichard, Ala.). (South Dakota: Misfiled.)

a loose gown with big long sleeves to it, and then they have a piece of the long gown thrown up over the head if they want to, but it has eye holes, and all Christendom could not tell who was inside of it by seeing the eyes. What I call the Tennessee Ku Klux had a very good rig. They look pretty well, with a red coat trimmed off with black, and when they threw the piece up over it was lined with different color from the rest. They had a sort of rubber caps with fixings to come all over them in a rain-storm. They could wear that down.[72]

On occasions when it was not possible to formally attire in Klan regalia, impromptu disguises were made by the derangement of ordinary clothing, devised quickly and without previous preparation. One distinct advantage of this spur-of-the-moment garb was its economy, requiring only the ingenious use of common articles of clothing, such as a handkerchief or scrap of cloth. Impromptu disguises are frequently referred to in oral tradition. A situation utilizing this type of costuming is described by the following commentator:

There is one other feature of this monstrous klan to which I call your attention. It is the manner in which young men and boys are drawn into it. A proposition is made to them to go to see a little fun. Unsuspectingly they agree to it, and start off with a crowd not knowing or suspecting any thing wrong, get off to some old field or woods, all halt, some disguise themselves, others, who have no disguise, are directed to put their shirts and drawers over their pants and coats. In this situation a negro is whipped, in a few instances killed.[73]

Impromptu body disguises consisted of simply draping a blanket around the shoulders, or turning suit pants, jackets, or federal overcoats to the wrong side. Another homemade disguise was to wear old clothes, usually different from their normal dress; cloaks, white carpenter-type overalls, shawls, and white pantaloons were often worn. One variation used the type of pants worn by little

[72] KKK Report, Alabama, 919.
[73] John A. Minnis, Address, "Ku-Klux in Alabama," Montgomery, Ala., July 1, 1872, p. 22.

boys: "They had on common breeches, buttoned just as little boys wear them, and disguises over their faces—some red and some black."[74] Pants of this variety were sometimes stuffed in order to make the wearer appear exceptionally broad.[75]

One style of homemade disguise consisted of wearing women's dresses, often homespun or calico.[76] Men were known to borrow their wives' dresses and sons borrowed from their mothers. One bystander who saw a group of Klansmen so garbed said, "At first they looked like a parcel of women."[77] An eyewitness, who fled to safety under a house, gave this account:

> The men appeared to be dressed in different colors; when I was under the house I looked at the captain, and his dress appeared to be blue and yellow; he had horns on his head over a foot long, and something over his face that appeared to be of different colors; I didn't hardly know what it looked like, but I believe it was blue and yellow; he had a long gown that came pretty much down toward his feet; some of them had on dresses, as I saw while I was under the house, that appeared to be short dresses like half-grown girls wear, and seemed to come down to their knees; some of them had old handkerchiefs over their faces, with holes in them for their eyes; I think there were about twelve in the company, but I did not count them.[78]

Another type of women's garment was also utilized. It was referred to as "what looked like these tight sacks the ladies wear, trimmed in black, that are white."[79]

The top of the head was often covered with an old hat, usually black or gray, or a hat turned wrong side out. Other types of head coverings included knitted or coonskin caps.[80] Head disguises which left the face exposed consisted of binding the jaws by using a yard or so of cloth tied under the chin: "They had about a yard

[74] KKK Report, Georgia, 463.
[75] *Ibid.*, 598.
[76] *Ibid.*, South Carolina, 42.
[77] *Ibid.*, Georgia, 550–51.
[78] *Ibid.*, South Carolina, 1953.
[79] *Ibid.*, Mississippi, 667.
[80] *Ibid.*, South Carolina, 696.

of cambric. . . . It was tied over their faces in a kind of bonnet fashion. . . ."[81] In another instance, a "comfort" was reported as having been worn on the head in the same manner.[82]

Impromptu disguises were often partial, in the sense that only portions of the body, head, or face alone were covered. In addition, Klansmen often dressed in ordinary clothes and disguised only their guns. As one informant put it, "They had something long and black hanging down over their guns."[83]

Partial face disguises were a simple solution to achieving anonymity as well as a suggestion of grotesqueness. The lower portion of the face could be effectively covered with oilcloth patches, a knit cravat, a pocket handkerchief, or an old rag about seven or eight inches wide. The eyes remained visible—and, it was hoped, unrecognizable. The use of this relatively small piece of material as a mask had the additional utility of allowing Klansmen to be able to lift the material in order to spit.[84] As one eyewitness said, "They had their mouths covered, and that's about all."[85]

Complete face disguises were often made of paper, with holes cut for the eyes and mouth, around which paint was used to define the openings. This type of mask was known as a "dough face." Lampblack was sometimes used to completely blacken the face. It was presumed the onlooker would not be able to discern if the face underneath the coloring was Negro or white. Tangled hair added another dimension of supposed grotesqueness: "They were not colored; they were as white as you are; but they had their faces blacked and hair tangled."[86] Witness after witness testified in a simple, straightforward way of having seen Klansmen so disguised: "The men were blacked or in disguise."[87] "Some had paper faces on, and some were just blacked and marked up."[88] ". . . those persons came in with their faces blacked, or were black men."[89] "That

81 *Ibid.*, Georgia, 218.
82 *Ibid.*, 667.
83 *Ibid.*, 665.
84 *Ibid.*, 376.
85 *Ibid.*, South Carolina, 694.
86 *Ibid.*, Georgia, 376.
87 *Ibid.*, Alabama, 240.
88 *Ibid.*, Georgia, 598.
89 *Ibid.*, Alabama, 3.

was Connor. His face was blackened."[90] "Wilson had his wife's dress on. My wife is well acquainted with them, and she knew that he had on his wife's dress, and an oil-cloth patch over his face, and his face blacked up."[91]

Disguises carried over even to their voices. Every effort was made not only to alter one's natural speaking voice, but to create the impression of supernatural animals:

> They were whistling when they came there, making all kinds of fuss —some hollering like owls, some whippoorwills, and some talk I could not understand. They talked while they were getting me out of the house in broken language.[92]

This kind of altered speech pattern was referred to by the folk as "talking Ku Klux." The folk referred to the type of unfamiliar language the Klansmen used as either French, Dutch, or Irish. Speaking rapidly, simulating a deep, gutteral tone, or adapting a high-pitched shrill were techniques for disguising the voice.

Often, however, Klansmen's voices were not heard, as silent, spectral movements became a traditional practice for some units. Others carried noisemakers that emitted weird, unearthly sounds, or used horns, whistles, and bells. "The whistle is made with a small piece of cane, with a shot inside of it, which vibrates and makes a shrill piercing sound."[93]

Klansmen also costumed their horses, ranging from the elaborate to the simple. An elaborate rig was described: "The horses had on fittings over the heads, mighty nice, and the ears were red, and a kind of speckled new calico covered all of one horse, and the other had a kind of tent-cloth covering him."[94] Simple disguises included covering horses with a black cloth[95] or "white sheets tied over them that came down under the belly and were tied."[96] Sometimes a blanket was simply thrown over the horse.[97] Partial cover-

---

[90] *Ibid.*, South Carolina, 290.
[91] *Ibid.*, Georgia, 519.
[92] *Ibid.*, Mississippi, 771.
[93] *Ibid.*, 1160.
[94] *Ibid.*, Alabama, 669.
[95] *Ibid.*, 528.
[96] *Ibid.*, 680.
[97] *Ibid.*, Georgia, 376.

ing usually meant that "The horses were half covered, back to the saddle; the head and neck were covered."[98] The horses also wore masks, with openings for the eyes and nostrils, and their hoofs were muffled. Often they were painted: "They were disguised and their horses painted, so that it was impossible to recognize any of them."[99]

Because color played an important role in the psychology of control, men who wore black robes often appeared on horses dressed all in white, which may have been designed to give the effect of a riderless horse. Describing how the Klansmen were disguised, one witness recalled: "I believe most of them were disguised in black, the horses were covered in white. They had a mule in the bunch that was not covered at all."[100]

While one can read full descriptions of Klan costumes, the details of their transportation, storage, and construction are seldom discussed in published Klan literature. Congressional testimony reveals that individual Klan members carried their garb in saddlebags when out on a raid, or concealed the costume about their person, depending on the bulkiness of the garb.[101] After they got through riding, the costumes were hidden in their houses[102] or about the barn or shuck house; several reports were made of finding Klan garb in the latter location.[103] Caves were also employed for hiding costumes: "We found a cave on a plantation where they hide their disguises. As a general thing, they dig a hole somewhere in the ground at the head of a gully, and cover it over with boards or pine-tops to hide their disguises. We found two caves of that description within two miles of our house."[104]

If not contrived on the spur of the moment, simple disguises were made principally in families. More elaborate costumes were often made by professional seamstresses in local towns. Under

[98] *Ibid.*, Mississippi, 771.
[99] *Ibid.*, Alabama, 352.
[100] *Ibid.*, Georgia, 577.
[101] *Ibid.*, Mississippi, 814.
[102] *Ibid.*
[103] *Ibid.*, Georgia, 245, 3, 6.
[104] *Ibid.*, 419.

careful Congressional questioning, three such seamstresses con-
fessed only to making disguises for masquerade parties, known as
domino parties (the disguises were called dominoes). But even
these witnesses would not deny that the disguises were the exact
duplicates of the local Klan costume. Tailors were contacted by
letter or note left on the owner's "gate directing him to make some
garments in some particular way; to put them back there; that
the price for making them would be left when they were taken
away."[105]

In view of all the devices the Klan employed to camouflage the
body, voice, and horses, how effective were the disguises?

A cross-section of testimony from the WPA material and Congressional testimony indicates that in many instances the wearers
of the regalia were successfully concealed. As one informant stated
when asked if he knew any of the men who paid him a midnight
visit: "No sir; and the mothers that suckled them could not have
known them."[106] Another victim testified that under normal circumstances he might have been more observant, but: "I could not
say that I knew any of them. I might have known them, but they
took me in an excitement, and in the night disguised; that would
disturb a man's mind so he could not tell."[107] Sometimes victims
were provided with a full view of Klansmen's faces when masks
accidentally dropped off, or were snatched off in unplanned scuf-
fles. "He would not tell me who he was, and I up with a rail and
knocked his dough-face off, and then I knew him. He then swore
he would Ku-Klux me."[108]

There is considerable evidence, on the other hand, that many
cool, collected souls were able to recognize individual riders (or
sometimes the whole parcel) by such things as body size, voice,
or unusual personal characteristics—such as missing front teeth,
walk, general appearance, behavior—or by their horses. Of these
identifying characteristics perhaps the one that most frequently

---

[105] *Ibid.*, Mississippi, 855.
[106] *Ibid.*, South Carolina, 1093.
[107] *Ibid.*, Alabama, 573.
[108] *Ibid.*, Georgia, 867.

gave away an individual Klansman was his voice: "I work with these boys every day. One of them I raised from a child, and I knew them. I have lived with them twelve years. . . . They came a-talking by me and I knew their voices."[109]

Poorly made or defective face pieces often exposed some feature of the anatomy that was known. Distinctive beards and whiskers were easily recognized: "I could see the whiskers through the mouth-holes; that is the way I knew one man. . . ."[110] In another instance a man was recognized by a bright red birthmark which ran from his neck to his face.[111] Even disguised with a robe and cap, one Klansman was known by an observant bystander:

> I asked her how she could know him under such circumstances, and she said that the mouth-holes around his mouth were extremely large and she could see his lips, and that the eye-holes were large and exhibited all the brow. She was outspoken, and said she knew him as well as she knew anybody; that she had known him about fifteen years.[112]

No manner of costume could conceal movements:

> . . . I could not tell any other way only from the movements—that one of them must be Henry Anderson. I went to school with him, and he moved very peculiar, and I thought it was him, though I did not believe he would be caught in such a place as that.[113]

Some distinctive clothing feature, perhaps an unusual garment, sometimes exposed the culprit. In South Carolina a Klansman was recognized by the black, white, and red-striped lining of his coat that had been turned wrong side out. It was such a flashy lining that he was the only one in the area to have one like it.[114]

A nocturnal encounter with fully outfitted Klansmen was an experience few freedmen forgot. Alice Duke's comment about the Klan garb is typical of folk opinion: "Dey was so scary looking dat I ain't never fergot dem. Dem's de awfulest 'boogers' I is ever see'd

[109] *Ibid.*, South Carolina, 605.
[110] *Ibid.*, Georgia, 547.
[111] *Ibid.*, Mississippi, 274.
[112] *Ibid.*, Georgia, 1009.
[113] *Ibid.*, Mississippi, 663.
[114] *Ibid.*, South Carolina, 543.

befo' or since."[115] Gabe Hines described the traumatic experience of facing an unexpected gathering of robed Klansmen:

> We was a'sittin' dar befo' de fire, me an' my ol' woman, when we heard a stompin' like a million horses had stopped outside de do'. We tipped to de do' an' peeked out an' li'l Missy what we seed was so turrible our eyes jes' mos' popped out our haid. Dere was a million horses all kivered in white, wid dey eyes pokin' out and a-settin' on de hosses was men kivered in white too, tall as giants, an' dey eyes was a-pokin' out too. Dere was a leader an' he heldt a bu'nin' cross in his hand.[116]

Intimidating, indeed, were the costumed Klansmen who capitalized on folklore to control the newly freed Blacks.

Supernatural Practices

During the first stage of its development the Klan employed a number of supernatural tricks to intimidate Blacks. Most of these tricks had been used earlier by slave masters, overseers, and the ante-bellum patrols: the belted-sheet costume, the practice of using stilts to make the "ghost" appear to be walking above the ground, and the gimmicks of the rotating head and the collapsible rubber bag. The latter device was now used to convince Blacks that Klansmen were thirsty dead returning from hell. The Klan refined and embellished many supernatural practices from earlier slavery times, making them the basis for extending supernatural control over Blacks.

For the most part, supernatural practices were built around two central ideas: the familiar dead returning to haunt former acquaintances; and the Klan's prodigious supernatural powers, "such as the ability to take themselves to pieces at will, rattle their bones, and drink whole pailfuls of water."[117] The returning-dead theme

---

[115] WPA Files, "Slave Narratives" (Alice Duke, Gaffney, S. C., Sept. 16, 1937).

[116] *Ibid.* (Gabe Hines, Eufaula, Ala.).

[117] James Wilford Garner, *Reconstruction in Mississippi* (New York, 1901), 338.

was played over and over again in various forms, re-emphasizing the same idea with which the slaves had earlier been indoctrinated. It was not enough for Klansmen to be considered as ghosts by the Black population; they liked to be referred to as "ghosts of the Confederate dead."[118] They were especially fond of telling Blacks, at whose houses they stopped for nocturnal visits, that the white-sheeted figures were former masters or specific people the Blacks had known. Jessie Brown stated: "They would profess to be from some nearby cemetery, you see, and they would say that they were an individual that you knew of who had died. In other words the whole thing tends to this ghost idea."[119]

The concept of the returning Confederate dead was meant to suggest that the slave regime had not ended, though the South was subdued, and that former controls were still being perpetrated Indeed, mortal masters who through death became supernatural were even more powerful than before. No longer limited by mortal flesh, the ghosts of the Confederate dead could follow freedmen anywhere, appearing at any time, any place.[120]

The hideous and grotesque Klan disguises were calculated to operate upon and exploit superstitious fears of Blacks.[121] When one witness was asked whether the Klan's members claimed to be spirits of Confederate dead, the reply was:

The negroes are very superstitious; they say the Ku-Klux are the spirits of confederate soldiers. I have talked with negroes sometimes who say they leave holes in the ground like the seventeen-year lo-custs; that they can see where they come up out of the ground. The negroes are very superstitious; they are very much afraid if they see anything white in the night.[122]

In order to establish credulity concerning their roles as ghosts, Klansmen found it necessary to use strange, far off, or super-natural places from which they had returned. Famous battlefields known to have taken a terrible toll in dead were a favorite choice;

118 Horn, 18.
119 Interview, April 23, 1964.
120 Annie Cooper Burton, *The Ku Klux Klan* (Los Angeles, 1916), 11.
121 KKK Report, Alabama, 627.
122 *Ibid.*, Georgia, 239.

Manassas Gap and Shiloh were the most frequently mentioned in oral tradition. An informant related:

> said they had come from Manassas Gap to see that the poor widows are not imposed upon. They also said that the rebels were not going to let the taxes be paid. From the two things you would infer that they were rebels killed at Manassas. They said they were risen from the dead, and that they were rebels, too.[123]

Klan horsemen, riding silently by, were known to drop or turn their heads when the squadron leader said "Shiloh":

> Sometimes we would meet one or two people and they'd ride right on by, and nobody would speak or say nothing, but just keep straight forward; just the foremost ones that would see them would say, "Shiloh," and then they'd all hang their heads, or turn their heads, and nobody would say anything.[124]

One variation of the battlefield theme involved impersonating a well-known hero who had died in battle. "One man in particular will tell you that one of the disguised men came up to him and asked if he knew who he was. The man said 'No'; and then the disguised man said, 'I am ———,' giving some name, 'from the battlefield of Shiloh.' "[125]

> . . . They dressed a fellow in white clothes—that is the story I was told about it—and they set him at the door, and brought the negroes out one at a time. He was standing at the door, and they would call him Stevens—that was the name of the man whom these prisoners had murdered. They would say to him, "Was this one of your murderers, Stevens?" They would say that to the man who personated Stevens' ghost, and he would say, "Yes." And they would say, "Well, take him off," and another would be brought out and he would answer ,"Yes," and they would take him off.[126]

Having established that these were ghosts returning from the dead, it became vitally important to associate them with some definite place of horror. The very idea of "returning ghosts" suggested

[123] *Ibid.*, Mississippi, 663.
[124] *Ibid.*, 813.
[125] *Ibid.*, Georgia, 512.
[126] *Ibid.*, South Carolina, 802.

some physical location to which they would ultimately return. Hell was one. Sometimes the journey from hell had a sense of mission: "They said they came from hell for Wright. They were the boys that carried Owens to hell and now they were going to carry Alfred Wright to hell, for company for Owens."[127]

The moon in the nineteenth century was certainly a remote place to have returned from. However, according to one witness, "They said they were just out of the moon."[128] And sometimes both places were used, as one intended victim recalled: " 'By God, we are just from hell; get up and open the door.' I said, 'No one who goes to hell ever returns back again'; the voice said, 'By God, we have come out of the moon tonight, and are come to kill you.' "[129]

Masked and garbed figures were also associated with strange or far-off places, about which ex-slaves would have misconceptions. "We are Yankees from the Federal City, and we will have you in hell before tomorrow night this time."[130]

Having established supernatural credentials, the Klansman in the next phase assumed extraordinary and inordinate thirst. A robed Klansman would call at the house of a Black and ask for water. " 'We have not drank any water in thirty days. We come all the way from old Virginny, and want some water. We want two buckets.' I went and brought them two or three buckets of water. They told me they had just risen from the dead . . . ."[131]

Commonly, the ghost said it was the best drink he had had since he was killed at Shiloh,[132] the battle most frequently referred to because of its proximity to Pulaski; the Blacks, too, had been deeply impressed by stories of how wounded men there begged for water.[133] One witness said of the Klan: "I have heard people say that they never saw persons who could drink so much water; that one of them could drink a whole bucket."[134]

[127] *Ibid.*, 1174.
[128] *Ibid.*, Alabama, 574.
[129] *Ibid.*, 1186.
[130] *Ibid.*, Georgia, p. 732.
[131] *Ibid.*, Mississippi, p. 894.
[132] Fleming, *Documentary History of Reconstruction*, 365.
[133] Romaine, 11.
[134] KKK Report, Alabama, 432.

It is interesting that the trick Klansmen most enjoyed playing on freedmen was the one talked about most in Black oral tradition. It would also appear that the ex-slaves were not quite as unsuspecting as the Klan members thought. Frederick Ross remembered:

> One time the Ku Klux come aroun. They knock on the doah, then they say, "Please give me a drink, Ah aint had a drink since the battle o' Shilo." What fo' they say that? My, you see, they wants us tuh think they's the spirits a' the sojers killed at Shilo an they been in hell so long they drinks all the water they kin git. This one man make us carry him five buckets of water, an' it look like he drink em but nex mahnin' theys big mud puddle side the doah.[135]

The water trick was played with seemingly endless variations. Sometimes it was performed by a lone Klansman, other times by a group. At times the water consumption was the main attraction, and at other times this feature was combined with other theatrics and an admonition to the freedmen to carry out Klan instructions. The following shows how supernatural tricks were tied in with Klan warnings:

> Us lef' de plantation in '65 or '66 and by '68 us was havin' sich a awful time with de Ku Klux. First time dey come to my mamma's house at midnight and claim dey sojers done come back from de dead. Dey all dress up in sheets and make up like spirit. Dey groan 'roun and say dey been kilt wrongly and come back for justice. One man, he look jus' like ordinary man, but he spring up 'bout eighteen feet high all of a sudden. Another say he so thirsty he ain't have no water since he been kilt at Manassas Junction. He asks for water and he jes' kept pourin' it in. Us think he sho must be a spirit to drink dat much water. Course he not drinkin' it, he pourin' it in a bag under he sheet. My mamma never did take up no truck with spirits so she knowed it jes' a man. Dey tell us what dey gwine do iffen we don't all go back to us massas and us all 'grees and den dey all dis'pear.[136]

---

[135] WPA Files, "Slave Narratives" (Frederick Ross, Commerce, Mo.).
[136] *Ibid.*, (Lorenza Ezell, Beaumont, Tex.). (C–F. Texas: Slave Interviews, Duplicates.)

Another version of this trick was for the Confederate ghost to assert that he had no food since the battle of Shiloh, or had never seen meat since he was straight from hell.[137] Ann Ulrich Evans recalls:

> Den some time dey come on in de house, tear up everything on the place, claim dey looking for somebody and tell us dey hungry 'cause dey ain't had nothin' to eat since de battle of Shiloh. Maybe twenty of 'em at a time make us cook up everything we got, and dey had false pockets made in dere shirt, and take up de skillet with de meat and hot grease pipin hot and pour it every bit down de front of dem shirts inside de false pockets and drop de hot bread right down dere, behind de meat and go on.[138]

Finally, the Confederate-dead idea was applied even to crop raising. Freedmen who were not particularly industrious were sometimes visited at night by Klansmen who pretended not to know what cotton was because "We jess from Hell. We ain't got no cotton there." Hammett Dell described such a Klan visit:

> The onlies sperience I had myself wid the Ku Klux was one night fo Grandma and Auntie left. Somebody wrap on our cabin door. They opened it. We got scared when we seed em. They had the horses wrapped up. They had on white long dresses and caps. . . . They say, "Who live next down the road?" I tole em Nells Christian. They say, "What he do?" I said, "Works in the field." They all grunt, m-m-m-m. Then they say, "Show us the way." I nearly run to death cross the field to keep outer the way of the white horses. The moon shining bright as day. They say, "Nells come out here." He say, "Holy Moses." He comes out. They say, "Nells what you do?" "I farms." They say, "What you raise?" He say, "Cotton and corn." They say, "Take us to see yo cotton we jess from Hell. We ain't got no cotton there." He took em out there where it was clean. They got down and felt it. Then they say, "What is dat?" feelin' the grass. Nells say, "That is grass." They say, "You raise grass too?" He said, "No. It come up." They say, "Let us see yo corn." He showed

[137] *Ibid.*, (Lee Guidon, Clarendon, Ark.). (E–G. Arkansas: Slave Interviews, Duplicates.)
[138] *Ibid.* (Ann Ulrich Evans, St. Louis, Mo.). (Missouri: Slave Interviews, Duplicates I.)

em the corn. They felt it. They say, "What this?" Nells say, "It grass." They say, "You raise grass here?" They all grunt m-m-m-m everything Nells say. They give him one bad whopping an' tell him they be back soon to see if he raisin' grass. They said, "You raise cotton and corn but not grass on this farm." They moan, "m-m-m-m." I heard em say his whole family and him too was out by daylight wid their hoes cuttin' the grass out their crop.[139]

Hammett Dell referred repeatedly to the moaning sound the Klan members made during this episode. Imitating ghost sounds came to be a rather standard practice of Klansmen. Sometimes a kind of howl was effected by saying, "O-O, O-O."[140] At other times Klan members murmured, "Ku Klux, Ku Klux, Ku Klux, Ku Klux," in a fine soft voice while performing their antics.[141]

Special effects designed to support the belief that Klansmen were Confederate dead returned from hell were later added to their tricks. If a Black was on trial, Klan members sprinkled a little powder which they called "hell fire" on the floor beforehand. When the Black defendant looked down at the floor, one of the Klansmen would run his foot over the powder line, causing a fiery-looking trail.[142] Sometimes an immense volume of flame was blown from the nose.[143]

Klansmen literally had a captive audience when making nocturnal visits to freedmen, who were forced to watch their antics or suffer consequences. One Black said:

We lived in a log house during the Ku Klux days. Dey would watch you just like a chicken rooster watching for a worm. At night, we was skeered to have a light. Dey would come around wid "dough faces" on and peer in de winders and open de do'. Iffen you didn't look out, dey would skeer you half to death.[144]

[139] *Ibid.* (Hammett Dell, Brasfield, Ark.). (C–D. Arkansas: Slave Interviews, Duplicates.)
[140] *Ibid.* (Mattie Lee, Fredericktown, Mo.).
[141] *Ibid.* (Kitty Hill, Raleigh, N. C.). (D–H. North Carolina: Slave Interviews, Duplicates.)
[142] Burton, 11.
[143] John Moffatt Mecklin, *The Ku Klux Klan: A Study of the American Mind* (New York, 1924), 73.
[144] WPA Files, "Slave Narratives" (Brawley Gilmore, Union, S. C., Dec. 3, 1936).

The second theme constantly reemphasized by Klansmen was the possession of extraordinary powers. To dramatize their supernatural nature, some tricks made Klansmen appear able to take themselves to pieces whenever they wished. For example, some of the members carried skeleton hands made of bone or wood with a handle long enough to be concealed by the gown sleeve.[145] The idea was to offer a friendly handshake and leave the startled victim holding on to what appeared to be a skeleton hand! A chapter in Nashville, made up of university medical students, actually used fingers or hands taken from corpses.[146]

Another dismembering trick was to ride up to a Black, dismount, and stretch the bridle reins toward him as if the Klansman desired him to hold his horse. When the frightened Black extended his hand to grasp the rein, the ghost appeared to remove his head and place that also in the victim's outstretched hands.[147] One freedman's reaction to the false head was this: "Some time they put sticks in the top of the tall thing they wear and then put an extra head up there with scary eyes and great big mouth, then stick it clear up in the air to scare the poor Negroes to death."[148] Removal of the head was a trick frequently practiced by the Klan. Headless disguises were generally effected by wearing a gown fastened by a drawstring over the top of the wearer's head. Over this was worn an artificial skull made of a large gourd or pasteboard. This, with the hat, could be readily removed, and the man would appear to be headless.[149] "Here, hold my head a minute," the Klansman would say, thrusting the masked gourd at the Black.[150]

The freedmen told about some previously unreported Klan tricks, such as parading in a donkey skin. One Black said, "They had another thing they call 'Donkey Devil' that was jes as bad.

[145] J. C. Lester and D. L. Wilson, *Ku Klux Klan* (New York, Washington, 1905), 98.
[146] Burton, 11.
[147] Lester and Wilson, 97.
[148] WPA Files, "Slave Narratives" (W. L. Bost, Asheville, N.C.). (A–C. North Carolina: Slave Interviews, Duplicates.)
[149] Lester and Wilson, 97.
[150] Horn, 19.

They take the skin of a donkey and get inside of it and run after the pore Negroes."[151]

> Theatrics often included acting like farm animals. Sometimes they pretended to be talking cows. There were some shook their heads and horns at me, and acted like cows. . . . They had horns, and they shook their horns at me when I was in the door. They were just leaving, though, when they said, "Woe unto that back of yours."[152]

Designating certain places as haunted, which had been practiced by masters and overseers during slavery, was also used by the Klan. For example, "A few figures wrapped in sheets and sitting on tombstones in a graveyard near which Negroes were accustomed to pass would serve to keep the immediate community quiet for weeks and give the locality a reputation for 'hants' which lasted long."[153] Indeed, "graveyards were a favorite meeting place for rural Ku Klux, the old-fashioned box tombs providing an ideal hiding place for their regalia."[154] Certain strategic country roads were also paraded at night with hosts of white-sheeted figures, and meeting places were visited[155] as well as abandoned houses and wooded areas.

Ghostly noises were produced by carrying chains,[156] reminiscent of the tin cans overseers formerly dragged around the slave quarters. Cow bones in a sack were rattled within earshot of Blacks,[157] supporting the belief that the Klansmen could shake their own bones. Cow horns were frequently used to announce that the Klan was riding. From this instrument came an eerie sound, especially frightening in the stillness of night. As one freedman said, "[I] never will forget de way dat horn soun' at

[151] WPA Files, "Slave Narratives" (W. L. Bost, Asheville, N. C.). (A–C. North Carolina: Slave Interviews, Duplicates.)
[152] KKK Report, Mississippi, 663.
[153] Fleming, *Sequel of Appomattox*, 256.
[154] Horn, 19.
[155] Fleming, *Sequel of Appomattox*, 255–56.
[156] Lester and Wilson, 96.
[157] Fleming, *Sequel of Appomattox*, 256.

night when dey was a-goin after some mean nigger."[158] Minnie
Bell Fountaine added:

> I have heard that they do that, make strange noises that would
> frighten them such as a weird holler, you know. And then another
> thing that they, that I have heard that they used . . . if someone
> killed a beef, they would take the cow horn or the bull's horn . . .
> crooked like that, and they would fix it in such a way that they
> would blow the horn and it would make a strange weird sound.
> Now that I know. That was one of their tricks, I've heard people
> say. I've heard that would be one of their ways of letting you know
> that they were out. In fact, I think that was the way they could call
> each other together . . . that that would be a signal to one another.
> But it was used as a frightening thing, something to frighten you.[159]

A Congressional witness recalls a completely acted out skit,
including costumes, dialogue, and plot:

> I had not been in bed twenty minutes until it went like thirty
> geese all around the outside of the house, making with their bills
> and coming to the door, "Hilloo! Hilloo!" . . . and they came in . . .
> and stooped about with their gowns on; stooped down so they could
> just cleverly walk, and went about over the house stooping, with a
> great white face and a black-looking beard, as well as I could
> recollect when they twisted their mustaches. One was black and the
> other white. One stood in the door; the others sauntered around
> the house. At last they came to the bed; one came to the foot and
> the other to the head; and the one at the foot smelled all around at
> the foot of the bed, and he says, [in deep bass], "He's a damned old
> rad." The other one said, [in sharp treble], "Is he fat?" The other
> answered, [in bass] "Yes." The other said, [in treble], "Well, we'll
> eat him then; get out of the bed." I raised on my elbow and says,
> "Look here, gentlemen, you will have tolerably tough eating; I
> am getting tolerably old now, and it looks to me like I would be
> tolerable tough eating." They ordered me again to get up. By this
> time the bolt of the middle door flew open, and the man of the house
> came into the room. He says, "Now, look here, the like of this
> shan't be done here." They said, "By God, we'll eat you." He says,

---

[158] WPA Files, "Slave Narratives" (Dora Franks, Aberdeen, Miss.).
[159] Interview, April 22, 1964.

"Well, cut in on me; but when travelers puts up, they are not to be imposed upon." They jawed a while and the coarse-talking one says, [in bass], "Let's go," and they jerked out of the door, and all of them jumped on their horses, and you would have thought there was a hundred whistles; they jumped on their horses and they went off. . . . They had horns about that long, [18 inches] and they had long gowns.[160]

Perhaps the most effective method used by the Klan to impress the community with its mysterious power was the nightly parade, a method still used with great effect by the revived Klan.[161] Klan parades were silent and arranged to give the impression of very large numbers. A great deal of marching and countermarching through the streets, doubling back and forth, gave the appearance that their numbers far exceeded the actual count.[162] In the regular drills held in town and country the men showed that they had not forgotten their Confederate army training. Commands were given in a very low tone or in a mysterious language, and usually only signals or whistle signals were used.[163] Their horses' feet were always muffled, making their approach completely noiseless.[164] To prevent recognition while on parade, Klan members often stayed out of the parade in their own town, freely and conspicuously mingling with the spectators.[165]

One explanation for the skill with which Klan drills and maneuvers were handled was this:

There were in Greene County a large number of soldiers from the confederate army, both cavalry and infantry, a very large number, and it is not at all improbable that the capacity to perform these military evolutions was obtained while in the confederate army. If it was not, then of course they must have had some practice. But it seems to me altogether incredible that they should have had practice

[160] KKK Report, Alabama, 729. The brackets above appear in the original record and do not indicate editorial comment. "Rad" in the skit is a short term for radical.
[161] Mecklin, 75.
[162] Romaine, 14.
[163] Fleming, *Sequel of Appomattox*, 256–57.
[164] Burton, 11.
[165] Fleming, *Sequel of Appomattox*, 256–57.

anywhere in Alabama, either in daylight or night-time, for a sufficient time to have become as expert as they were represented to be on that day, without being seen before or since.[166]

Blacks were seldom visited by fewer than fifty Klansmen, and the number was usually reported to be two to three hundred,[167] every man carrying a small whistle and a brace of pistols for protection.[168] For added safety, fabricated stories were circulated about the consequences of trying to fire on Klan members. Blacks were told that it was impossible to hurt a Klansman, and if he were shot at, the bullet would rebound and kill the shooter.[169] The Blacks were told that if they attempted to shoot Klansmen they would fall dead themselves.[170] Another tale was that any physical contact with Klansmen would result in the immediate death of ex-slaves. Alice Hutcheson explains: "Ma allus tole us dat if one of dem Kluxers tetched a Nigger, dat Nigger was gwine to die, and us was so skeered us stayed out of deir way so dey didn't ketch none of us, but dey sh' did wuk on de hides of some of dem other Niggers what dey did git a holt of."[171]

To some extent the Ku Klux Klan never entirely got away from the original purpose of the organization—to amuse members by terrorizing the Black population. For example, Brawley Gilmore stated that Klan members used to ride Blacks by climbing on their backs and forcing them to crawl on their hands and knees: "When I was a boy on de Gilmore Place, de Ku Klux would come along at night a riding de niggers like dey was goats. Yes, sir, dey had 'em down on all-fours a crawling, and dey would be on dere backs."[172]

Forcing Blacks to dance was a common Klan practice, of which the patrollers, too, had been guilty. Madison Griffin re-

166 KKK Report, Alabama, 352.
167 Garner, 340.
168 Fleming, *Sequel of Appomattox*, 254.
169 Howe, 30.
170 Charles Woodward Stearns, *The Black Man of the South and the Rebels* (New York, 1872), 423.
171 WPA Files, "Slave Narratives" (Alice Hutcheson, Athens, Ga.).
172 *Ibid.* (Brawley Gilmore, Union, S. C., Dec. 3, 1936).

ported, "Dey caught a nigger preacher once and made him dance, put him in muddy water and walloped him around in de mud."[173] Willis Winn recalled an experience in which Klansmen made him dance and stand on his head: "I's been cetched by them Ku Kluxers. They didn't hurt me, but they have lots of fun makin' me cut capers. They pulls my clothes off once and made me run four hundred yards and stand on my head in the middle of the road."[174] Another Black stated that he lacked first-hand knowledge of Klan practices of this sort, but he added: "They run my uncle in. He was a big dancer. One time they made him dance. He cut the pigeon-wing for them. That was the name of what he danced."[175]

Suddenly surprising Blacks while dressed in ghostly garb, in order to watch them run away in terror, continued to be a favorite form of Klan amusement. One ex-slave remembered:

> I was going down the road in the moonlight and I heard a hog grunting out in the bushes at the side of the road. I jest walk right on and in a little ways I hear another hog in some more bushes. This time I stop and listen, and they's another hog grunts across the road, and about that time two men dressed up in long white skirts steps out into the road in front of me! I was so scared the goose bumps jump up all over me 'cause I didn't know what they is! They didn't say a word to me, but jest walked on past me and went back the way I had come. Then I see two more mens step out of the woods and I run from that as fast as I can go![176]

Ante-bellum Patrol Duties Assumed by the Klan

Many Southern whites apparently believed that the Reconstruction Klan was a substitute for the old patrol system, [177] func-

---

[173] *Ibid.* (Madison Griffin, Whitmire, S. C., June 18, 1936).
[174] *Ibid.* (Willis Winn, Marshall, Tex.). (Texas: Duplicates 2.)
[175] *Ibid.* ("Cat" Ross, Brasfield, Ark.). (N–R. Arkansas: Slave Interviews, Duplicates.)
[176] *Ibid.* (Joanna Draper, Tulsa, Okla.).
[177] KKK Report, Alabama, 451.

tioning to control Blacks and keep them in their places. "It was a follow-up of the old slave system of patrolling. It originated in that. It may have merged into other things."[178]

While the Klan may have descended from the slave patrols, its power was considerably widened. During slavery the patrols were authorized by law to prevent the free movement of Blacks out after nine o'clock at night without a pass. Offenders were punished by whipping. The Klan, on the other hand, acted as a sort of police patrol, guarding against excesses in Black behavior and acting to curb moral excesses against whites:

> Patrols did not punish petty offenses; but they would not allow negroes to be out where they could commit petty offenses after 9 o'clock at night, unless they had a pass. The master of the negro could give him a pass, so that he could stay out all the year round if he wanted to, and the patrol could not interrupt him. But the negro who was disposed to thieving could not get a pass to be out after 9 o'clock. They did not undertake to punish a negro for petty crimes, but for being out after that hour without a pass. That was the extent of the punishment by the patrol. And men generally through the country subject to military duty were subject also to patrol duty.[179]

As one link in the chain of continuity between the slave patrol and the Klan, disguised men were know to ride in parts of Georgia before the Civil War.[180]

> Before the war they were men selected by the justices of the peace in precincts, whose duty it was to visit negro quarters and chastise, not to exceed thirty-nine lashes, any negro caught off the premises of his master without a permission in writing; probably after a time it got down to fifteen lashes; and they went from one house to another. Probably there would be two companies, six in each company, with a captain, confined to a precinct of say ten miles square; hardly that, say six miles.[181]

[178] *Ibid.*, Georgia, 877.
[179] *Ibid.*, 242.
[180] *Ibid.*, 240.
[181] *Ibid.*, Alabama, 489.

In answer to questioning, a Congressional witness said these patrols performed their duties at night, the frequency ranging from once a week to once a month: "I think they were required probably to go around once a month." Of their officers, he said, "I heard that there was an officer called the officer of the night, or something in that way, who seemed to control them just the same as the captain of the patrol of the night." [182] When asked how long the Klan patrols had existed, an informant replied:

It has been about three years this goober-digging time, as well as I can remember. I was at Jefferson one day selling some goobers, and some fellows were standing around there. Two men said to another one, "Ku-Klux boys." They had been telling about the dead rising out of the ground. I said to old Mr. Whitehead, "They tell me that people have got to rising out of the ground." He said, "Prince, that is not so; it is just like the old patrollers. It was first in South Carolina and then it came here." After these men got around in the settlement, they had a tale on me that I had seen these men; but I said I had not. I said, "It is curious to me that they will say they are our friends, Mr. Whitehead, and then they go and do like they are doing." After telling me the year before that they were patrollers, when that got around they said they are something that comes out of the ground. [183]

In matters other than the supernatural control of the Black the Klan also patterned itself after the old slave patrols. For many freedmen the Civil War made little, if any, difference in their daily existence. One ex-slave testified that she "stayed right there where we was at home, working in the fields, living in the same old cabins just like before the War." [184] All prewar slave controls were still in effect. All freedmen assemblies were forbidden, as well as travel after dark without written permission from white employers. The Klan more and more assumed the role of the old slavery patrols in enforcing these prohibitions.

---

[182] *Ibid.*
[183] *Ibid.*, Georgia, 649.
[184] WPA Files, "Slave Narratives" (Emma Turner, Pine Bluff, Ark.). (S–T. Arkansas: Slave Interviews, Duplicates.)

In Reconstruction days, nightfall marked the beginning of curfew time for the Black. One Black said: "Dem Ku Klux—you dassent be out after dark. But Sunday night they didn't bother you when you went to church."[185] And another Black commented: "After slavery we had to get in before night too. If you didn't, Ku Klux would drive you in."[186]

According to oral sources, passes were still required in order for freedmen to move around unmolested after dark. Written permission to travel had to come from either former owners or the Black's present employers. As one ex-slave stated:

> De Ku Kluckers start riding 'round at night, and dey pass de word dat de darkeys got to have a pass to go and come and to stay at de dances. Dey have to git de pass from de white folks dey works for, and passes writ from de Northern people wouldn't do no good. Dat de way de Kluckers keep the darkies in line.
>
> De Kluckers jest ride up to de dance ground and look at everybody's passes, and iffen some darkey dar widout a pass or got a pass from de wrong man dey run him home, and iffen he talk big and won't go home dey whop him and make him go.
>
> Any nigger out on de road after dark liable to run across de Kluckers, and he better have a good pass! All de dances got to bust up about 'leven o'clock, too.[187]

Another freedman said: "Dem old Ku Klux was a bad lot of mongrels. Dey catch you out widout a pass dey cut you 100 lashes, and you feel like you ain't able to go no where again wid a pass or widout one."[188]

The Klan discouraged all nocturnal assembly of free Blacks, for as one Black said: "One thing the Ku Kluxes didn't want much big gatherings among the black folks. They break up big gatherings."[189] Black meetings were viewed suspiciously because they provided opportunity to air mutual grievances and hatch plots (a

185 *Ibid.*
186 *Ibid.* (Henry Blake, Little Rock, Ark.).
187 *Ibid.* (Charley Williams, Tulsa, Okla.). (M–Y. Oklahoma: Slave Interviews, Duplicates.)
188 *Ibid.* (James Wilson, St. Louis, Mo.).
189 *Ibid.* (Vergil Jones, Brinkley, Ark.). (I–J. Arkansas: Slave Interviews, Duplicates.)

feeling that had long influenced white thinking). In addition, extracurricular night meetings were believed to make Blacks less productive day workers. This was hardly a new point of view, but the Klan intensified efforts to make the freedmen more industrious. As one ex-slave stated, "Ku Klux made them work, said they would starve and starve white folks too if they didn't work."[190] In this regard, Jessie Brown recalled an experience in which the Klan broke up some church meetings until after the crops were harvested:

> My great-grandfather built a church right after slavery and he started this church from a brush arbor. . . . My grandmother remembers this, they were at a summer meeting, and they all were afraid of these things they call ghosts or hants. Of course the white man found out that his Negroes wasn't given him a whole days work because he was at this church until 11 and 12 o'clock at night. So what he did, about three or four of them, dressed in these whites came right down there and walked right into the church door and the church got completely—everybody left. . . . They didn't have any more church service at night until the crops were in.[191]

Whippings were still the punishment inflicted on freedmen caught away from home without passes, but the Klan generally dispensed more beatings to Blacks than did the ante-bellum patrols. A freedmen commented, "De Niggers got more beatin's from 'em dan dey had ever got from deir Old Masters."[192] One reason for this, aside from the sadistic element, was that the Klan, as a regulatory body, performed many of the duties of the former slave masters in controlling Black's behavior, so that whippings were freely administered to freedmen accused of theft, laziness, leaving the plantations in order to seek work elsewhere, and, as one Black said, "they got whoppin's for doin' too much visitin'."[193]

Besides maintaining continued surveillance over the activities

---

[190] *Ibid.* (Phyllis Hicks, Edmondson, Ark.). (H. Arkansas: Slave Interviews, Duplicates.)

[191] Interview, April 23, 1964.

[192] WPA Files, "Slave Narratives" (Willis Cofer, Athens, Ga.).

[193] *Ibid.* (Robert Wesley, Holly Grove, Ark.). (V–Y. Arkansas: Slave Interviews, Duplicates.)

of former slaves, the Klan patrols now had a new task—to prevent the establishment of Black schools. Learning and education had always been discouraged among Blacks, but now white efforts to maintain this ignorance were redoubled. The experience of Wesley Graves' father was shared by many others—black and white—in the post-Civil War South:

> The pateroles made my father do everything but quit. They got him about teaching night school. That was after slavery, but the pateroles still got after you. They didn't want him teaching the Negroes right after the War. He had opened a night school, and he was doing well. They just kept him in the woods then.[194]

And another freedman reported:

> Dere was a school after freedom. Old Man Tilden was de teacher. One time a bunch of men dey calls de Klu Klux come in de room and say, "You git out of here and git 'way from dem niggers. Don't let us cotch you here when we come back." Old Man Tilden sho' was scart, but he say, "You all come back tomorrow." He finishes dat year and we never hears of him 'gain. Dat a log school house on Williamson Creek, five miles south of Austin.[195]

Clearly the Reconstruction Ku Klux Klan relied heavily on folk traditions in its name, costume, and operating procedure as it sought to intimidate and coerce by means of the supernatural.

Officially launched in 1865, the famous "Pulaski Six" deliberately selected a name that had already been circulating in oral tradition with some degree of awe and fearfulness. Co-Cletz thus became Ku Klux, while conveniently retaining the original sounds. Though the origin of the name has become obscured by political rhetoric and historical dust, even the founders admit to utilizing white sheets in an effort to simulate ghostly garb. Later embellishments in the direction of more ornate, custom-made costumes, elaborate accessories, and impromptu disguises effected by disarrangement of clothing or donning inappropriate apparel—all aimed at concealing identity through the appearance

194 *Ibid.* (Wesley Graves, North Little Rock, Ark.). (E–G. Arkansas: Slave Interviews, Duplicates.)
195 *Ibid.* (Clarissa Scales, Austin, Tex.).

of other-worldliness. Finally, by employing crude tricks, border-line practical jokes, and improvised skits centering on traditional themes, early Klan members attempted through burlesque to keep Black folks and white outcasts in political line.

5

THE KU KLUX KLAN IN THE EYES OF THE BLACK

My grandmother used to tell me how [the patrollers] would patrol the countryside and if they caught the slave out without a pass, what they would do to him, and see that he returned to his master. And then immediately after slavery they called them Ku Klux Klans. —THE REVEREND EARL L. HARRISON

Black Folk View of the Klan

TO THE BLACK FOLK, the Ku Klux Klan was simply a later form of the ante-bellum patrols. Since both groups engaged in exactly the same activities—maintaining curfew regulations, administering the pass system, and meting out whippings to truant Blacks—there was every reason to justify this opinion. As one ex-slave said, "The Ku Klux and the pateroles were the same thing, only the Klan was more up to date."[1] And another observed, "I allus pronounced de patterollers and the Ku Kluxers 'bout de same."[2] Earl Harrison recalled the similarity between the patrols and the Klan:

I heard a good deal about them during slavery and immediately after the surrender, that is, after the slaves had been set free. Yes,

[1] WPA Files, "Slave Narratives" (W. L. Bost, Asheville, N.C.). (A–C. North Carolina: Slave Interviews, Duplicates.)

[2] *Ibid.* (George Owens, Beaumont, Tex.). (N–S. Texas: Slave Interviews, Duplicates.)

154

they called them Klans. And they would do the thing what they do now, call themselves keeping the Negro in his place. They would catch them out and they would whip them and do other things to them such as lash them up, and take them and send them back to wherever they belonged, and run them. And in fact they were afraid to travel at night in some, certain areas of Texas where they were. . . . Of course during slavery they didn't have to robe themselves, but after slavery they robed themselves just as the Klans do now, disguise themselves. And it is felt that in many instances it was the poor class of white people and maybe some who had been their overseers who had lost their jobs as overseers. They didn't think that their own masters had done it but they approved of it, as society approves of certain areas in the same sort of thing going on today.[3]

The main point to be considered here is that the patrols and the Klan were viewed by Black folk as two separate, distinct groups, though they operated in exactly the same way. In historical publications the Civil War draws a temporal line of demarcation between the patrol system and the Ku Klux Klan, but Black folk do not have this same neat chronology in their oral tradition. They agree that the patrol system was in effect in the South before the Civil War, but they also maintain that postwar patrols (as distinct from the Klan) operated in many Southern states. Further, the folk argue that while the Ku Klux Klan was organized after "surrender," the "Ku Klux" existed before the war.

The operation of postwar patrols is, to some extent, historically verifiable. Historians mention briefly the secret reorganization of ante-bellum patrols to deal with feared slave insurrections. Informal vigilance committees were formed in every community after the Civil War and in many of them before the war ended.[4] But what a few historians casually refer to, Blacks frequently mention in their oral tradition. One said, "The patrols carried on

[3] Interview, March 6, 1964. The ellipsis in this extract indicates, in part, the omission here of that part of the testimony which began this chapter.
[4] Fleming, *Sequel of Appomattox*, 244–45.

their work for a good while after slavery was over and the Civil War had ended."[5] The following testimony refers to the postwar patrols and reflects the sharp distinction made between the two groups:

> You had to get a pass from owners to go out at night. If you had a pass and the pateroles found you, it was all right if you hadn't overstayed the time that was written on it. If you didn't have a pass or if you had overstayed your time, it was still all right if you could outrun the pateroles. That held before freedom and it held a long time after freedom. The pateroles were still operating when I was old enough to remember those old quarters. They didn't break them up for a long time. I remember them myself. I don't mean the Ku Klux. The Ku Klux was a different thing altogether. The Ku Klux didn't exist before the War. I don't know where they got the name from—I don't know whether they give it to themselves or the people give it to them. But the Ku Klux came after the war and weren't before it.[6]

The operation of these postwar patrols is often spelled out in detail by Black folk. Though their techniques and methods were essentially the same, the rationale for the existence of patrols after the Civil War had changed somewhat; their goal now was to keep the Black in the South and on the plantation of his former master. Randall Lee said on this point: " 'Paddyroles' as the men were called who were sent by the Rebels to watch the slaves to prevent their escaping during war times, were very active after freedom. They intimidated the Negroes and threatened them with loss of life if they did not stay and work for their former masters."[7]

Passes were still required by these latter-day patrols in order to leave the plantation for any reason. Francis Bridges stated: "I 'member more after de War. I 'member my mother said dey had patrollers, and if de slaves would get passes from de Master to

[5] WPA Files, "Slave Narratives" (F. H. Brown, North Little Rock, Ark.). (B con. Arkansas: Slave Interviews, Duplicates.)

[6] *Ibid.* (G. W. Hawkins, Little Rock, Ark.). (H. Arkansas: Slave Interviews, Duplicates.)

[7] *Ibid.* (Randall Lee, Palatka, Fla.).

go to de dances and didn't get back before ten o'clock dey'd beat 'em half to death."[8] And chasing truant freedmen home was very much a part of the patrol's continued operation. An Arkansas Black recalled: "I have heered my father talk about the pateroles too. He talked about how they used to chase him. But he didn't have much experience with them, because they never did catch him. That was after the war when the slaves had been freed, but the pateroles still got after them."[9]

The second assertion, that the Ku Klux operated before the Civil War, cannot be corroborated by historical sources. But the insistence is so strong and recurring that it merits further investigation. One freedman said, "I know the Ku Klux must have been in use before the war because I remember the business when I was a little bit of a fellow. They had a place out there on Crowley's Ridge they used to meet at."[10] In the following testimony Joseph Badgett drew a clear distinction between four confusing words in common usage by the Black at the same time: "patrollers," "jayhawkers," "Ku Klux," and "Ku Klux Klan":

> Pateroles, jayhawkers, and the Ku Klux Klan came before the war. The Ku Klux in slavery times were men who would catch Negroes out and keep them if they did not collect them from their masters. The pateroles would catch Negroes out and return them if they did not have a pass. They whipped them sometimes if they did not have a pass. The jayhawkers were highway men or robbers who stole slaves among other things. At least, that is the way people regarded them. The jayhawkers stole and pillaged, while the Ku Klux stole those Negroes they caught out. The word "Klan" was never included in their name.[11]

Samuel S. Taylor was the WPA worker who interviewed Badgett and a number of other ex-slaves in Arkansas. More discerning than many of the other workers, Taylor noticed the recurring

[8] *Ibid.* (Francis Bridges, Oklahoma City, Okla.). (A–L. Oklahoma: Slave Interviews, Duplicates.)

[9] *Ibid.* (Oscar Felix Junell, Little Rock, Ark.). (I–J. Arkansas: Slave Interviews, Duplicates.)

[10] *Ibid.* (William Brown, North Little Rock, Ark.).

[11] *Ibid.* (Joseph Samuel Badgett, Little Rock, Ark.). (A–B. Arkansas: Slave Interviews, Duplicates.)

assertion among many of the Blacks of the Klan's pre-Civil War existence. He felt that the term "Ku Klux" as distinct from "Ku Klux Klan," might have been a colloquial term applied to jay-hawkers or patrollers. Concerning Badgett's testimony just given, Taylor wrote:

> Badgett's distinctions between jayhawkers, Ku Klux, patrollers, and Ku Klux Klan are most interesting.
>
> I have been slow to catch it. All of my life I have heard persons with ex-slave backgrounds refer to the activities of the Ku Klux among slaves prior to 1865. I always thought that they had the Ku Klux Klan and the patrollers confused.
>
> Badgett's definite and clear-cut memories, however, lead me to believe that many of the Negroes who were slaves used the word Ku Klux to denote a type of person who stole slaves. It was evidently in use before it was applied to the Ku Klux Klan.[12]

The idea that Ku Klux is a folk term meaning slave stealers is supported by other former slaves. Eliza Hays, for example, said:

> I've heard of the pateroles and Ku Klux. I thought they said the Ku Klux was robbers. I think the Ku Klux came after the war. But there was some during the War that would come 'round and ask questions. "Where's yo' old Master?" "Where's his money hid?" "Where's his silverware?" And on like that. Then they would take all the money and silver and anything else loose that could be carried away. And some of them used to steal the niggers theirselves 'specially if they were little childrens. They was scared to leave the little childrens run 'round because of that.[13]

Unlike the patroller, who was the source of derision and scorn and whom they looked upon as "poor white trash," the image of the Klansman was that of a "shadowy," evil figure who committed great wrongs against Black people. While the patrollers

---

[12] *Ibid.* William Lynwood Montell made a similar assumption concerning one of his collected texts in his book *The Saga of Coe Ridge: A Study in Oral History* (Knoxville, 1970), 48. Montell noticed that an informant had assigned the name "Ku Klux" to a pre-Civil War patrol under discussion and assumed that an error had been made.

[13] WPA Files, "Slave Narratives" (Eliza Hays, Little Rock, Ark.). (H. Arkansas: Slave Interviews, Duplicates.)

emerge in Black oral tradition as a "type" of character—sadistic, but fun-loving and mischievous—the Klansman's individuality is submerged beneath an era in which racial injustice and social violence were a part of the Southern way of life.

Interestingly enough, the crimes of which the Klansmen are accused in Black oral testimony far exceed their patroller counterparts in brutality and viciousness. A few of their more serious crimes include cruel whippings (for no given reason), drownings, mutilations, castrations, rapes, and lynchings. Illustrating the heinousness of their deeds, one Black man said: "De Ku Klux uster stick de niggers head on er stake alongside de Cadiz road en dar de buzzards would eat them till nuthin' was left but de bones. Dar was a sign on dis stake dat said, 'Look out Nigger You are next.' "[14] Another Black told of Klan drownings in South Carolina in which the victims were tied to their own guns:

> The Ku Klux made a boat twenty-five feet long to carry the negroes down the river. They would take the negroes' own guns, most of them had two guns, and tie the guns around their necks in the following manner: The barrel of one gun was tied with wire around the negro's neck, and the stock of the other gun was fastened with wire around the negro's neck. When the captain would say, "A-M-E-N," over the side of the boat the negro went, with his guns and bullets taking him to a watery grave in the bottom of Broad River. The wooden parts of the guns would rot, and sometimes the bodies would wash down on the rocks at Neal's Shoals what was then Jeter's Old Mill. Old gun stocks have been taken from there as mementoes.[15]

The humor that is clearly present in Black testimony concerning the patrollers is almost totally absent in discussions of the Klansmen. There was nothing funny about Klan terrorism, either in its supernatural manifestations or in its physical brutality. Diminished, too, were the retaliatory measures which the slaves had used so effectively on the ante-bellum patrols. Reports do appear in oral testimony of freedmen having used the "grapevine," "live

---

[14] *Ibid.* (Mary Wright, Christian Co., Ky.).
[15] *Ibid.* (Charlie Harvey, Union, S. C., Aug. 18, 1937).

coal," and "red pepper" tricks against Klansmen; apparently, however, these practices were now less frequently employed. It was now the Klansmen who used the "grapevine" trick against the Yankees. A freedman reported:

> Directly atter de surrender, de Ku Kluxes sho' was bad atter de Yankees. Dey do all sorts of things to aggivate 'em. Dey's continual' tyin grape vines crost de road, to git 'em tangled up an' make 'em trip up an' break dey own necks. Dat was bad too, 'cause dem poor Yankees never s'picioned sompin.[16]

Several interesting folk names were used by Blacks to designate the Klan organization. "Night riders" was a favorite term since the Klan rode at night, usually between midnight and dawn.[17] This organization was also familiarly known to Blacks as Ku Klux, a word which could be used as a noun or a verb. As a verb, the present participle was formed by adding "ing." Thus "Kluxing" or "Ku Kluxing" denoted any Klan activity such as parading, whipping, frightening Blacks, etc. The past tense was formed by adding "ed." For example, one Black stated, "I heard 'em say lots of niggers was took down in Sabine bottom and Kluxed, just 'cause they wanted to git rid of 'em."[18] A proper noun was formed from Ku Klux by simply adding Mister. To illustrate, Nicey Pugh answered a Klansman's question concerning her destination by stating, "Us is jus' atter de cows, Mr. Ku Klux, us say. Us ain't up to no debilment."[19]

Some regional Klan names are also commonly used in oral tradition. In some Southern states, such as Virginia, this organization was known as the "white caps," a name derived from the hoods with which the group came to be identified. In some parts of Virginia the Klan robe was black and only the hood portion was white. This fact may account for the folk singling out the hood for special designation.

16 *Ibid.* (Aunt Cheney Cross, Evergreen, Ala.).
17 Howe, 29.
18 WPA Files, "Slave Narratives (Jordon Smith, Marshall, Tex.). (Texas: Slave Interviews, Duplicates 2.)
19 *Ibid.* (Nicey Pugh, Prichard, Ala.). (Misc. Slave Excerpts, Duplicates. Alabama Folder 3.)

To some Blacks, however, the name "white cap" does not indicate a regional term of reference to the Klan, but the name of
an earlier group which later evolved into the Klan. To this way
of thinking, the ante-bellum patrols and the "white caps" were
distinct groups which preceded and later merged with the Klan.
Thomas L. Henry explains:

> But see now, in those days, those men that rid in groups, and
> was called white caps. But now they changed, in these days and
> times they changed the name. The Ku Klux Klan, they are the
> same things, the same thing that it was back there when I first
> growed up. The only thing back there they was called white caps
> and now they called the Ku Klux Klan.[20]

Another regional name for the Ku Klux Klan is "night thiefs."
Many Blacks insist that Klansmen robbed them of money, horses,
and other valuable goods after the Civil War. One Black said
that Klan members "come sneaking up and runned you outen
your house and take everything you had."[21] Another freedman
recalled:

> Whar us lived, Ku Kluxers was called "night thiefs." Dey stole
> money and weepons [weapons] f'um Niggers atter de war. Dey
> tuk $50 in gold f'um me and $50 in Jeff Davis' shinplasters f'um
> my brother. Pa and Ma had left dat money for us to use when us
> got big enough.[22]

Fear of being robbed by the Ku Klux Klan was so serious that
some Blacks killed their horses rather than let the Klan take them
away. Some freedmen also hoped that a dead horse in front of a
house might convince Klansmen that the owner's home had already been robbed. Anthony Dawson tells of killing his horse
for this purpose.

> These bunches that come around robbin' got into our neighbor-
> hood and Old Master told me I better not have my old horse at the
> house, kase if I had him they would know nobody had been there

[20] Interview, March 15, 1964.
[21] WPA Files, "Slave Narratives" (Boston Blackwell, North Little Rock, Ark.).
(B con. Arkansas: Slave Interviews, Duplicates.)
[22] *Ibid.* (Charlie Hudson, Athens, Ga.).

stealin' and it wouldn't do no good to hide anything kase they would tear up the place huntin' what I had—and maybe whip or kill me.

"Your old hoss aint no good, Tony, and you better kill him to make them think you already raided on," Old Master told me, so I led him out and knocked him in the head with an axe, and then we hid all our grub and waited for the kluckers to come most any night, but they never did come. I borried a hoss to use in the day and tuck him back home every night for a year.[23]

Black Connections with the Klan

An interesting and little-known aspect of Klan activity also described by oral tradition is that Blacks sometimes accompanied night-riding patrols. In some cases it was a matter of an old Southern custom prevailing—the loyal servant constantly attending his master. When a Black informant was asked by the Congressional committee if a group of forty Klansmen who had intimidated him were disguised, he replied:

> The whole was covered, excepting one old colored man that my wife concluded was a servant of my old regular master—an acquaintance ever since she was a child—forty years back; and he is dead; I believe the Almighty God took him out of the world as soon as he got through.[24]

The role played by Blacks in Klan activity deserves more investigation. It is reported that Blacks sometimes served as informers, pointing out the residence of a particular Black and assisting in gaining entrance. A Black victim, after testifying that he had been Ku Kluxed by a group of white men, added:

> A black man brought them to my house and showed them how to get into it. I have learned that since court was over, and it can be

---

[23] *Ibid.* (Anthony Dawson, Tulsa, Okla.). (A–L. Oklahoma: Slave Interviews, Duplicates.)

[24] KKK Report, Mississippi, 899.

pretty well proved . . . me and him was just the same as two brothers when he staid down there. I don't know whether they forced him to do it or how it was done.[25]

Allen W. Trelease discusses the participation of Blacks in Klan raids in his extremely well-researched and documented book *White Terror*. He cites evidence of Blacks joining in raids in York County, South Carolina, and in Monroe County, Mississippi.:

> Monroe County claims the rare distinction of having Negro Ku Klux—not initiated members, to be sure, but hangers on who participated in raids. Apparently there were five such men; three were forced to go along against their wills (two of them later turning state's evidence against their captors), and two were Democratic Negroes who went voluntarily.[26]

Verbatim testimony indicates that these night-riding Blacks whipped, intimidated, and threatened whites and Blacks, men and women. It would appear that a number of these Blacks were mulattoes, as they were referred to as being yellow. The following testimony makes this reference:

> One of them had on a doughface; the other had his face blackened. The yellow man was not in disguise. He came in with them. He gathered my wife in her chemise and stood over her with a drawn knife, threatening to kill her, until they had taken me clean off. That was the first occasion. He stood and held her by the bosom, and with a drawn knife stood over her, telling her to hush or he would kill her; that if she alarmed the neighborhood he would have to kill her and the whole of us.[27]

In a black-face routine in reverse, the Blacks were often disguised to imitate whites. A South Carolina witness told the Congressional committee: "I understood that they had put something white over their faces, and afterward put on a disguise. I do not

[25] *Ibid.*, Alabama, 583.
[26] P. 296.
[27] KKK Report, South Carolina, 289.

know what it was; some white substance put on their faces."[28]

Although frequently identified as Democrats, some of the night-riding Blacks were not formally associated with regular Klan groups or with the Union or Loyal Leagues, but roamed in small parties of disguised men, committing various anti-social acts. It appears they were imitating Klansmen in an effort to get away with illegal acts:

> Everybody who commits any offense disguises himself in some way. Night itself is a mask. I have heard of robberies being committed by disguised men—sometimes Negroes disguised—sometimes white men disguised—worthless scoundrels who undertake to commit depredations, but whose acts are not political in any sense.[29]

Another informant reiterated the nonpolitical nature of these marauding groups who imitated Klan garb:

> Ku-Klux outrages have been committed by persons who have simply used the occasion to accomplish private ends, for plunder and robbery sometimes, without any politics in view. There are some instances in which we know that the disguised parties when detected have turned out to be negroes.[30]

Other groups of masquerading Blacks had a more specific goal—theft:

> There was a colored band went to the house of a merchant in the country some time ago, in disguise, drove the clerk off, broke the house open, and took all the money they could get and some goods. They were all disguised. They followed them the next day and caught them; and I understand that there are nine of them now in jail, and they got some of the disguises they had.[31]

Sometimes Blacks turned to Ku Kluxing when they became fed up with harrassment:

28 *Ibid.*, 209.
29 *Ibid.*, Alabama, 431.
30 *Ibid.*, Georgia, 788.
31 *Ibid.*, South Carolina, 209.

He said they had been on him and had abused him, the Ku Klux had, and he intended, and had a crowd made up, and, damn them, he could be a Ku Klux too. . . . He turned to a negro boy staying there and asked him if he wouldn't go into it with him to go Ku-Kluxing.[32]

Personal grievances or assumed injury were sometimes settled by Blacks against Blacks. One case in point is that of a group of incensed Black women who found masquerading a simple, expedient means of bringing justice to an offending husband:

A black man and his wife had some difficulty, and his wife went off and got up some six or eight colored women, and I think his statement was that there was a white man among them. They dressed up in men's clothes, and disguised themselves every way, and then went to the house of her husband, took him out and gave him a most terrible whaling, beat him very badly with rocks and sticks.[33]

This entire party was later arrested. Evidence suggests that Black imitators of Klan methods were more often apprehended than their white counterparts. The reasons for this higher arrest rate among Blacks is found in the Congressional testimony. First, it was theorized that Blacks "were not so sharp"[34]—presumably "sharp" in the sense of being able to elude the sheriff and his posse. Another explanation is that "the white men prepared a better disguise. The Blacks did not do it up so artistically as the others."[35] A final explanation for the fact that disguised Blacks were so promptly met by the authorities was that "they recognized the negroes, and did not recognize the white men."[36]

What was the effect of the early Klan activities? Undoubtedly, more through fear of physical violence than supernatural occurrences, Blacks and whites stayed indoors at night or hid in nearby woods: ". . . they are afraid to go out of doors at night; colored

[32] *Ibid.*, 652.
[33] *Ibid.*, 210.
[34] *Ibid.*, 219.
[35] *Ibid.*, Alabama, 488.
[36] *Ibid.*, Georgia, 240.

men and white men both. You cannot find a man scarcely riding on the roads at night."[37] In addition, there was a generalized fear of provoking Klansmen by any type of "improper act."

> There was a fear, when it first started, an awful horror was manifested of these disguised men. It was reported currently everywhere that if you said anything against one of them they would visit you, and if anything was said derogatory of any act they did they would take you out. These reports being circulated—I do not pretend to say whether they were correct or not—it put the whole body-politic under fear. They were afraid of them.[38]

Sleeping in the woods was one of the few alternatives Blacks could exercise. Some men hid out for months at a time, unable even to change clothes. "I had laid out in the woods for months like I was a dromedary or a hog or a cow afraid to go into the house; that was hard, I think, for poor negroes."[39] In some cases Blacks from a whole region were known to be sleeping in the woods because they could not rest at night for fear of Klan intimidation.[40]

Another recourse was to move, even temporarily, into nearby towns. Landowners, in touch with the abundant labor supply in towns, tried to persuade Blacks to return to rural areas for jobs. Most refused, citing fear of Ku Klux activities as the reason. Southern whites, of course, preferred to believe that Blacks enjoyed town life because of the opportunities it presented for stealing and marauding.[41]

> Well, a negro is mighty fond of the town. I tell you he loves to stand up against a house and look up and down the street, the best of anything in the world. I have frequently said to them, "Don't you want to go out and work?" They would say, "O yes; but I am afraid of the Ku-Klux." I tell the people there that it is too bad that the Ku-Klux do not come into town and run them out. Hundreds of negroes will stay in town and almost starve to death.[42]

---

[37] *Ibid.*, South Carolina, 288.
[38] *Ibid.*, Alabama, 720.
[39] *Ibid.*, South Carolina, 598.
[40] *Ibid.*, 599.
[41] *Ibid.*, Georgia, 271.
[42] *Ibid.*, 916.

It appeared to the whites that the supposedly ignorant and superstitious freedmen actually believed that the white-robed Klansmen were ghosts. As one ex-slave said: "Was not long after dat fore de spooks wuz a gwine round ebber whar. When you would go out atter dark, somethin' would start to a haintin' ye."[43] But the Blacks were not so ignorant or superstitious that the Ku Klux Klan versions of supernatural subterfuge would actually deceive them. To some extent whites were observing surface behavior of Blacks, which they interpreted as real, genuine feelings. Appearing to believe what whites wanted them to believe was a part of wearing the mask and playing the game. When one Congressman queried a white informant about whether Blacks really believed that the Klansmen were spirits of Confederate dead, the reply was: "I do not know whether they believe it or not; they pretend to."[44]

In another instance, an ex-slave who heard rumors of strange riders in his neighborhood went to his former master for information. The master told him, "There are Ku-Klux here; are you not afraid they will get among you?" The Black said, "What sort of men are they?" The reply: "They are men who rise from the dead." According to the Congressional committee's report, this informant gave the matter considerable thought and rejected it. In his own words: "I studied about it, but I did not believe it."[45] Clearly, this informant resisted the Reconstruction Klan's technique of psychological intimidation, which along with their costume and ritual had long been a part of Southern custom. Their general operations were intended to paralyze with fright any miscreant whose attitude or behavior did not conform to Southern ways of thinking.

It is significant that the early Klan made such great efforts to frighten and terrorize Blacks through supernatural means. Though many of their devices had been used by earlier authority groups, the Klan pulled out all stops in ferreting out, re-creating, polishing up, adding to, and refining every means of supernatural

[43] WPA Files, "Slave Narratives" (Millie Bates, Union, S. C.).
[44] KKK Report, Georgia, 239.
[45] *Ibid.*, 599.

disguise imaginable. Even this early stage of the Klan employed physical violence; it was certainly no novelty to see a masked figure whipping Blacks or whites during the ante-bellum or post-bellum periods. The collective and intensive efforts to terrorize through fear of the supernatural are perhaps unparalleled in our history.

The whole rationale for psychological control based on a fear of the supernatural was that whites were sure that they knew Black people. They were not only firmly convinced that Blacks were gullible and would literally believe anything, but they were equally sure that Blacks were an extremely superstitious people who had a fantastic belief in the supernatural interwoven into their life, folklore, and religion.

Such thinking had obvious flaws: the underestimation of Black intelligence and the overvaluation of existing superstitious beliefs. Blacks were frightened, no doubt, but not of ghosts. They were terrified of living, well-armed men who were extremely capable of making Black people ghosts before their time. The bulge under the white sheet was correctly identified as a pistol, and the face under the grotesque mask was recognized as being all too human. But a careful examination of oral tradition and Congressional testimony leads one to an inescapable conclusion: as long as Blacks kept up a pretense of belief—it was safer to feign fright than feel pain—they felt that perhaps a more violent form of intimidation could be averted. It is a classic case of who was manipulating whom!

By 1867 the Klan had already entered a more brutal phase of its operations, in which intimidation of the Black was based on fear of violence rather than fear of the supernatural. But violence and brute force had never completely dominated the slaves, and these techniques did not completely break the will of the newly freed Blacks.

The post-Civil War migration of Blacks to Northern cities caused a final white effort to control the Black by subterfuge. Trading on the Black's known superstitions, his fear of ghosts, and his supposed ignorance, the Klan updated old ante-bellum patrol tricks to psychologically coerce the freedman into obedience. As the supernatural theme wore thin, still another idea took its place—fear of a horrible death at the hands of mythical night doctors who trafficked in living bodies for purposes of medical experiments. Thus began the final phase of the efforts to control the Black psychologically.

6

THE NIGHT DOCTORS:
A FINAL PHASE IN THE
PSYCHOLOGICAL CONTROL
OF THE BLACK

*In later years they were-he'd [father] say
that you musn't go out to visit people in the
other cottages because the night doctor get
you and "sect" your body, cut you up to see
how you are made. And they believed that,
too. Well, all that was originated from the
whites.*   —WILLIAM H. HENDERSON

Historical Background and Genesis of Belief in Night Doctors

THE SO-CALLED "Tuskegee Study," initiated by the Public Health
Service in 1932 on six hundred poor, uneducated, Black men
from rural Alabama, touched off a wave of controversy and in-
dignation thirty years later. The purpose of this now celebrated
study was to determine the effects of syphilis on the human body.[1]
Exposure of this medical project authenticates a conviction basic
to Black folk: that Blacks have been used as subjects for medical

[1] A compilation of available facts concerning the nature of the Tuskegee
experiment can be found in a four-box set of working documents, volumes 1–10,
located in the National Library of Medicine, Bethesda, Maryland. A concise
summary of details regarding this study is also available there in a document entitled "Final Report of the Tuskegee Syphilis Study Ad Hoc Advisory Panel,
United States Department of Health, Education and Welfare, Public Health
Service." Additional references can be found in the *Washington Star-News*, July
25, 1972; *Washington Post*, March 4, 1973; *Wall Street Journal*, Thursday, Nov.
2, 1972; *Medical World News*, "The Forty Year Death Watch," Aug. 18, 1972;
Ebony, "Condemned to Die for Science," Nov. 1972.

experimentation. The conviction arises from a belief in night doctors, a belief that dates back to slavery times.

Many Blacks are convinced that Southern landowners fostered a fear of "night doctors" in the post-Reconstruction period in order to discourage the migration of Blacks from rural farming areas to Northern and Southern urban centers. One informant stated:

> The people that owned the farm in those days, why actually they would dress like that [as night doctors] to keep the fellows that worked on the farm and lived there, you know, and they would practically live there all of their life. And to keep them from leaving, why they would dress like that to frighten them, to keep them from going away, leaving the farm going to the city.[2]

The term "night doctor" (derived from the fact that victims were sought only at night) applies to both students of medicine, who supposedly stole cadavers from which to learn about body processes, and professional thieves, who sold stolen bodies—living and dead[3]—to physicians for medical research. Night doctors were also known to Black folk as "student doctors" (referring specifically to apprentice physicians), "Ku Klux doctors," "night witches," and "night riders."[4]

The period of the night-doctor scare coincides with the great

[2] Informant Fred Jackson, March 26, 1964.

[3] This chapter is not concerned with the grave-robbing tradition among Blacks. The strong belief in the kidnapping and murder of living people by night doctors completely overshadows Black narrative tradition about grave robbing. Preoccupation with murder by body-snatchers, however, is not unique to the United States. Kenneth Goldstein, director of the Folklore Program at the University of Pennsylvania, has collected oral stories that still circulate in Scotland concerning the "Burkers," who are believed to kidnap living people for eventual sale to doctors for medical experimentation. Few, if any, such stories exist for the rest of Europe. The Archives of the Irish Folklore Commission contain, for example, many texts of narratives about newly buried corpses being taken up and sold to the doctors, but nothing about the kidnapping of living persons for this purpose. Sean O'Sullivan, chief archivist, stated in a private letter to the author (dated Oct. 26, 1965): "I know the material fairly well, and I can say that I have never come across any tradition about attempts to capture or abduct *live* persons for medical experiments."

[4] The terms "night doctors" and "body-snatchers" are often used synonymously by Blacks to refer to both students of medicine and professional body thieves.

migration of Blacks to industrial centers, which lasted from about 1880 to the end of the First World War. Discussing this movement, shortly after the war, Donald H. Henderson observed that since 1880 the Black population had increased considerably in Boston, New York, Philadelphia, Chicago, Cincinnati, Evansville, Indianapolis, Pittsburgh, and St. Louis.[5]

The outbreak of World War I and the curtailment of immigrant labor from abroad created a severe labor shortage in Northern industrial centers. Not only were few laborers coming in from abroad, but thousands already established in the United States went back to their native countries. To alleviate this situation, Northern employers, such as tobacco growers, railroads, and steel mills, sent labor agents throughout the South promising free transportation to the North and talking enthusiastically of the high wages and better living conditions there. As the news spread among the Black population, thousands of them sold their possessions and went North. "Instances are given showing that Negro teamsters left their horses standing in the streets or deserted their jobs and went to the trains without notifying their employers or even going home."[6]

The mass movement of Blacks from the rural South to urban centers of the North, West, and South seriously affected the Southern economy. Emmett J. Scott described the effects of this movement on the South: "Homes found themselves without servants, factories could not operate because of the lack of labor, farmers were unable to secure laborers to harvest their crops."[7]

Southerners made strenuous efforts to check the Black exodus by legislation, by the use of force, and by circulating false rumors about the fate Blacks suffered at the hands of labor agents in the North. Severe laws were passed in some Southern states (Alabama, Arkansas, Mississippi, and Georgia) to curtail the activities

[5] "The Negro Migration of 1916–1918," *Journal of Negro History*, 6 (Jan. 1921), 383–498.
[6] *Ibid.*
[7] *Negro Migration During the War*, Carnegie Endowment for International Peace, Preliminary Economic Studies of the War, No. 16 (Washington, D. C., 1920), 86.

of labor agents. Licenses were required of all agents and then made prohibitively expensive. If labor agents failed to observe the license laws they were often arrested and heavily fined. Added to this form of legal intimidation was the physical abuse and injury inflicted on many of these labor agents.[8] When discriminatory legislation and physical force against labor agents failed to diminish the number of Blacks leaving for Northern centers, white Southerners resorted to creating false rumors about the perils Blacks would face in the North. According to one author, "Blacks were then warned against the rigors of the northern winter and the death rate from pneumonia and tuberculosis."[9] Another rumor that traveled throughout the Southeast was that Blacks were being enticed to the coast, where they were loaded on ships, taken to Cuba, and sold into slavery.[10]

Perhaps the most effective rumor deliberately circulated by Southern whites among the Blacks concerned the kidnapping and murdering of city people by night doctors. At least this is the assertion the Black folk make in their oral tradition. The following statement concerning night doctors appears in an 1896 issue of the *Journal of American Folklore*:

> On dark nights negroes in cities consider it dangerous to walk alone on the streets because the "night-doctor" is abroad. He does not hesitate to choke colored people to death in order to obtain their bodies for dissection. The genesis of this belief from the well-known practice of grave-robbing for medical colleges, several of which are located in Southern cities, is sufficiently evident.[11]

Though the author of this article failed to specify which medical colleges in Southern cities were referred to, the South Carolina Medical College, located in Charleston, reportly advertised in *The Charleston Mercury* for diseased and disabled "living"

[8] *Ibid.*, 250.
[9] *Ibid.*, 253.
[10] E. Merton Coulter, *The South During Reconstruction 1865–1877* (Baton Rouge, 1947), 98.
[11] Ruby Andrews Moore, "Superstitions of Georgia, No. 2," *Journal of American Folklore*, 9 (July–Sept. 1896), 227.

slaves to be used for medical experimentation. This advertisement, which Thomas Wentworth Higginson identified as having appeared as early as 1831, read: [12]

> Some advantages of a peculiar character are connected with this institution, which it may be proper to point out. No place in the United States offers as great opportunities for the acquisition of anatomical knowledge. Subjects being obtained from among the coloured population in sufficient numbers for every purpose, and proper dissections carried on without offending any individuals in the community! [13]

Such blatant advertising may have been extreme even for the times, for this same ad was reprinted by two nineteenth-century writers. The first was Theodore Douglas Weld, an indefatigable antislavery worker who culled from thousands of Southern newspapers printed between 1837 and 1839 the excerpts reprinted in his classic monograph *American Slavery As It Is*. Weld not only printed the advertisement, but passionately responded to it concerning the inhumanity implicit in the language of the prospectus. He clearly realized that the slaves would be subjected to experiments conceived by inexperienced students who thought of their patients as subhuman property.

This advertisement for prospective students was not the only one concerned with the use of slave bodies for medical experimentation. Another ad Weld cited as being placed in *The Charleston Mercury* between 1837 and 1839 gave notice of the establishment of a special clinic for the treatment of Blacks:

> Surgery of the Medical College of South Carolina, Queen st.— The Faculty inform their professional brethren, and the public that they have established a Surgery, at the Old College, Queen street, FOR THE TREATMENT OF NEGROES, which will continue in operation during the session of the College, say from first November, to the fifteenth of March ensuing.
> The object of the Faculty, in opening this Surgery, is to collect

---

[12] "Nat Turner's Insurrection," *Atlantic Monthly*, 8 (Aug. 1861), 185.
[13] Theodore Douglas Weld, *American Slavery As It Is* (New York, 1968), 169.

as many interesting cases, as possible, for the benefit and instruction of their pupils—at the same time they indulge the hope, that it may not only prove an accommodation, but also a matter of economy to the public. They would respectfully call the attention of planters living in the vicinity of the city, to this subject; particularly such as may have servants laboring under Surgical diseases. Such persons of color as may not be able to pay for Medical advice, will be attended to gratis, at stated hours, as often as may be necessary.

The Faculty take this opportunity of soliciting the co-operation of such of their professional brethren, as are favorable to their objects.[14]

Weld observed that on November 12, 1838, this same college placed a supporting advertisement in which it was stated that "interesting cases" of disabled slaves would be treated free of any professional charges.

Supporting evidence that Charleston may well have been a busy center for traffic in slave bodies is a third advertisement, again placed in *The Charleston Mercury*, by a Dr. T. Stillman who, in the interest of improved medical techniques, decided to operate his own infirmary stocked with slaves having interesting and unusual diseases:

To Planters and Others—Wanted fifty negroes. Any person having sick negroes, considered incurable by their respective physicians, and wishing to dispose of them, Dr. S. will pay cash for negroes affected with scrofula or king's evil, confirmed hypocondriasm, apoplexy, diseases of the liver, kidneys, spleen, stomach and intestines, bladder and its appendages, diarrhea, dysentery, etc. The highest cash price will be paid on application as above.[15]

The second nineteenth-century writer to reprint the advertisement for slave bodies was William Wells Brown in his 1853 edition of *Clotel*. While Brown may have seen the advertisement in Weld's *American Slavery As It Is*, he identified the source of his prospectus as the *Free Trader*. In his characteristic style, Brown combined newspaper accounts with elaborations from oral tra-

[14] *Ibid.*, 170.
[15] *Ibid.*, 171.

dition. One of his fictional characters stated after reading the ad that slaves would be kept on hand at the college until needed, at which time they would be bled to death.[16]

Charleston was certainly not the only Southern city that may have utilized slaves for medical experimentation. It was rumored that Nat Turner in his prison cell was forced to sign a release in exchange for food granting permission for his body to be turned over to doctors for dissection after his death.[17] Hampton Roads, the locale of Nat Turner's capture, was very near Richmond, where another famous Southern medical school was located. The Medical College of Virginia regularly placed official advertisements for students in several Southern newspapers, including *The Charleston Mercury*, though no mention was made in their ads of having an available supply of slaves for dissection.

Because of the absence at this time of anatomical laws in England and America providing for the legal acquisition of human bodies, the medical profession often resorted to illegal means of procuring cadavers for instructional purposes in medical schools. Medical students and teachers were known to either engage in grave robbing themselves, or to depend on the services of professional thieves to supply them with cadavers.

Bodies were illegally obtained by exhumation from graveyards, by purchase or theft of cadavers before interment, and by murder.[18] Of these three, grave robbing was the most popular. The acquisition of bodies before burial was infrequently reported, and murder by body-snatchers occurred in only a relatively few cases in the British Isles and in the United States. The most sensational murders of this type were committed in Edinburgh by two Irishmen, William Burke and William Hare.[19] The verb "to burke" (meaning to murder so as to leave few marks of violence —for example, by strangulation) was derived from the technique Burke perfected on his victims:

[16] *Clotel, Or The President's Daughter* (New York, 1853; rpt. 1969), 123–24.
[17] Higginson, 185.
[18] Allan F. Guttmacher, "Bootlegging Bodies," *Society of Medical History of Chicago*, 4 (Jan. 1935), 353–402.
[19] James M. Ball, "Resurrection Days," Lecture given before the Mayo Foundation, Rochester, Minn., April 17, 1928.

With diabolical cunning, however, Burke had invented a method which made a quiet and sure end, and at the same time left on the body no traces that might arouse suspicion when it came to be laid on the table for dissection. Burke was a man of heavy build and immense muscle, and his method was first to throw his victim down, then to leap on the breast with the whole weight of his knees, and at the same moment grip the mouth and nose with both hands like a vice, thus producing suffocation in a moment or two.[20]

The only case of reported burking in the United States occurred in Baltimore in 1886. A medical historian, Allan Guttmacher, related this information:

> It was the famous case of Emily Brown. Emily was the daughter of a respectable innkeeper who lived on the eastern shore of Maryland. She is said to have been a charming southern belle and well educated. After her father's death she moved with her brother to Richmond and kept house for him until he died some eleven years later. Eventually, at the age of 50, she drifted to Baltimore and was seen trudging the streets in a lamentable state, frequently under the influence of drugs and liquor. Her condition became so forlorn that this white woman finally resided with a Negro family in one of the squalid alleys of the eastern part of the city. Among the other members of the household was a Negro who was a porter in a dissecting room at the University of Maryland and who saw in the person of the dejected Emily a salable corpse. He, with the aid of another Negro, strangled her, took the body to the University of Maryland and received $15 for it. Strangulation was suspected by a member of the staff, and this suspicion was corroborated by a police investigation. The murderers were convicted and hanged.[21]

Certainly Washington, D. C., was not the scene of the many lurid body-snatching murders the Black folk tell about in their oral testimony. The District of Columbia has had an anatomical law since 1902 which stipulates that bodies to be buried at public expense are to be turned over to city medical schools. The former head of the Anatomy Department at Howard University, Dr.

[20] Alexander MacPhial, "The After-Math of Body Snatching: A Plea for Anatomy," *St. Bartholomew's Hospital Journal*, 24 (Dec. 1916), 28–34.
[21] Guttmacher, 400.

W. Montague Cobb, maintains that before the passage of this law bodies were unofficially obtained in the same manner:

> Well they got them the same way. They didn't have to steal them. But it would take considerable research to find out just what was done, but there was no shortage of bodies before that time. And I'm quite sure that they were legitimately obtained. We would call them potter's field bodies in those days.[22]

Dr. Cobb labeled the idea of night doctors murdering victims in the District "utterly ridiculous" and "a complete myth."

> There never was any case of murder for the sale of a body to a medical school in the District of Columbia. As I told you, I'm a native of Washington. I've been associated either through the eight years my father worked at Freedmen's Hospital while a small boy, and during various associations during high school and college. And I've been over 30 years on the faculty here, and Secretary of the Anatomical Board of the District of Columbia since 1951. In addition, I've been particularly interested in this field. So that I think if there had been any actual case of burking, as we call it, it would have come to my attention.[23]

Night Doctor Tradition in the Rural South

Among the Black folk, oral accounts testify to the influence of night-doctor beliefs in the rural South. Based on the same principle of psychological control that had been in earlier use, the action to be avoided (in this case residence in the city) was made an object of fear. Rumor spread the idea, according to an informant, "that there was a scarcity of dead bodies, and that in order to get one for dissection they [doctors] would sometimes kidnap people."[24] Landed proprietors pictured cities to their Black tenants as dangerous places in which people were daily being kidnapped and murdered by night doctors. Southern farms

[22] Interview, April 20, 1964.
[23] *Ibid.*
[24] Informant J. L. S. Holloman, March 4, 1964.

were made to appear as havens of security and serenity by contrast. An informant explains the fear some Blacks had of city life:

> I have heard many stories about the night doctor, but it usually related to the fear of the city. From my experience this is the story that the elders in the country would tell about city life. You see the hospitals were there, and these are the places where the doctors were to be found, and it was there that one was apt to be caught and, well, eventually killed, as it were, for the purpose of medical inspection or investigation. You were safe in the country. [25]

The old theme of impending danger was played by the same group of labor-conscious whites on an old instrument, the Black, but to a new tune, the night doctors. In this new phase of psychological control the supernatural elements were combined with certain scientific overtones, exploiting the new interest in education in general and medical science in particular that had developed in the post-Civil War South. Body-snatching, as it related to the struggling young discipline of anatomy, made a natural addition to the pattern of psychological control. Southern white landowners played on both the superstitions of the Black and his suspicion of science, realizing that the uninformed and the uneducated were naturally suspicious of all things scientific. As the focal point of a new interest in science, doctors and hospitals represented a strange phenomenon to Black folk, who had had little contact with either during slavery or Reconstruction.

Ignorance enforced on the Blacks since slavery again paid dividends as they began more and more to express their fear of traveling at night because of the danger of encountering night doctors. References by informants to fear of night travel were often short and pointed, but they all carried the same general meaning. Mildred Green recalled, "They used to say, 'You'd better not go out, the night doctors will catch you.' "[26] Mary Johnson said, "When night come I was in my place because I was afraid of

[25] Informant James Daniel Tymes, March 25, 1964.
[26] Interview, March 26, 1964.

them."[27] Mamie Law remembered, "Some people was afraid to walk the streets, especially at night."[28] Henry Lewis Brown added: "Now the only thing that they [night doctors] could do if they spot you in the day time, well they'd come around at night. If you ever leave home and go somewhere, you won't never return."[29]

When whites first began to masquerade as night doctors in the rural South, their performance was not essentially different from the ghost routines acted out by slaveholders and overseers. In order to keep Blacks indoors at night, and therefore less able to escape undetected to the city, landowners regularly visited Black ghettoes dressed as night doctors. William Henderson said on this point:

> They [whites masquerading as night doctors] traveled singularly. And they would make a noise saying, "I'm looking for a man, I'm looking for a man." And of course they [Negroes] would huddle themselves together and peep out at him, you know. They had no weapons if they come in. They had no weapons. They always saw to that, that they didn't have weapons.[30]

While the whites circulated a rumor among the Blacks that the new and mysterious night visitors were called night doctors, the disguised landowners, dressed very much like ante-bellum and Reconstruction Klan ghosts, were faced with the old problem of reinforcing a belief by producing evidence of it. Fred Jackson said about this practice:

> To keep them from leaving the farm, see, they'd tell them all of the ghost stories, you know, and then they got them to believe that, and those that didn't believe it, why, they would make them believe it by dressing that way, see. Tell them what a ghost looked like, and how they was dressed. Some of them dressed black, some of them dressed white, but still they would say white. They were

[27] Interview, March 7, 1964.
[28] Interview, March 24, 1964.
[29] Interview, April 11, 1964.
[30] Interview, March 3, 1964.

dressed in white, and they would stay on the farm, see? They wouldn't stay out late if they left. Why if they go out, they'd come right back.[31]

Often the night-doctor garb was simply a white sheet. One informant described the whites "dressed in white . . . like a white sheet over them, a gown or something like that."[32] Another Black stated that in Virginia whites disguised as night doctors wore white "hoods with long robes."[33] The Ku Klux Klan in that state wore black robes. Thus it can be fairly certain that this informant did not confuse body-snatchers with Klansmen. He also said of the Klan in Virginia: "Oh, yes, there were real Ku Klux Klan. Yes, I've seen them. They'd come around, and all of them was dressed in black. And when you hide behind those hoods like that, you don't know what color they were, you know."[34] At least within this state whites made it easy for Blacks to distinguish between a Klan ghost and a night doctor. But in other localities the general similarity in apparel may well have led to one folk term for body-snatchers, "Ku Klux doctors."[35]

In the early stages of this new control device (fear of body-snatchers) the label "night doctor" was almost the only new element since old forms of subterfuge based on the supernatural were still largely used by Southern whites. Even the names "ghosts" and "night doctors" were to some extent used interchangeably by Blacks. One Black said: "They called them [night doctors] ghosts, you know like. . . . Just when you're walking around at night you would walk up on something like that."[36] And Ella Davenport, who heard of body-snatchers in South Carolina, said of them:

> They [whites] didn't have much of a technique because I think they always would put something over them and go like a ghost,

---

[31] Interview, March 26, 1964.
[32] Informant William H. Henderson, March 3, 1964.
[33] Informant Fred Jackson, March 26, 1964.
[34] *Ibid.*
[35] Informant Lucille Murdock, April 11, 1964; and informant Alice Virginia Lyles, March 16, 1964.
[36] Informant Fred Jackson, March 26, 1964.

or something, and catch you like that. They'd act like a ghost or something, you know, and catch you. But you never could tell who they were.[37]

Frightening and chasing Blacks were still very much in vogue. Rachel Jenfier stated, "All I heard about was them running people, but I never saw them run nobody."[38] And Laura Reed even told of being chased home from dances by the night doctors:

Them doctors would run you at night if you was out until late, twelve or one o'clock. They used to run me a many a times, going from the halls. I used to go to dances. Go to Odd Fellows Hall and all around to different dances and things. They'd get behind you, child, and have you flying.[39]

Making sudden and dramatic appearances dressed in ghostly garb at Black places of assembly was still used to discourage group meetings. When asked if he had heard about night doctors, Jessie Brown stated:

Well, one of the things I've heard about the night doctors and the ghosts was that they would, according to some of the tales of my grandfather and my great-grandfather whom I remembered vaguely, was that they would at times come in the settlements where the Negroes were even at their church, in order to keep them afraid of ghosts. It would be the owner of a plantation. That was one of the ways where he was able to keep them in check.[40]

Night Doctor Tradition in Washington, D.C.

The belief in body-snatching, deliberately fostered by Southern landowners, was transported to the city by Blacks either courageous or desperate enough to brave those terrifying rumors and flee from the rural to the urban environment. While many Black

[37] Interview, April 2, 1964.
[38] Interview, March 26, 1964.
[39] Interview, March 27, 1964.
[40] Interview, April 23, 1964.

informants believe that body-snatching occurred in a number of major cities of the North and South—Chicago, New York, Atlanta, Augusta, and Baltimore, to name a few—discussion in this section will center on Washington, D. C., where most of these interviews were conducted.

The belief in night doctors, active enough in rural areas, not only flourished in Washington but, fanned by rumor and exaggeration, actually mushroomed there. One factor which partially explains the extraordinary strength of body-snatching lore in this area is that Washington is bounded on two sides by rural Southern states (Maryland and Virginia) from which thousands of Blacks migrated in the first two decades of the twentieth century. The majority of informants who were not native Washingtonians came originally from either one or the other of these two states. In addition to the constant stream of immigrants from Maryland and Virginia, large numbers of Blacks had been immigrating into the District since before the Civil War. They came from many parts of the Deep South, first as contraband and later as freedmen. Although lacking perhaps in worldly goods, each newcomer brought with him a wealth of folklore traditions, among which was a strong belief in bodysnatching. Each new variation was added to the general store of Black night-doctor beliefs until Washington became a kind of repository of the myriad traditions drawn from isolated hamlets and large communities all over the South and the Middle Atlantic Seaboard. It is no wonder that the entire Washington area is fertile ground for the collection of night-doctor traditions.

Another reason why body-snatching lore flourished in the District is that the city actually contained the very things rural Blacks had been taught to fear: doctors and hospitals. Darwin Smith commented: "Well, there was a lot of it here in Washington because they had a lot of hospitals here in Washington. They had a lot of medical students."[41]

Neighborhoods in the vicinity of hospitals were especially feared by local Blacks after dark because of the supposed activi-

[41] Interview, March 25, 1964.

ty of night doctors in these areas. Three hospitals in the District were singled out by the folk for special mention in their oral tradition: the old Naval Hospital, said to have been located on E Street, N.W.; the former Homeopathic Hospital on Kirby Street, N.W.; and the old Freedmen's Hospital at 4th and Bryant Streets, N.W.

Eva Francis Parker was raised near the old Naval Hospital and said concerning it: "Have you ever heard talk of the Naval Hospital on E Street? Well, the doctors, the student doctors used to go there, you know, and most of these people were so scared, scared to go out at night. Afraid the doctors might catch them, you know."[42] Bruce Powell lived for a time near the former Homeopathic Hospital on Kirby Street, and he remembered that his family finally moved out of this neighborhood because of its being too often frequented by body-snatchers:

People were captured and caught, as I say, in these isolated areas. Now I'll give you an example. Now at one time I used to be over—you know where Dunbar High School is, don't you? When I was living across where the stadium is, there used to be a row of houses, oh, about eight, just above Dunbar High School, on the same side of the street. On N Street. And all of the rest of that was lots—open area. And as you know across the street from Dunbar is a playground. And on Kirby Street there is a hospital, Homeopathic Hospital.

Well, that made that area rather isolated after dark in the evening, winter time and summer time, very quiet. Week ends the same way. And as a result, you often heard of night doctors being in that area. There was quite a bit of talk about it even up until I got to be, oh, some 15 or 16 years old, or maybe a little better. And that's when we left. My mother and them moved out of that neighborhood.[43]

Of the three hospital neighborhoods, however, the one most often discussed by the folk was the old Freedmen's. "I've heard lots of tales about them [night doctors]," one Black said. "The main tales was that up by Freedmen's Hospital, up there, it was

42 Interview, March 19, 1964.
43 Interview, April 3, 1964.

widely known to be a bad place for the night doctors."[44] A Black woman testified: "You couldn't go through Bryant Street. And a lot of times you'd start through there and you never would get to where you was going. And they would wonder where these people go. That's the reason so many people disappeared."[45] Another informant remembered the experience of a friend whose child was threatened by a supposed night doctor near Freedmen's Hospital:

> Now a girl friend of mine had a little girl. Course she's grown now. But, however, they said they were walking up near Freedmen's Hospital. Of course at that time there was a fence along, and her little girl was playing back of her. And all of a sudden they saw a man grab, and they looked back. And after they looked back, why, the man stopped, they said, you know. But she said if they hadn't looked back, why she thinks they would have been minus of a child.[46]

Perry Randolph, on the other hand, boasted of being able to move freely in this neighborhood, unmolested by the night doctors. Notice the reason for his lack of fear: "Of course, after I got to be a man around about 1914, I used to go all around about Freedmen's Hospital and nobody never did bother me because I carried a gun."[47]

The existence of Howard University's medical school in proximity to Freedmen's Hospital was an added reason for the special fear of this neighborhood, for kidnapped victims were often believed to have been taken to medical schools for dissection. One informant said, "They claimed that it was dangerous to walk around Howard University Medical School."[48] Another explained, "Howard boys would catch you, you know, and take you off."[49] The broad lot which formerly lay between Freedmen's Hospital and Howard's medical school was considered by young

[44] Informant Walter Scriber, March 26, 1964.
[45] Informant Gaynelle Fagin, April 10, 1964.
[46] Informant Mary H. Mercer, April 10, 1964.
[47] Interview, March 24, 1964.
[48] Informant Matthew H. Hurley, March 12, 1964.
[49] Informant Elizabeth Wheeler, March 24, 1964.

boys to be a good hiding place for lurking night doctors of this area. A native of Washington formerly on Howard University's medical staff stated:

> I shall be 60 a year or so in October. When I was a small boy, I would say between 7 and 10, the area where our present medical building in which we are sitting now stands, was occupied by the old medical school. And the dissecting room then was almost in the same site in which it is now. There was a broad lot, or field, between here and Freedmen's Hospital. The present Tuberculosis Chest Annex now stands on that lot. This lot was covered with tall grass, across which there were a number of paths. A good bit of this grass, because it was never cut, used to grow quite high, and young boys could hide in it.
> Now Freedmen's Hospital was where it is today, the central wing, the central unit. And back of Freedmen's Hospital was a hill, and on that hill there was also part of the University campus undeveloped. That had tall grass in it, too. And it was the firm belief of the boys whom I knew, that if you got caught out after dark out there, the night doctors might get you.[50]

Aside from the haunts just mentioned, Washington contained other places unique to city life which night doctors were believed to frequent. A few public buildings close to the center of the city, for example, were said to have attracted night doctors. Lincoln Court House and the Union Station were two of these. One Black informant learned about body-snatching activities around Union Station through his white supervisor in the federal government:

> Well, this man happened to live, was reared right here in the vicinity of Washington, and he talked about it being, oh, around the Union Station area, before they really had all of that building up over there. It used to be a famous place for night doctors, he said.[51]

City parks in general were usually feared by the Blacks after dark because night doctors could conveniently hide in a number of places. Fred Manning remarked: "I heard that they catch peo-

[50] Informant W. Montague Cobb, April 20, 1964.
[51] Informant Henry Oliphant, March 28, 1964.

186

ple in the parks and it happened to me. Run after me but couldn't catch me."[52] Lincoln Park was considered to have been a favorite night-doctor haunt. Laura Reed commented concerning it:

> The doctor's place would be right on the corner of East Capitol, 15th and East Capitol Street. Where the Lincoln Park is. Yes, right there. There's where they used to hang out right there. And I worked right there [living in] the janitor's apartment, at 1447 East Capitol Street, N.E.[53]

Near Lincoln Park there was also a car barn (a terminal station for a street-car line usually built some distance from houses), and the area was relatively isolated. Consequently, Laura Reed said: "Out at 1447 East Capitol Street, why you know, the night doctors was awful bad out there. Out there by the car barn."[54]

The collection in one urban center of many variations of the night-doctor tradition is one reason for its strength in the Washington area. The concentration in the city of medical facilities and special features unfamiliar to the immigrant Black is another. Relocation, however, significantly affected these beliefs in that the supernatural element was dropped. The emphasis was completely shifted to science by the Blacks, who structured a detailed system of beliefs concerning every aspect of the body-snatching business. They described in detail such things as the types of dress employed; the kinds of victims body-snatchers sought; techniques of capturing people; methods of abduction, i.e., the use of blindfolds and anesthetics; types of conveyances used to transport kidnapped victims; places where the bodies were taken; and the manner of death people were supposed to

[52] Interview, March 26, 1964.
[53] Interview, March 24, 1964.
[54] Interview, March 24, 1964. This informant's assertion that a place frequented by night doctors was located at the corner of East Capitol and 15th Streets has some basis in historical fact. According to Dr. Llewellin Eliot, who admitted robbing graves himself at one time, a group of professional grave robbers operated from a shanty on East Capitol Street, near the old Lincoln Hospital. Such articles as clothing, shrouds, and other graveyard things were stored there. For additional information about grave robbing in the District of Columbia see Dr. Llewellin Eliot's article, "A History of Bodysnatching," *Washington Medical Annals*, 15 (May 1916), 247–53.

have suffered. In other words, from the moment of a person's capture to his slow, torturous death at the hands of body-snatchers, they described every step—often with numerous variations.

Apparel of the Night Doctors

At present there seems to be no consensus among the folk concerning the wearing apparel of night doctors. Three schools of thought predominate—that they wore white robes or suits, black robes or suits, or plain clothes. Concerning the first, one group of informants insists that night doctors wore the traditional physician's attire, either white intern suits[55] or long white coats. An eyewitness who "used to see them here in town," gave the following description: "Well, most of them used to be dressed in a long white coat like these doctors wear, long like that, straight down to the ankles."[56] Other informants stated that the doctors wore white robes[57] or a covering like a sheet. William Henderson recalled that "They usually come dressed in white . . . like a white sheet over them, a gown, or something like that."[58]

A good number of informants support the second opinion, that night doctors wore black robes,[59] suits, or coats[60] for the same reason that the patrollers and some Klansmen had chosen this color: it allowed them to take their victims unaware. As Fred Manning said: "All of them dressed in black. You can't see where they are dressed in black."[61] Henry Lewis Brown vividly described a night doctor's black garments:

They called themselves night doctors and they had a black cape over their heads, all the way down. And around their eyes they had

[55] Informant Lucille Murdock, April 11, 1964.
[56] Informant James H. Morrison, March 27, 1964.
[57] Informant Florence E. Smith, April 3, 1964.
[58] Interview, March 3, 1964.
[59] Informant Elizabeth Wheeler, March 24, 1964.
[60] Informant Perry Randolph, March 24, 1964.
[61] Interview, March 26, 1964.

a white circle right around where, you know, you see through the eyes there. And they would only come out at night. When they got a hold of you that was it. [62]

The third view expressed by informants was that the night doctors just dressed in plain clothes,[63] or that "they dressed ordinary, like ordinary people dress." [64] The rationale for this opinion is that the doctors did not want to be singled out as body-snatchers by dressing in any special outfits. Mary Johnson explains:

They couldn't because people would know who they was, see? They didn't wear no certain outfit. Now these here night doctors, they had the name but they wasn't supposed to do that, because that was killing people, you know. Catching them and killing them. [65]

Supporters of this school of thought argued that white was an unlikely color for night doctors because it "could be seen a pretty long ways off, and if you saw that, you wouldn't continue to contact with it. You'd change your course. You can see white a long ways off, you understand." [66] A "colored" night doctor purportedly seen by Rachel Jenfier was wearing plain clothes. She described him as "tall, dark, wore dark clothes, and a black striped hat." [67]

Most informants agreed that masks or hoods completed the night-doctor outfit. In fact, it was the one item most frequently mentioned by informants in their description of night-doctor attire and was often the only article of clothing described. One Black woman said, "They described that they wore masks over their face." [68] The mask she referred to was a surgical type of mask used in this instance to conceal the wearer's identity. According to Elizabeth Wheeler, "You could only see their eyes, you know." [69] A

[62] Interview, April 11, 1964.
[63] Informant John Green, March 24, 1964.
[64] Informant Russell Burke, March 24, 1964.
[65] Interview, March 7, 1964.
[66] Informant Robert Henson, March 24, 1964.
[67] Interview, March 26, 1964.
[68] Informant Mamie Ardella Robinson, April 2, 1964.
[69] Interview, March 24, 1964.

night-doctor headpiece similar to the Klan hood was described by Henry Lewis Brown: "[They wore] those black hoods and round white eyes that was a white circle around the eyes. And you couldn't tell who they were. And they wore gloves and they was all clothed in black."[70]

Another night-doctor accessory most often agreed upon by informants was their rubber-soled shoes.[71] These were worn to facilitate "sneaking up" on victims. Some felt that the entire shoe was rubber (similar to rain boots), while others thought that canvas tennis shoes were worn by night doctors. Concerning the latter, Gaynelle Fagin snapped, "She [mother] didn't say nothing but just said that the men wore rubber shoes . . . so you couldn't hear them walk. Everybody know that."[72]

Kinds of Victims Sought

The folk also differ on the kinds of victims sought by night doctors. One idea is that night doctors were interested in obtaining any available body. As one informant said: "I gathered that they were chasing anybody. In other words, you wasn't supposed to be on the street at a certain hour."[73] Laura Reed commented, "Oh, they'd get anybody."[74] Many informants were of the opinion that body-snatchers especially preyed on helpless people because they offered less resistance to capture. The aged, infirm, drunk, and physically disabled fell in this general category.

The second school of thought believed that the night doctors were only interested in people with special medical problems, such as those deformed in some manner, excessively fat, or of some unusual height (abnormally tall or short). Concerning the interest of night doctors in deformed persons, Gaynelle Fagin said:

They wasn't nothing but like interns is now. [They wanted people who were] afflicted or ill formed, or something like that. Like they

70 Interview, April 11, 1964.
71 Informant Laura Reed, March 27, 1964.
72 Interview, April 10, 1964.
73 Informant Henry Oliphant, March 28, 1964.
74 Interview, March 27, 1964.

call children now who have water heads. Their heads too big. Well, they take those and experiment on them and find out what was really wrong with them.[75]

Many Blacks share this point of view. Henry Lewis Brown stated that his grandfather was especially fearful of body-snatchers "because he was a little man and he said he thought perhaps they might want to find the reason why he was so little, why he didn't grow some more."[76] A great deal of fear was based on the belief that the night doctors were interested in deformed people. On this point Brown stated:

And he [grandfather] also said they had quite a time with what you call these night doctors. They were a group of people that came around looking for unusual born people, like ill deformed. Like if you was afflicted of any kind they would come in and hit you in the arm with a needle. Soon as they catch you alone, they'd stick a needle in you that numbs you. Well, they'd take you away, and then that was in the beginning of medical science, and use you as they use animals for experiment. They would use you to experiment, find out what reason that you were born that way, and could that have been corrected, if it was possible, and all such things as that.[77]

Obese people represented another kind of abnormality equally interesting to body-snatchers, according to Black folk opinion. The cities held special dangers for stout people, and many such persons were often afraid to visit urban areas because of a fear of being captured by the night doctors. Lucille Murdock avoided New York for this reason: "And they in all these big cities. That's the reason I stayed off from New York so long before I even went there because I weighed 220 pounds when I started thinking about going up there, upper country, to see my sister."[78] Messiah King told of a three-hundred-pound woman who was believed to have been abducted by the night doctors in Washington, D. C.[79]

[75] Interview, April 10, 1964.
[76] Interview, April 11, 1964.
[77] *Ibid.*
[78] Interview, April 11, 1964.
[79] Interview, April 10, 1964.

Methods of Ensnarement and Abduction

Whether the doctors looked for such easy prey as children or only people having special medical problems, the techniques of capturing victims have been greatly detailed by Black folk in their oral tradition. Although one informant said, "Oh, they used to catch people all kinds of ways in them days,"[80] most informants describe two basic methods. Either a person would be captured while walking alone on the street at night, or he could be lured to a special house and seized there by the waiting doctors.

The first technique required a great deal of teamwork and stealth. The doctors were believed to have operated in pairs: "two goes together."[81] Sometimes a third man was added. As one informant stated, "They said it would be more or less two or three of them together at one time."[82] Stealth was accomplished by body-snatchers in two ways: sometimes the doctors walked noiselessly behind people (in their rubber-soled shoes) and surprised victims from behind; at other times night doctors hid conveniently out of sight and sprang out at their prey. Walter Scriber said about the latter method, "They would be out late at the hour, would be hiding some place and see you and run and catch you and grab you."[83]

Another body-snatching method described was to lure people into especially designed street traps, from which no one emerged alive. There were two kinds of these outdoor traps: manholes and cellar doors which opened out from the ground. James Daniel Tymes explained the manhole trick:

Well no, for me it was always a thing that was to be feared if one found themselves in the city. Take for example the manhole. A common part of the fear was that walking along the way, one might find himself dropping down, being dropped down in a manhole. And this was all a part of a trick, you see, of the doctor. The manhole itself was a design, you see, to capture persons for this purpose.[84]

80 Informant John Johnson, April 4, 1964.
81 Informant Perry Randolph, March 24, 1964.
82 Informant Henry Lewis Brown, April 11, 1964.
83 Interview, March 26, 1964.
84 Interview, March 25, 1964.

A second trap described was the old-fashioned cellar door equipped with springs. Generally these were thought to lead to the basements of stores. Sara Gatewood said of these doors:

> As a kid we were never to walk over a trap door. You know it used to be here in the streets, a trap door that would lead down in the cellar. So we were always told never to walk on those trap doors because we might get caught. Somebody might take you.[85]

Sometimes these trap doors were said to have led to the sewer system to which night doctors supposedly carried their victims. Louise Hopkins testified:

> In Chicago years ago they had springs on these [cellar doors], and of course whenever you called a cop or something like that, why, they would go under there where you say your child disappeared, but they would never be able to follow because [it] led down to the sewer to something.[86]

Catching people either as they walked down a dark street or over a hidden trap were ways night doctors were thought to have captured people outside in the open, but they were also supposed to have lured people to certain houses or office buildings where medical experiments were conducted. Several tricks were used to entice people into these houses. Sometimes individuals were offered a temporary job cleaning a particular house, and when they showed up for work they were ushered inside by their employer, only to disappear forever.[87] Another lure was to offer a stranger a sum of money if he would deliver a note to a particular address. When the note was delivered to the stipulated address the messenger disappeared. John Johnson said of this practice: "Fool people in your house with a note. 'Mister, I'll give you ten cents if you take this note across the street.' He'll go in there and never come out no more."[88]

These houses were said to have been equipped with many different kinds of traps. As one informant said: "These traps were

[85] Interview, April 10, 1964.
[86] Interview, March 31, 1964.
[87] Informant Gaynelle Fagin, April 10, 1964.
[88] Interview, April 4, 1964.

anywhere you walked. Think you were walking on natural floors and you'd go down through it."[89] Sometimes the bearer of a fake message disappeared beneath a trap door. Perry Randolph explains:

> And another thing they used to do was to take kids and give them a note. They got certain houses in town. They say, "Go to such and such a house and go to the vestibule." Houses have vestibules, you know, and step in the vestibule and they got a trap door go right down to the cellar. Of course my mother always told me not to take no note from nobody.[90]

The trap doors frequently led to the basement of the night doctor's house, the supposed scene of the experimental operations they were believed to have performed. Morgan Ward stated:

> I've heard my daddy say that the doctors, for experimenting, they would trap these men at night. They would catch them. They would have trap doors in the houses. You go in a house, and you, maybe you would be sent to this house, and when you go in you step on a trap door and down you'd go into a basement. And that's when you'd be in an enclosure and nobody would see or hear from you anymore, and the doctors would take you and experiment. Would take this person and experiment on them. Evidently, you know, trying medicine on them and taking their lives, cutting them open, dissect them like.[91]

The manner in which people were silenced and carried off by the doctors is also the subject of a great deal of oral speculation. The consensus is that most of the victims captured outdoors were not immediately killed, but only temporarily silenced for their trip to the place of experimentation. For some reason not explained by informants, it was essential that the victim not "die until they got you to the hospital."[92] As one Black said, "then I suppose they would experiment on you, but I don't know."[93]

According to oral tradition there were many ways to silence

[89] Informant Robert Henson, March 24, 1964.
[90] Interview, March 24, 1964.
[91] Interview, March 6, 1964.
[92] Informant Minnie Bell Fountaine, April 22, 1964.
[93] Informant Darwin Smith, March 26, 1964.

victims. A simple, but crude way was to "Steal up on top of you and knock you in the head, and tie your hands and foot, and put you in a bag and go on about your business to the medical school or somewheres."[94] Another commonly reported way to keep victims from making a noise was to either "gag you by putting something in your mouth,"[95] or to throw "a sack,"[96] "sheet,"[97] or "hood"[98] over the victim's head. Concerning the use of the hood, C. T. McLain said:

> Anything to keep you from making a noise, you see? And you couldn't see, naturally. It's just like these hoods like the Ku Klux Klan wear now. And naturally if you put it over your face, you can't see nothing but the eyes. But when they put that thing over your head and you get in that wagon, you didn't know nothing, because you were scared to death anyway.[99]

Whatever the type of head covering used by night doctors, "If it ever went over your head, no matter how you screamed, you were not heard by anyone."[100]

Blindfolds were said to have often been used instead of a cloth covering the entire head.[101] Blindfolded victims were simply threatened not to yell or to scream. Ida Mitchell stated:

> Seemed like to me he said they wore masks over their face so you couldn't tell who it was that grabbed this man. And it would be a mess of them grabbed him. And blindfolded him, what they called blindfolded him, so you couldn't tell where they were taking him. And they would tell you not to holler or not to scream.[102]

Hoods and blindfolds, while supposedly effective enough, were often replaced by more certain means of keeping victims quiet. Night-doctor victims were frequently rendered unconscious and thus completely helpless in a number of ways:

[94] Informant John Johnson, April 4, 1964.
[95] Informant Walter Scriber, March 26, 1964.
[96] Informant Henry Oliphant, March 28, 1964.
[97] Informant Minnie Bell Fountaine, April 22, 1964.
[98] Informant C. T. McLain, March 10, 1964.
[99] *Ibid.*
[100] Informant Minnie Bell Fountaine, April 22, 1964.
[101] Informant Florence E. Smith, April 3, 1964.
[102] Interview, March 10, 1964.

They used to carry things in their pocket and if they got near to you, see, whatever they would do to you, see, you couldn't holler or nothing. I imagine it was some kind of morphine or something, you know, they'd carry. And then they'd put this on you, and you couldn't holler and they would just take you on, see, wherever they chose, see?[103]

The "things" this informant referred to are described by others as anesthetizing needles and chloroform caps and plasters.

Needles, presumably filled with some type of anesthetic, were forced into various parts of the victim's body. "They say they used to stick needles in your back,"[104] one informant said. Another informant stated: "Some say they had a needle that would stick you and you would pass out. Then they would cover you and put you in the wagon."[105] Mildred Green talked about "flying needles" which immediately anesthetized victims:

They'd say they'd [night doctors] throw some kind of a needle, or something, and it would stick you and that's the way they would catch you. They'd throw something. I guess it was a needle, I don't know. They'd say you'd stop right there and you wouldn't move another peg.[106]

Aside from the use of needles, another means of anesthetizing victims was to put a rag or hood soaked with chloroform or ether over a person's face. Russell Burke said of this practice, "They tell me they used to sneak up on you from behind and put something, I mean chloroform you and carry you off."[107] Katherine Brooks Robinson referred to the chloroform cap night doctors used. "They put," she said, "chloroform caps or hoods over their heads, and this would knock them out."[108] Concerning the use of chloroform-soaked rags, Perry Randolph said: "See, they got a rag soaked with ether, chloroform, whatever you call it. Some call it chloro-

[103] Informant Alice Williams Duvall, April 12, 1964.
[104] Informant Benny Hawkins, April 4, 1964.
[105] Informant Mary Blue, April 12, 1964.
[106] Interview, March 26, 1964.
[107] Interview, March 24, 1964.
[108] Interview, April 20, 1964.

form, and some call it ether. And they get close to you and slap it over your mouth."[109]

Anesthetizing plasters are also spoken of by the Black folk as a means used by night doctors to render victims unconscious. Gaynelle Fagin stated simply, "They would throw a plaster over their face."[110] Rachel Jenfier explained how the plaster technique antedated the use of needles:

> Once there, I heard them say, years ago, that they used to put plasters over their mouth. Then they tell me they would stop doing that and would go by and stick needles. Stick needles in their arms. I don't know no more than what I heard.[111]

Laura Reed related an incident in which this trick was used unsuccessfully by night doctors on a friend:

> One of my girl friends, they caught her and was gonna stuff a plaster on one side of her face. They didn't get her in the mouth, but just got her right on the face. And she, Sarah Primrose, she lived right out in South East, and [they] caught, grabbed at her and smacked at her. And she just did get in the house in time.[112]

Conveyance of Victims and Manner of Death

Horses and wagons were commonly reputed to have been used to transport kidnapped victims and were considered by the folk as an important part of the night doctors' equipment. "They used," as one informant said, "horses and wagons and horses and buggies."[113] Such wagons were believed either to stay a block or so behind the doctors or to lurk out of sight around the corner from a possible victim. As one Black commented, "They got a wagon somewheres close around, working all the time."[114]

[109] Interview, March 24, 1964.
[110] Interview, April 10, 1964.
[111] Interview, March 26, 1964.
[112] Interview, March 27, 1964.
[113] Informant Darwin Smith, March 26, 1964.
[114] Informant John Johnson, April 4, 1964.

Most descriptions of wagons used for kidnapping were of vehicles built like hearses, completely closed in on all sides. C. T. McLain described such a wagon: "I don't know whether they picked up children or what they did, but in those days they had a wagon going around just like a undertaker's wagon, you know. It was all covered over and you couldn't hear them."[115] Perry Randolph's niece told him of being chased by a similar hearselike wagon: "She said it was a black wagon. Looked like a hearse. And the horses got rubber on the shoes. She looked around and saw the black wagon creeping up on her and she run, run to her house."[116]

On the other hand, Mary Blue claimed to have seen a night doctor's wagon as a child and she remembered it a little differently: "The wagon that I saw was an ordinary old dark wagon. Looked like it was black and these horses were dark horses. And I knew they weren't no milk drivers or no trash collectors."[117]

Informants generally made a point of mentioning the rubber tires with which these wagons were believed to have been equipped. Such tires were apparently not standard equipment on carriages at the time, and their use by the night doctors was considered extremely unusual. Henry Lewis Brown comments about this practice:

> And at that time he said they had a little wagon with a rubber wheel on it so it could roll easily, and they could roll around at night over the roads and around places where no one could hear them traveling. And had the horses; you know they would keep them walking on the sandy part of this road. And if they knew where you were they could come on in there and get you. Just like ordinarily you would hear a wagon rolling on the road out here. If it's a hard gravel road you would hear it at night. But at night you couldn't hear that, because . . . he said before it come to the time for the rubber wheels on those little wagons, they would take the iron tie off the wheel of the buggy and leave nothing but the wood; and they would wrap that wood section of that wheel in a burlap,

[115] Interview, March 10, 1964.
[116] Interview, March 24, 1964.
[117] Interview, April 12, 1964.

and it rolls just as easily as if it had rubber on it. That's how they traveled at night so the people couldn't hear them.[118]

Not only did the wagons have rubber wheels, but the horses were believed to have been shod with rubber shoes[119] or to have had pads on their feet[120] in order to operate as noiselessly as possible. Concerning the practice of using rubber to deaden the sound of horses and wagons, Thomas L. Henry states:

> They tell me they had rubber shoes on their horses and they had rubber tires on the buggies, on the wagons or whatever they carried, and you didn't hear them run at night. Because they, that's the time they said they always come out at night time. And they never made no fuss because they said the horses had rubber shoes on and you couldn't hear.[121]

Most Black folk believed that people captured by night doctors were taken in a wagon directly to a local hospital, laboratory, or medical school where they were murdered so that their bodies could be used for experiments. Concerning the use of hospitals as depositories for the victims of body-snatchers (by far the more popular belief), Robert Bowie said: "They used to tell me they'd catch you and carry you to some doctor's hospital, or something like that. People was experimenting on people in them days, you know. Wasn't no good doctors then, and wasn't no whole lot of hospitals."[122] An interesting variant opinion of where captured victims were taken was expressed by one informant, who felt that night doctors took intended victims "down to the Smithsonian grounds and experiment on you. All kinds of skeletons and things down there."[123]

Washington residents (primarily children) also believed in the existence of a "curfew wagon," which was very similar in description to the ones night doctors allegedly used. The "curfew wagon" patrolled Washington streets after nine o'clock at night in order

118 Interview, April 11, 1964.
119 Informant Thomas L. Henry, March 15, 1964.
120 Informant Laura Reed, March 27, 1964.
121 Interview, March 15, 1964.
122 Interview, March 26, 1964.
123 Informant Perry Randolph, March 24, 1964.

to pick up truant children. It was believed to have been operated by the city. Jessie Richardson remembered: "That was [the curfew] when I was a small boy going to school. And at that time you wasn't allowed out no later than 9 o'clock at night. They used to have a night wagon that come around and pick us up. Children, you know."[124] According to oral tradition, children picked up by the wagon were taken to the House of Detention, formerly located at 26th and E Streets, N.W., and were held there until a two-dollar collateral was paid for the children by their parents.[125] Alice Williams Duvall, who claimed to have seen the wagon, "just like I'm looking at you," said of it:

> And then we used to have something here like the 9 o'clock cab. It was a cab, like. [It] had glass and you could look out, but of course you couldn't get out because the door would be locked. And it was kind of a low vehicle, and the man sit up front. And inside it, see the door, it opened in the back, and it had brass balls on the inside. . . . [The horses] wore rubber soles and the cabs had rubber tires. And if they catch you out after 9 o'clock, children, they would take you down to 26th and E, and your mother would have to pay two dollars for you.[126]

Based on historical evidence, the existence of a "9 o'clock wagon" is highly questionable. Police records contain nothing about a curfew operating in the District after 1865 or a detention wagon of the type described by Black folk. Neither do the files of one of Washington's leading newspapers, *The Evening Star*, contain any information about these subjects.[127]

Regardless of the method of transportation, victims of the notorious night doctors supposedly suffered bizarre and terrifying deaths. It is a common belief among Blacks that night doctors bled their victims to death, usually by making an incision at the bottom of the foot. The blood so obtained was then believed to have been used by whites in the preparation of various medicines.[128] Accord-

---

[124] Interview, March 26, 1964.
[125] Informant Alice Williams Duvall, April 12, 1964.
[126] *Ibid.*
[127] Letter from *The Evening Star* Information Bureau, May 25, 1964.
[128] Informant William Allen Stokes, April 3, 1964.

ing to a dispatch from Columbia, South Carolina, which appeared in the *Boston Herald*, May 23, 1889:

> The Negroes of Clarendon, Williamsburg, and Sumter counties have for several weeks past been in a state of fear and trembling. They claim that there is a white man, a doctor, who at will can make himself invisible, and who then approaches some unsuspecting darkey, and, having rendered him or her insensible with chloroform, proceeds to fill up a bucket with the victim's blood, for the purpose of making medicine. After having drained the last drop of blood from the victim, the body is dumped into some secret place where it is impossible for any person to find it. The colored women are so worked up over this phantom that they will not venture out at night, or in the daytime in any sequestered place. One old colored woman insisted that she knows the white men make castor oil out of negro blood, and that in slavery times a negro would die before he would take a dose of castor oil. [129]

Many informants referred to the alleged practice of night doctors bleeding their victims. Minnie Bell Fountaine, for example: "I have heard that they start at the bottom of your feet and begin to bleed you. Those were the tales that we heard. It would take a long time to die because they would bleed you from the bottom of your feet." [130] There were several variations as to the manner in which the bleeding was accomplished; one informant described an ironic laughing death:

> They would stand them on something that would cut the nerves of the feet and they'd laugh themselves to death. Under the bottom of the feet there is a nerve that when you hit it, or when you cut it, you begin to laugh and you laugh until the blood is gone, and then you fall out. [131]

Another bleeding technique involved a special water solution: "They would slice you and put you in water and would draw your blood." [132]

---

[129] Stewart Culin, "Concerning Negro Sorcery in the United States," *Journal of American Folklore*, 3 (Oct.–Dec. 1890), 281–87.
[130] Interview, April 22, 1964.
[131] Informant Clara Cherry, April 12, 1964.
[132] Informant Alice Williams Duvall, April 12, 1964.

Once the blood was drained from a person, the corpse was then used for experiments by the doctors. During the course of these experiments the bodies were believed to have been mutilated. "They'd kill you and cut you up and they'd experiment on you."[133] James Morrison added:

> The first thing they'd do, they'd cut you in different places and bleed you to death. That's what they study, see. The doctors studied that. And from that they chop you up and do what they wanted to do with you, burn you up or anything else, expose you. But they'd never find you.[134]

A Notorious Washington Night Doctor

The most infamous professional body-snatcher in Washington, D.C., according to oral tradition, was a Black named Sam Mc-Keever.[135] Most informants who knew anything at all about night doctors had heard of McKeever, and a few even professed to have seen him in person. One of these was John Johnson, who said: "I've seen him, too. Many a times he would go all around Washington City, all around buying rags."[136] Another informant said, "Everybody knowed him, everybody."[137]

Sam McKeever became a kind of bogeyman around Washington during the period between 1880 and 1910.[138] The simple mention of his name was usually sufficient to send adults and children

---

[133] Informant Lucille Murdock, April 11, 1964.

[134] Interview, March 27, 1964.

[135] Sam McKeever was not the only Black body-snatcher in Washington. An unidentified Black preacher was known for burying the dead of his congregation and later stealing the corpses for sale to local doctors. See Frank Baker, "A History of Bodysnatching," *Washington Medical Annals*, 15 (May 1916), 251.

[136] Interview, April 4, 1964.

[137] Informant Laura Reed, March 24, 1964.

[138] Another body-snatching bogeyman was William Cunningham, a famous Cincinnati, Ohio, grave robber of the same period as McKeever. Cunningham pretended to be a drayman in the daytime and robbed graves at night. See Linden F. Edwards, "Cincinnati's 'Old Cunny,' A Notorious Purveyor of Human Flesh," *Ohio State Medical Journal*, 50 (May 1954), 466–69.

scurrying home. As one Black woman commented, "All you had to say was 'Sam McKeever,' and Lord we—oh, we would move out!"[139]

During the daytime McKeever was ostensibly a rag dealer who pushed a hand cart all over the city collecting and buying old cloth for resale to junk yards. Rachel Jenfier stated: "He would go around in the daytime and pick up rags with a push cart. And in the night time, they'd tell me he used to go around catching people."[140] John Johnson added supporting testimony concerning McKeever's rag business: "Everybody knowed Sam McKeever, much as he run people all hours of the night, and used to buy rags in the daytime for a sham and run people at night and catch them for the doctors. Everybody knowed him uptown, all around there."[141]

Sam McKeever was described by the Black folk as being a tall, heavily built, dark brown-skinned man, who may have been around sixty years old in the period between 1900 and 1910.[142] Most informants said that he usually wore old clothing, the cast-off garments he presumably collected around Washington. Laura Reed, who claimed she saw McKeever, described him and his customary attire:

> He was a tall, brown-skinned man. Yes, just about your color, he was [pointing to author]. Great big, heavy set. Wore old time overcoat and things. At night time, old big shoes. You would never know he had rubber shoes, old rubber shoes. You wouldn't know it.[143]

McKeever is supposed to have lived with his wife and three daughters[144] at Hughes Court, an alley dwelling near 25th and I Streets, N.W.[145] Laura Reed described herself as a former neighbor of McKeever in this Hughes Court:

[139] Informant Alice Williams Duvall, April 12, 1964.
[140] Interview, March 26, 1964.
[141] Interview, April 4, 1964.
[142] *Ibid.*
[143] Interview, March 27, 1964.
[144] *Ibid.*
[145] Informant Rachel Jenfier, March 26, 1964.

Yes, certainly I know him. I know him well. I lived right there by him. I ought to know him. I lived right around there in that neighborhood where he lived at. He would come out his back gate and go right down by the alley over me.[146]

Of all of Sam McKeever's reputed exploits, the accidental kidnapping of his own wife for sale to a local medical school is his most celebrated deed, told with many variations. She supposedly left home one night on an errand—some say it was to get coal oil[147] or water from an outdoor hydrant,[148] or to deliver some freshly laundered clothes to a customer.[149] McKeever is said to have spotted her—a tall woman—and not realizing it was his wife in the dark, kidnapped and sold her body to some local physicians. After his transaction with the doctors was completed, McKeever returned home. Noticing the absence of his wife, he inquired from his children where she was. When the children explained where their mother had gone, McKeever is supposed to have realized his mistake and rushed back to the hospital to save his wife's life, but he arrived just as she was dying. James Morrison told the most commonly accepted version of this episode:

> He sold his wife and didn't know it. She had been carrying clothes and was sitting in the park. And he stole up there and throwed that mask on her. A big footed fellow like that. And then, he got home and asked his children where their mama at. They said, "I don't know." Then it come to him what he had done, you see. He run to the doctors. She was breathing her last breath.[150]

In some versions of this narrative, McKeever is supposed to have killed his wife outright, with full knowledge of her identity, and then delivered her body to the physicians himself. Bessie Smith told the story this way:

> Sam McKeever, he caught his wife and killed her. He went out to the hydrant to get a bucket of water. That's where his wife was. That's where he caught her and he killed her, and made out he

---

146 Interview, March 27, 1964.
147 Informant Alice Williams Duvall, April 12, 1964.
148 Informant Bessie Smith, March 19, 1964.
149 Informant James H. Morrison, March 27, 1964.
150 *Ibid.*

didn't know it was her. But he did know it, they say. Because he was after people, you know, and sent them to the doctors.[151]

Another form of this story contains a happy ending, at least for Mrs. McKeever. The physicians to whom she was sold while still alive recognized her jewelry and turned her loose with the admonition never to return to her husband. Laura Reed told this version:

> Everybody knowed him in Washington, Sam McKeever. He was the one who used to go—he lived on Virginia Avenue down in South West. Well, his wife used to take in washing. She was a laundress. Much like you would take in washing, like you'd stay home and wash and iron. Well, she went out to get her clothes, carry her clothes home, and that's the time they got her. He caught her when she was going to—they would never know it was his wife, only by the rings and jewelry that the doctors taken off of these people's hands, what they had carried there. And he got his wife, too, but they let his wife go on account of they found the rings on her fingers. And they turned her right on aloose and told her to go on home and never come back, go ahead and wash and go on to her sister's. So she went on away with her people and never did come back no more.[152]

Sam McKeever died simply and quietly, apparently of natural causes, according to oral testimony. He may have succumbed to infirmities of old age since the folk tell of nothing that might have prematurely terminated his body-snatching career. Despite his reputed infamous deeds in life, the Blacks paid scant attention to his death. There was an occasional comment, such as one informant's statement, "He's dead and gone on to the—the devil's got him now,"[153] but little else was said concerning McKeever's death. His burial, however, was said to have been carried out with dispatch. One informant said on this point: "When he died they carried him through Georgetown to the undertaker's shop just as quick as that horse could go across the K Street Bridge. He was dead. They were glad to get rid of him."[154]

[151] Interview, March 19, 1964.
[152] Interview, March 27, 1964.
[153] *Ibid.*
[154] *Ibid.*

Very possibly McKeever may be buried in Mt. Zion Slave Cemetery located in Georgetown; the cemetery is now undergoing restoration by the Afro-American Bicentennial Corporation. It can be historically verified that a man named Samuel McKeever actually resided in the District during the night-doctor scare, roughly from 1880 to 1920. The main facts of the real McKeever's life which can be pieced together coincide so completely with folk oral testimony that there can be little doubt that he was the same man the folk tell about. Whether the real McKeever was a body-snatcher or a grave robber will have to remain a matter of conjecture.

Information concerning the actual existence of Samuel McKeever was obtained from *Boyd's Directory of the District of Columbia,* a city directory published annually and listing alphabetically the name, occupation, and home address of each adult resident. Scanned over a thirty-six year period for the name of Sam McKeever, *Boyd's* first listed McKeever in 1883. The entry read as follows:

> McKeever, Samuel, laborer
> 85 Clark Alley, N.W.[155]

From this date until the last entry of his name in 1918, the McKeever family name appeared in most of the issues, being occasionally omitted for intervals of a year or two. The names of Samuel and Eliza McKeever (of the same address and presumably his wife) were listed either separately or together, forming almost a pattern, until 1907, when a sharp break occurred—for this is the last date Eliza McKeever's name appears. For ten years no member of the McKeever family was listed in the directory. When the family name reappeared in 1917 only Sam's name and his children's names were entered as follows:

> McKeever, Samuel, laborer
> Rear 1518 O Street, N.W.
> McKeever, Armenia, nurse
> Rear 1518 O Street, N.W.

---

[155] Judah Delano, *The Washington Directory* (Washington, D.C., 1883), 581.

> McKeever, Essie, laundress
>> Rear 1518 O Street, N.W.
>
> McKeever, Exter, laborer
>> Rear 1518 O Street, N.W.
>
> McKeever, Laura [no profession listed]
>> Rear 1518 O Street, N. W.[156]

Eliza had now either died or moved out of town. Oral tradition carried both alternatives. Sam's daughter Laura was the last Mc-Keever to be entered in the directory, appearing alone in 1931. This corroborates oral testimony that Sam McKeever's daughters married and moved away.[157]

All additional information listed in the directory agrees completely with oral testimony concerning the McKeever family. Sam's occupation is variously referred to in the annual listings as laborer, rags, junk, buyer, and elevator operator. The latter career was listed in 1917 when Sam was apparently too old to engage in his former activities (whatever they might have been). Eliza McKeever listed her occupation at various times as washer, midwife, and nurse. The McKeevers had three daughters, a fact previously stated in oral testimony. Their son, Exter, was never mentioned in oral sources.

Finally, the directory listed 912 Hughes Court, a secluded Foggy Bottom alley, as one of the McKeever family home addresses. Significantly, this is the alley frequently referred to in oral tradition, and it is also the one place the McKeevers lived the longest —seven years. All other dwellings listed were vacated after one or two years.

Legal Basis and Demise

The Black's extraordinary fear not only of night doctors in general, but of specific practitioners such as Sam McKeever, was undoubtedly reinforced by an accompanying belief that a law existed in the District, enforced by the city government, which

---

156 *Ibid.*, 877.
157 Informant Laura Reed, March 27, 1964.

allowed student doctors to capture a stipulated number of people per year to be used for medical experiments. There was one catch to the law—the doctors could not be caught in the act of body-snatching, presumably by either the police force or local citizens. One informant said, "You're allowed to have so many bodies every year, but you ain't allowed to be caught with them."[158] Another informant's comment was: "In them days the law used to allow menses to catch people if they didn't get caught. If they caught you it was a penitentiary act."[159] This is the substance of Thomas Henry's remarks, which also philosophize about why such a law is not enforced today:

> If they caught you, why it wasn't nothing nobody done about it because they were supposed to catch different people, so many folks a year. But they had to catch them in secret and not let nobody know. And if they could catch you and nobody know nothing about it, well, and then . . . well, they'd take you. . . . But they would get so many, many people a year. They said the law, the government would allow them to catch so many a year. Of course now they claim that they don't go by that no more because they have too many dead bodies, and too many folks just dies now. They don't have to chase nobody now.[160]

Whether legally or illegally, a number of people were believed to have disappeared every year in the District (and elsewhere for that matter) because of the activity of night doctors. A Black woman told me, "Of course you would hear so many people was missing and it wasn't nothing but that."[161] Another woman said, "You would just disappear and it was supposed that you were taken in by the night doctors."[162] Missing persons were often the subject of conversations, and it was automatically assumed that the individual under discussion had been abducted by night doctors. Darwin Smith didn't know of any specific people who were

[158] Informant Laura Reed, March 27, 1964.
[159] Informant John Johnson, April 4, 1964.
[160] Interview, March 15, 1964.
[161] Informant Gaynelle Fagin, April 10, 1964.
[162] Informant Minnie Bell Fountaine, April 22, 1964.

captured, but as a child he often heard older people talking about people who disappeared under strange circumstances:

> No, I don't remember any specific cases. All I heard was hearsay, see? "And he must have been," or if somebody disappeared, "He must have been, the night doctors must have gotten him." That was at the turn of the century, you know. And just a kid, they would be listening to what the old people would say, and if they turned around and saw him listening, they'd run him on off.[163]

The folk agree about very little concerning the various phases of the body-snatching business, except that night doctors are no longer in existence and have not been operating for a long time. They tell about the demise of the body-snatching business in their own way. One said, "I haven't heard about them for a long time";[164] and another, "I don't think I've heard about them now. They used to have them years ago."[165] Anna Cooper Roy said, "But now that's all done away with."[166] A number of informants don't bother to speculate about the end of body-snatching. When queried concerning this subject, one Black woman simply stated, "So finally, I don't know, it just died down and they stopped doing things like that."[167]

But a few of the more speculative Black folk feel that the condition which originally gave rise to body-snatching—a scarcity of bodies—no longer exists. As one informant theorized:

> The law allowed them men for to catch the people in them days, yes, ma'am. But you don't never do it now because they use animals and unclaimed bodies, and all like a that, and dogs and cats now. They has enough now. They don't have to bother.[168]

The reason why unclaimed bodies and dogs and cats were not available for medical research during the night-doctor era was not explained.

[163] Interview, March 25, 1964.
[164] Informant Benjamin Dozier, March 24, 1964.
[165] Informant Russell Burke, March 24, 1964.
[166] Interview, April 2, 1964.
[167] Informant Gaynelle Fagin, April 10, 1964.
[168] Informant John Johnson, April 4, 1964.

The idea held by many informants is that hospitals now have enough unclaimed bodies on which to experiment. As Robert Bowie said: "You don't hear no more talk about no night doctors now. Hospitals is night doctors now."[169] Alice Williams Duvall explained it this way:

> You see, the doctors used to get their experience in them days, see. Whereas now you are in the hospital and it's so much diseases now in the hospitals, see, they don't need you now. Because there are so many diseases in the hospital.[170]

In view of the systematic denial of the existence of night doctors by trained physicians, and lack of solid historical evidence of murder for the purposes of obtaining bodies to sell, how does one explain the very real fear of being kidnapped and used for medical experimentation?

One explanation is that whites deliberately fostered a fear of night doctors among rural Southern Blacks (and perhaps whites) in order to discourage their migration to urban industrial centers. Such a view would explain the parallel existence of the night-doctor tradition among Blacks and whites. Another view, perhaps too long overlooked, is that living people were, indeed, victims of scientific experiments while bona fide patients in approved hospitals, at least during the early part of the nineteenth century. To what extent slaves before the Civil War and the poor, downtrodden, and disadvantaged after the war were openly used to try out unproven medical techniques has to remain an intriguing conjecture.

Historians and scientific minds aside, to the folk it was a dreary, dreadful business in which the night doctors were supposedly engaged. Not only did one have to fear a mysterious kidnapping and sudden death, but the terrifying thought of having one's blood drained, drop by drop—only to wind up in dismembered parts carefully scrutinized by overeager medical students, or scattered around an anatomy laboratory—was enough to give the average man pause. And it did. At least until the 1930s a number of dis-

[169] Interview, March 26, 1964.
[170] Interview, April 12, 1964.

advantaged people chose to avoid certain cities altogether, certain parts of cities in the daytime (areas adjacent to hospitals), and many avoided traveling at all at night unless accompanied by small groups. Whether fact or simply fear, the night doctor had certainly captured the imagination of the folk.

EPILOGUE

The Preservation of Oral Stories in Black Culture

THAT SLAVE OWNERS knew about—and tried to prevent—clandestine meetings of the Blacks is a historical fact. Masters perceived these nocturnal gatherings as an organizing force for the slaves, a very real threat to the slave system. What the master did not understand, or perhaps even know, was that many of these secret meetings were no more than the continuation of a practice deeply rooted in the Blacks' African heritage and, in this strange land, the only way to preserve the continuity with the past that would sustain them in the future. The Blacks needed to talk to each other; quite simply, they met to tell stories. In so doing, they continued their oral tradition, now the basis of this book. A former slave recalled to this author the moving about at night from one plantation to another for storytelling sessions at designated cabins:

> They used to sit nights and tell tales. One or two of them would come to the quarters, steal there after old marster and old mistress gone to bed. They would steal to the quarter and sit down and tell tales.[1]

During slavery, these gatherings for storytelling acted as a kind of clearinghouse of news concerning family members who had been sold or who had stolen away from the plantation. Slaves learned of births, deaths, illnesses, and separations, as well as of approaching secret meetings and social events. Indeed, information concerning every facet of life, from the private world of the slave compound to the outside arena of local and national events,

---

[1] Informant Alice Virginia Lyles, March 16, 1964.

was verbally disseminated in the quarters. Equally important, however, was the function of these sessions in helping to preserve the slave's sense of self-identity, of knowing who he was and how he perceived his world and objectified his experiences. These slaves who risked so much to attend forbidden secret assemblies were driven by a strong need to remember the past. Moments of conversation—fleeting though they must have been at times— offered one of the few opportunities for transported Blacks to form a verbal link with a long-remembered African past.

Stories told in the slave quarters were the first link in the storytelling tradition in the newly formed Black community. In the post-Civil War period, Black descendants channeled their need to remember their own side of the slavery experience—the perspective of the victims rather than the perpetrators—into frequent storytelling sessions at predetermined sites. Sometimes the storytelling situation was occasioned by social events, such as a church revival, a housewarming, or a lull at a frolic. Indeed, any type of gathering sooner or later spontaneously turned to storytelling.

> I recollect a good many stories told by my grandparents. As a matter of fact, when I was a child, my grandparents and other relatives of mine and people from the neighborhood used to go to my grandfather's house, and they would sit and talk on Saturdays and Sundays about what slavery was like, and I would sit and listen to them.[2]

These were frequent sessions open to a closely knit group of tellers. Within the family unit, time was often set aside nightly for reminiscences and stories. Such accounts either accompanied boring and tedious household routines or were the basis of afterwork leisure. Oral stories which provided an escape from stark reality were usually told while some form of food was being prepared, such as roasting sweet potatoes or chestnuts, pulling molasses candy, or cranking the ice-cream freezer.

Slave narratives frequently refer to the supernatural stories told by the fireside during the long winter months. The eerie light cast by burning embers, the puffs of curling smoke, and the crackling

[2] Informant Floyd Wardlaw Crawford, Feb. 8, 1964.

213

timbers provided a dramatic setting for stories about ghosts, witches, Jack o' Lantern, "the evil eye," and Raw Head and Bloody Bones. Listeners, especially those who had come from some distance, were known to have become so distressed by these stories that they refused to leave the security of the hearthside until morning. The Reverend Earl L. Harrison remembered that

> My grandfather's sons would sit up until the wee hours of the night telling these stories. And they would tell some of the awfullest, most terrible ghost stories. Of course our houses would be built up on stilts, up off of the ground, where dogs slept under the house, and hogs too. We didn't have a fence at night. And there'd be cracks in the floor, like those down there, some of them bigger than that. And I've sat up many a night with my feet up on the chair like this, afraid that something would get me through those cracks. And then they would tell me to go to bed. We'd all be sitting before a fire, you know, a fireplace with logs on the fire. Just one fireplace and you had to go out in the cold room to go to bed. And I was scared to death.[3]

Whatever the storytelling situation, it was the constant repetition of these stories, year after year, that accounts for their tenacity in the memories of many Blacks. Individual members of the Black community became known as "good talkers" and were often identified with particular repertoires of stories. As the occasion required, these stories were repeated again and again in flawless and meticulous detail. The audience, acting as an unconscious preserving force, helped to maintain some stability of texts by calling attention to such story changes as substitutions of detail and omitted passages. Borrowing and exchanging stories occurred freely, with the storyteller usually beginning the borrowed story with the opening formula, "Old Man So and So used to tell the story about. . . ."

The role of children in these storytelling sessions is an aspect of folk tradition too long overlooked. Stories about the past seemed to have had a special kind of appeal for children of slave descendants, for they listened by the hour, fascinated by the history of their family. James C. Evans recalls that

[3] Interview, March 19, 1964.

> In the evenings, we'd sit around. If it was the cool part of the weather, we'd sit around the fire, and if it was the warm summer time, just sit around the yard, and there would be two hours or more of just family talk. Maybe five of us there, maybe twenty-five of us. With the senior one always being respected as the moderator, or whatever it was. And this would go on every night.[4]

Old people, including favorite grandparents, were especially sought out by children because of their storytelling abilities. Such a person was

> Old man Ben Jeanes [who] came up in slavery, and he used to have a lot of children to be around him. He was very amusing, and he'd tell stories about white folks and how they did him, and how he outplanned them.[5]

In public gatherings, however, children learned to sit as quietly as possible while their elders held forth. Assuming and maintaining an inconspicuous posture was essential, for there were certain types of sensitive stories which were felt by adult Blacks to be too delicate for children's ears. But older Blacks, often caught up in the atmosphere of re-created experience, simply forgot that children were present. These children then, listening mesmerized to countless tellings and retellings of a remembered past, learned of the fears, the horrors, the whole of the Black slave world. They learned, too, the storytelling tradition and passed it on to their children, forging still another link in the chain of transmission between Africa, the slave situation in the New World, and the present Black experience. This is their book and theirs who before them lived the stories and told them.

[4] Interview, March 19, 1964.
[5] Informant Samuel Chappell, March 7, 1964.

APPENDIX A

Biographies of Informants

INFORMANTS WERE INTERVIEWED in their places of residence. The majority of interviews were conducted in Washington, D.C. Some collecting was done in Hyattsville, Maryland; Alexandria and Norfolk, Virginia; and Bloomington, Indiana.

Bing, Marie. Born in Aiken, S.C., in 1916; came to Washington, D.C., in 1954. Expressed gratitude for being able to discuss slavery reminiscences because she did not want to prejudice her only son by recalling the bitter slavery experiences of her great-grandparents. Domestic worker.

Blue, Mary Strother. Born in Washington, D.C., in 1903. Worked at the Pentagon as a special messenger in the Military Department during World War II. Currently in poor health and therefore unemployed.

Bowie, Robert. Resident of the District Home for the Aged. Born in Surrattsville, Md., in 1879. Came to Washington, D.C., about 1891. He was a maintenance worker for the city until his retirement. Never attended school in his life, though he can read.

Bradley, Lillian. Has lived in Norfolk, Va., since 1917. Born in Ward's Mill, N.C., in 1887. Worked as a dressmaker and domestic servant.

Brown, Henry Lewis. Lives in Hyattsville, Md. Born in Caroline County, Va., in 1912. Came to the Washington, D.C., area about 1934. Self-employed for 18 years driving a taxicab; now janitor in an apartment house in Hyattsville.

216

Brown, Jessie W. Born in Bennettesville, S.C., in 1920. Has resided in Washington, D.C., since about 1938. A self-employed barber.

Brown, Julia. Born in North Hampton, Va., in 1897. Came to Washington, D.C., in 1923. Formerly worked as a maid at the National Press Building; now retired.

Brown, Sterling. Born May 1, 1901. A Phi Beta Kappa graduate of Williams College in 1922, Professor Brown obtained his master's degree from Harvard in 1923. Aside from holding various academic posts, has written books, articles, essays, and reviews which have appeared in major publications. Now professor emeritus of Howard Univ., he was awarded two honorary degrees: Doctor of Humane Letters, Univ. of Massachusetts, May 30, 1971; Doctor of Literature, Howard Univ., June 5, 1971.

Burke, Russell. A native of Washington, D.C., born in 1903. Held a variety of unskilled jobs. Professes to be Afro-American, though he claimed that his father was white and his mother a full-blooded Indian.

Chappell, Samuel. Born in Lawrence, S.C., in 1882. A Baptist minister, pastored in Charlotte and Ellenburg, N.C., for about 45 years. Now lives with his son and daughter-in-law in Washington, D.C., and is semiretired from active ministerial duties.

Cherry, Clara. A housewife; lived in Washington, D.C., more than 50 years. Born in Windsor, N.C., in 1895. Her father, Wright Cherry, was a slave. His master did not allow patrollers on his property.

Chisholm, Frances White. Interviewed in Bloomington, Ind. Born in Lenoir City, Tenn., in 1928. Now lives in Tuskegee, Ala. Holds a master's degree in nursing education from Indiana Univ.

Cobb, W. Montague. Born in Washington, D.C., in 1904. Holds the following degrees: M.D., Ph.D., and Sc.D. Dr. Cobb is head of the Dept. of Anatomy in the College of Medicine, Howard Univ.

Cooper, William Mason. Lives in Norfolk, Va. Born in Hampton, Va., in 1892. Retired from Hampton Institute in 1958 as the school's registrar. Since 1962 has been employed at Norfolk Division, Virginia State College, as director of the Federal Demonstration Research Project for Re-education of Unemployed, Unskilled Workers.

Coppage, Samuel Francis. Lives in Norfolk, Va. Born in Durham's Neck, N.C., in 1886. A practicing dentist. Dr. Coppage's father was a slave; his grandfather was a white patroller.

Crawford, Floyd Wardlaw. Born in Forsythe, Ga., in 1900. Lives in Norfolk, Va. He holds a Ph.D. degree and is head of the History Department, Norfolk Division, Virginia State College. Grandparents were slaves; recalled many stories they told him about their slavery experiences.

Davenport, Ella. A resident of Stoddart Baptist Home in Washington, D.C. Born in Lawrence, S.C., in 1880. Came to the District in 1917. Worked as a cook at Emergency Hospital for 20 years. Her father was a slave.

Dozier, Benjamin. Has lived in Washington, D.C., all of his life. Born in 1887. Worked as a laborer before retiring to the District Home for the Aged.

Duvall, Alice Williams. Born in Washington, D.C., in 1896. Formerly employed as a maid in a federal government building; now retired. High school education.

Edmonds, Lucy. Born in Shenandoah, Va., in 1874. Has lived in Washington, D.C., since the mid-1930s. Worked at the Court of Customs, Patent Appeal, as a maid before retirement. Paternal grandmother, a slave, was killed by fellow slaves for tattling.

Egypt, Ophelia Settle. Born in Red River County, Tex., 1903. B.A., 1925, from Howard Univ.; M.A., Sociology, Univ. of Pennsylvania, 1928. Former Associate of Charles S. Johnson, Social Science Department, Fisk Univ. Retired from academic and government service; engaged full time in writing.

Fagin, Gaynelle. Born in Lynchburg, Va., in 1900. Worked in a tobacco factory and laundry in Lynchburg before coming to Washington, D.C., in 1927. Since that date Mrs. Fagin has been a housewife.

Fountaine, Minnie Bell. Born in Caroline County, Va., in 1894. Has lived in the District for more than 50 years. A beautician. Both of her parents were slaves.

Gatewood, Sarah Catherine Jones. Born in Washington, D.C. Uncertain about date of birth, but believes it was about 1897. Employed as an elevator operator before retirement.

Goines, Valmore. Lives in Norfolk, Va. Born in St. Louis, Mo., in 1921. Holder of Ph.D. degree in psychology; head of the Department of Psychology at Norfolk Division, Virginia State College. First informant to mention night doctors.

Green, John. Has lived in Washington, D.C., all of his life. Born in 1895. Has a fourth-grade education and worked as a laborer.

Green, Mildred. Born in Bedford County, Va., in 1897. Has lived in Washington, D.C., since she was six months old. Practical nurse.

Harrison, Earl L. Born in Cherokee County, Tex., in 1891. Former pastor of the Shiloh Baptist Church, one of the largest Negro churches of this denomination in the District. Father was a white Irish physician. Reared by maternal grandparents, who were slaves.

Hawkins, Benny. Has lived in Washington, D.C., since 1916. Born in Charles County, Md., in 1898. Has a third-grade education; worked as a truck driver and laborer.

Henderson, William H. Came to Washington, D.C., in 1894 at the age of 19. Born in Westmoreland County, Va., in 1875. Worked as a messenger in the War Department for 42 years, becoming supervisor of the messenger force before retirement. Mr. Henderson's father was the master's son.

Henry, Julia. Born in Farmville, Va. Though informant refused to state her age, she appeared to be in her eighties. Total formal education has been limited to three or four months of night school. Mrs. Henry can, however, read and write.

Henry, Thomas L. Lives in Alexandria, Va. Born in Bedford County, Va., in 1890. Father fought in the Civil War on the side of the Union. Has recently been working as a church janitor.

Henson, Robert. Born in Charles County, Md., in 1892. Came to Washington, D.C., about 1898. Now a resident of the District Home for the Aged.

Holloman, J. L. S. Came to Washington, D.C., in 1917 to accept a position as pastor of the Second Baptist Church. Former president of Washington Baptist Seminary. Born in Herford County, N.C., in 1885. Grandfather, Boston Holloman, was a slave.

Hopkins, Louise. Born in Xenia, Ohio, in 1922. Came to Washington, D.C., during World War II as a government employee. Still employed by the federal government. Has a high school education and one semester of college work completed at Wilberforce Univ. in Ohio.

Hurley, Matthew H. Came to Washington, D.C., in 1940. Born in Johnston, S.C., in 1910. Baptist minister with a B.D. degree from Howard Univ.

Jackson, Fred. Born in Culpepper, Va., in 1896. Has lived in the District since the mid-1950s. Has a fourth-grade education. Worked as a licensed barber in the Washington area for about 50 years.

Jenfier, Rachel. A native Washingtonian. Did not know her exact age, but apparently qualified for residence in the District Home for the Aged, her present home.

Johnson, Hayden C. Born in Washington, D.C., in 1908. Has lived entire life in the District, except for a tour of duty in the army in World War II. Now a practicing attorney. Maternal grandfather, Calvin Clutchfield, was the slave who helped carry Abraham Lincoln from Ford's Theater on the night of his assassination.

Johnson, John. Born in the District in 1875. Has a third-grade education. Worked as a day laborer before retirement.

Johnson, Mary E. Came to Washington, D.C., in 1909. Born in Crest Hill, Va., in 1892. She worked alternately as a federal government charwoman and beautician. Paternal grandfather was a runaway slave from the Deep South who successfully escaped to Pennsylvania.

Jones, Mary Elizabeth. Born in Clinton, S.C., in 1892; came to Washington, D.C., in 1922. Domestic worker. Reared by her ex-slave grandparents.

King, Messiah. Born in Pickings County, S.C., at the foot of the Blue Ridge Mountains, in 1881. Worked for 33 years as a federal employee. By avocation a writer of speeches, letters, sermons, etc.

Law, Mamie. Has lived in Washington, D.C., since her birth in 1879. Employed as a federal government charwoman before retirement. Has an eighth-grade education. Now a resident of the District Home for the Aged.

Lyles, Alice Virginia. At the time of this interview, she was an ex-slave, apparently 103 years old. Born in Charlotte Hall, Md., her father, Henry Stansberry, was manumitted by his owners, but fared

220

worse as a freedman than many of the slaves in the Tidewater area. Has a remarkable memory, able to recall in vivid detail several childhood experiences in slavery.

Lyles, Grace Singleton. Born in Edwards, Miss., in 1891. Has lived in Washington, D.C., since 1950. Manages a boarding house.

McKinney, Evelyn. Born in Carrien, Ga.; came to Washington, D.C., in 1932. A legal assistant, office manager, and notary public at a local law firm.

McLain, C. T. Born in Washington, D.C., in 1879. Retired army officer.

Manning, Fred. Born in Richmond, Va., in 1892; came to Washington, D.C., as a baby. Has a fourth-grade education. Employed as a furniture mover before he retired to the District Home for the Aged.

Mercer, Mary H. Born in Spencersville, Md. Refused to state her exact age, but stated that she is "just about a half-century." Has a high school education and works as a military pay clerk.

Mitchell, Ida. Born in Edgefield, S.C., in 1896; came to Washington, D.C., in 1929. Held a number of laundry jobs until the 1940s. At this time she became a charwoman in the federal government.

Mixson, Daniel. Has lived in the District since 1924. Born in Barnwell County, S.C., in 1892. Worked as a Redcap for the Washington Terminal Company until retirement.

Morrison, James H. Born in St. Mary's County, Md., in 1882; came to Washington, D.C., in 1904. Formal education limited to a few months in a public school. Worked as a laborer before retiring to the District Home for the Aged.

Murdock, Lucille. Born in Collarton, S.C., which she described as "way down in the country." Uncertain about her age, but reckons to be about 74 years old. Came to Washington, D.C., in 1939. Has a second-grade education. Worked primarily as a cook.

Neeley, Mary Howard. Born in Fayette, Jefferson County, Miss. Refused to give her age; appeared to be about 70. A retired school teacher. Grandfather, Merriman Howard, was sheriff of Jefferson County during Reconstruction. He left town when a mob determined to remove a Black prisoner from jail. Howard slipped the prisoner to a white man and fled to Washington, D.C.

Oliphant, Henry W. Has lived in Washington, D.C., since 1942. Born in Edgefield, S.C., in 1914. Works for the Navy Department in the Pentagon. Both grandmothers were slaves.

Parker, Eva Frances. Born in the District in 1893. Formerly employed as a domestic worker and laundress. Has a sixth-grade education. Now a resident of the District Home for the Aged.

Powell, Bruce. Born in Charlotte, N.C., in 1910. Came to Washington, D.C., in 1911. High school education. Employed at the Government Printing Office before retirement to the District Home for the Aged.

Purnell, Theodora Lee. The great Chicago fire was raging at the time of her birth there in 1871. Claims great-grandfather was the son of Light Horse Harry Lee and a slave mother.

Randolph, Perry. Born in Albemarle County, Va., in 1900. Came to Washington, D.C., in 1909. Has a fourth-grade education. Employed as a truck driver before retirement to the District Home for the Aged.

Reddick, Lawrence D. Born in Jacksonville, Fla. Received B.A. and M.A. from Fisk Univ. and Ph.D. from Univ. of Chicago. Has held various academic positions at Kentucky State College, Dillard Univ., Atlanta Univ., Johns Hopkins Univ., and is presently professor of history at Temple Univ. For nine years was curator of the Schomburg Collection of Negro Literature of the New York Public Library. Chief librarian of Atlanta Univ. for seven years.

Reed, Elizabeth. Has lived in the District since 1934. Born in Rockhill, S.C., in 1906. Worked as a charwoman in the federal government before retirement.

Reed, Laura. Uncertain about her age, but appeared to be at least 70. Born in Washington, D.C. A former domestic worker. Has a fifth-grade education.

Richardson, Jessie. Born in Washington, D.C., in 1889, and has lived there all of his life. Fourth-grade education. Formerly employed as a laborer.

Robinson, Katherine Brooks. Born in the District in 1926. College trained. Presently employed as an elementary school teacher in Washington. Daughter of C. T. McLain.

Robinson, Mamie Ardella. Born in Grainger County, Tenn., in 1887. Did not know her exact age, but remembered hearing people say as a child, "It's been forty years since slavery." Received no formal education, but became a self-taught speaker and elocutionist. Employed as a cook, practical nurse, and beautician before retiring to Stoddart Baptist Home.

Roy, Anna Cooper. Has lived in Washington, D.C., since her birth in 1884. A dressmaker. Grandmother was a slave who escaped on the underground railroad to Hartford, Conn.

Scriber, Walter. Has lived in Washington, D.C., since his birth in 1914. Formerly employed as an unskilled laborer. Now a resident of the District Home for the Aged.

Smith, Bessie. Born in the District in 1891. Received an eighth-grade education in local public schools. Now a resident of the District Home for the Aged and extremely senile. The only question she was able to answer coherently was about the night-doctor tradition in Washington. Was the first person to mention the name of Sam McKeever. The whole ward was shocked at her lucid responses concerning the night doctors.

Smith, Darwin Enoch. Born in Pittsburgh, Pa., in 1893. Came to the District in 1920. Retired army officer.

Smith, Ernest Clarence. Born in Cumberland County, Md., in 1897. Former pastor of Metropolitan Baptist Church, largest Black church of this denomination in the District. Has been a Baptist minister for 50 years, serving a number of churches in the Washington-Virginia area. Trained at Virginia Seminary, Union Seminary, Union Univ., and Columbia Univ. Holds following degrees: A.B., Th.B., B.D., A.M., D.D. and Li.D.

Smith, Florence E. Has lived in Washington, D.C., most of her life. Born in Baltimore, Md., in 1903. Worked as a waitress and elevator operator.

Smith, Rufer. Lives in Bloomington, Ind. Born and raised in Winchester, Ark. Came to Bloomington 21 years ago. A domestic worker.

Stokes, William Allen. Born in South Carolina, in 1905. Came to Washington, D.C., about 1946. Farmed in South Carolina and worked in a tobacco factory there for a number of years. Has a fifth-grade education.

Tolbert, James Maurice. Born in Dallas, Tex., in 1884. Came to the District about 21 years ago. A retired insurance agent.

Tymes, James Daniel. Born in Aberdeen, Miss., in 1905. Came to Washington, D.C., in 1934. Holds Ph.D. degree from Boston Univ. Entered the fifth grade at the age of 19 in Kansas City, Mo., having been denied public education in the rural Mississippi community of his birth. Now retired, was formerly professor of Religious Education and director of the Program of Graduate Studies in Religious Education at Howard Univ.

Ward, Morgan. Has lived in Washington, D.C., since 1960. Born in White Stone, Va., in 1923. Works as a watchmaker and repairman.

Wheeler, Elizabeth. Born in Bedford, Va., in 1875. Came to the District in 1891 at the age of 16. A domestic worker with a fifth-grade education.

Willis, William. Resides in Washington, D.C. Born in Westmoreland County, Va., in 1903. Employed as a computer operator for the Navy Department. Maternal grandfather, Solomon Dixon, "took up with Negroes," rather than go to the Civil War. He was a wealthy man who married two Black wives and had a number of children by them. Paternal grandfather, George Willis, was a slave, the son of his master.

APPENDIX B

WPA Informants

Adams, Rachel. Athens, Ga.
Allen, Jim. West Point, Miss.
Andrews, Samuel Simeon. Jacksonville, Fla.
Badgett, Joseph Samuel. Little Rock, Ark.
Baker, Georgia. Athens, Ga.
Bates, Millie. Union, S.C.
Blackwell, Boston. North Little Rock, Ark.
Blackwell, Willie, Fort Worth, Tex.
Blake, Henry. Little Rock, Ark.
Bost, W. L. Asheville, N.C.
Bridges, Francis. Oklahoma City, Okla.
Brown, F. H. North Little Rock, Ark.
Brown, William. North Little Rock, Ark.
Butler, Marshall. District No. 1, Ga.
Carder, Sallie. Burwin, Okla.
Cofer, Willis. Athens, Ga.
Colbert, Polly. Colbert, Okla.
Cooper, Mandy. Franklin, Ind.
Cross, Cheney. Evergreen, Ala.
Dawson, Anthony. Tulsa, Okla.
Dell, Hammett. Brasfield, Ark.
Dortch, Charles Green. Little Rock, Ark.
Draper, Joanna. Tulsa, Okla.
Duke, Alice. Gaffney, S.C.
Evans, Ann Ulrich. St. Louis, Mo.

Ezell, Lorenzo. Beaumont, Tex.
Franklin, Leonard. Little Rock, Ark.
Franks, Dora. Aberdeen, Miss.
Freeman, Henry. Mart, Tex.
Fulkes, Minnie. Petersburg, Va.
Gill, Frank. Mobile, Ala.
Gilmore, Brawley. Union, S.C.
Goodwater, Thomas. Charleston, S.C.
Graves, Wesley. North Little Rock, Ark.
Gray, Ambus. R.F.D. 1, Biscoe, Ark.
Griffin, Madison. Whitmire, S.C.
Guidon, Lee. Clarendon, Ark.
Harvey, Charlie. Union, S.C.
Hawkins, G. W. Little Rock, Ark.
Hayes, Eliza. Little Rock, Ark.
Hicks, Phyllis. Edmonston, Ark.
Hill, Kitty. Raleigh, N.C.
Hines, Gabe. Eufaula, Ala.
Holloway, H. B. Little Rock, Ark.
Holmes, Joseph. Prichard, Ala.
Horn, Josh. Livingston, Ala.
Hudson, Charlie. Athens, Ga.
Hunter, Elbert. Method, N.C.
Hutcheson, Alice. Athens, Ga.
Hutchinson, Ida Blackshear. Little Rock, Ark.
Jackson, Solomon. Evergreen, Ala.
James, Fred. Newberry, S.C.
Johnson, Richard. Waco, Tex.
Jones, Vergil. Brinkley, Ark.

225

Junell, Oscar. Little Rock, Ark.
Kyles, Preston. Texarkana, Ark.
Lassiter, Jane. Raleigh, N.C.
Lee, Mattie. Fredericktown, Mo.
Lee, Randall. Palatka, Fla.
McCullough, Lucy. Athens, Ga.
McQueen, Nap. Beaumont, Tex.
McWhorter, William. Athens, Ga.
Matthews, Ann. Nashville, Tenn.
Morgan, James. Little Rock, Ark.
Morris, Charity. Camden, Ark.
Owens, George. Beaumont, Tex.
Pattillo, G. W. District 5, Georgia.
Pugh, Nicey. Prichard, Ala.
Rimm, Walter. Fort Worth, Tex.
Rogers, Ferebe. Baldwin County,
  Milledgeville, Ga.
Ross, "Cat." Brasfield, Ark.

Ross, Frederick. Commerce, Mo.
Scales, Clarissa. Austin, Tex.
Smith, Berry. Forest, Miss.
Smith, Jordon. Marshall, Tex.
Sutton, Jane. Gulfport, Miss.
Thomas, Dicey. Little Rock, Ark.
Tims, J. T. Little Rock, Ark.
Turner, Emma. Pine Bluff, Ark.
Watkins, William. Beaumont, Tex.
Wesley, Robert. Holly Grove, Ark.
Williams, Andy. Waco, Tex.
Williams, Charley. Tulsa, Okla.
Williams, Millie. Fort Worth, Tex.
Wilson, James. St. Louis, Mo.
Winn, Willis. Marshall, Tex.
Wright, Mary. Christian County,
  Ky.

APPENDIX C

Texas Slave Narrative Informants

THE FOLLOWING INFORMANTS were a part of an ex-slave study conducted by James B. Cade with the help of Prairie View Extension Class students in Madison and Leon counties of Texas in 1935. These uncatalogued narratives are permanently housed in the Southern University Archives, Baton Rouge, Louisiana. Except for the two ex-slaves so indicated, no information was available concerning the place of residence of the remaining informants used in this study.

Anderson, The Reverend Reuben
   (San Antonio, Tex.)
Ford, Henry Ellis
Garrett, Tobe
Gilmore, Mrs. E.
Gober, Richard
Goff, Jim

Marshall, Matilda
Murphy, Bill
Reed, Charles (San
   Antonio, Tex.)
Roberts, I. B. R.
Williams, James

APPENDIX D

Tale Type Index

TALE TYPES are classified according to *The Types of the Folktale: A Classification and Bibliography*, Folklore Fellows Communications, No. 184 (Helsinki, 1961), translated and enlarged by Stith Thompson from Antti Aarne's *Verzeichnis der Märchentypen*, FFC, No. 3 (Helsinki, 1910).

Tale types which are also found in Ernest W. Baughman's *Types and Motif-Index of the Folktales of England and North America* (The Hague, 1966; Indiana University Folklore Series No. 20) are followed by an asterisk.

73	Blinding the Guard, 107–109
1676 A*	Big 'Fraid and Little 'Fraid, 77–78

Motif Index

Motif numbers are taken from Stith Thompson's *Motif-Index of Folk-Literature*, rev. ed., 6 vols. (Bloomington, Ind., 1955–58).

Motif numbers which are also found in Ernest W. Baughman's *Types and Motif-Index of the Folktales of England and North America* (The Hague, 1966; Indiana University Folklore Series No. 20) are followed by an asterisk.

A1210	Creation of man by creator, 50
C420.2	Tabu: not to speak about a certain happening, 58
D412.3	Transformation: swine becomes another animal, 80

D1274.1	Magic conjuring bag, 54
D1385*	Magic object protects from evil spirits, 77
D1385.5	Metal as defense against spirits, 55
D1402.31	Magic salt kills, 54
D1812.3.3*	Future revealed in dream, 42
D2061.2.2.7*	Animals abused or destroyed to cause death of person, 54
D2070.1	Magic hair-ball used for bewitching, 55
E200	Malevolent return from the dead, 135–36
E251.3.3*	Vampire sucks blood, 201
E261.4*	Ghost pursues man, 75–78
E266*	Dead carry off living, 64, 138
E272.4*	Ghost chases pedestrian on road, 76–78
E273*	Churchyard ghosts, 66
E275*	Ghost haunts place of great accident or misfortune, 67
E280	Ghosts haunt buildings, 66
E283*	Ghosts haunt church, 76
E323.5*	Mother returns to search for dead child, 68
E402*	Mysterious ghostlike noises heard, 120
E402.1.1.3*	Ghost cries and screams, 68–69
E402.1.1.4*	Ghost sings, 74
E421.1*	Invisible ghosts, 201
E422.1.1*	Headless revenant, 71
E422.1.3*	Revenant with ice-cold hands, 74
E422.1.11.4*	Revenant as skeleton, 119–20
E422.4.3	Ghost in white, 71
E423.1.1*	Revenant as dog, 76
E423.1.1.2.1*	Headless ghostly dog, 67–68
E423.1.3.3*	Revenant as headless horse, 65
E423.1.5*	Revenant as swine, 80
E423.1.8*	Revenant as cow, 65
E423.1.8.1	Revenant as calf, 80
E425.2.4*	Revenant as American Indian, 119–20
E434*	Magic protection against revenants, 77
E443.5*	Ghost laid by adjuring it to leave "in the name of God," 80
E497	Fighting warriors show the way of their past life and of their death, 120, 136–38

E542*	Dead man touches living, 76
E556*	Ghost drinks, 138
E581.2.1	Ghost jumps on horse behind man, 74
F441.3	Wild man as wood-spirit, 67
F470*	Night-spirits, 57, 61, 167
F491*	Will-o'-the-Wisp (Jack o' Lantern) light seen over marshy places, 68–69
G265.8.3.1.2*	Witch throws bullets back at shooter, 146
G303.4.8.1*	Devil has sulphurous odor, 62
G303.6.3.4*	Devil appears in an intense light and with strong odor of sulphur, 62
G303.9.8.11	Pranks played by devil, 62
G303.10.4.0.1	Devil haunts dance halls, 75
G350	Animal ogres, 65
J1789	Things thought at night to be other frightful object, 168
K621*	Escape by blinding guard, 107–109
K1682.1*	Big 'Fraid and Little 'Fraid, 77–78
K1810*	Deception by disguise, 79–80
K1823	Man disguises as animal, 142–43
K1825.1	Disguise as doctor, 171, 180, 188–90
K1833	Disguise as ghost, 82, 88–89
M312.0.1	Dream of future greatness, 42
N338	Death as a result of mistaken identity: wrong person killed, 204
S112.4	Attempted murder by live coals in garments, 108
T550*	Monstrous births, 115–17

Classification of Superstitions

Superstitions are classified according to the *Frank C. Brown Collection of North Carolina Folklore*, vols. 6 and 7, *Popular Beliefs and Superstitions from North Carolina*, Wayland D. Hand, ed. (Durham, N.C.: Duke Univ. Press, 1964).

97	Prenatal fears cause birthmarks on children, 115–17
5543	A spell was usually worked by means of a conjure ball buried in the victim's path, 54

5546 If you carry a lock of hair of a person, you will have power or control over that person, 55

5568 To prevent conjuring, wear a dime in the shoe, 55

5721 A horse can see a ghost and will balk, 67

5725 If you see a ghost coming toward you at night, say "What in the name of the Lord do you want with me?" and it will go away, 80

5730 A rabbit's foot carried in one's pocket will keep off ghosts, 77

5806 A mole's foot carried in the clothes will keep off evil, 77

LIST OF WORKS CITED
OR CONSULTED

Archives Housing Slave Materials

Folksong Archives of the Library of Congress: Supplementary and Duplicate WPA Slave Narratives Materials. Washington, D. C. Bound volumes of the WPA Slave Narratives Collection are deposited in the Rare Book Room of the Library of Congress. Supplementary texts are located in the Folksong Archives of this library. These texts are indicated in this book by the use of parentheses.

Hampton Institute Archives: Slavery Documents; Handbills on Slave Sales. Hampton, Va.

Harrison County Court House Records: Uncatalogued Will Books and County Records. Clarksburg, W. Va.

Indiana University Folklore Archives: Indiana Negro Material; Data and Copy for Guides, etc. Bloomington, Ind.

Samuel J. May Archives, Cornell Univ. Library: Underground Railroad and Antislavery Materials. Ithaca, N. Y.

Southern University Archives: "Texas Slave Narratives; The Story of Slavery as Told to Students of the Midway Extension Class by Ex-Slaves of Madison and Leon Counties in Texas, 1935." Ed. J. B. Cade. Baton Rouge, La.

West Virginia University Archives: Folk Narratives Assembled by the WPA Relating to Blacks.

Unpublished Slave Materials

Work Projects Administration, Federal Writers Project. "Slave Narratives, a Folk History of Slavery in the United States from Interviews with Former Slaves" (typewritten records), Library of Congress Rare Book Room, Washington, D. C., 1941.

Jackson, Margaret. "An Investigation of Biographies and Autobiographies of American Slaves Published Between 1840 and 1860." Diss. Cornell Univ., 1954.

Starling, Marion Wilson. "The Slave Narrative: Its Place in American Literary History." Diss. New York Univ., 1946.

Yetman, Norman R. "The Slave Personality: A Test of the 'Sambo' Hypothesis." Diss. Univ. of Pennsylvania, 1969.

Individually Published Slave Narratives

Anderson, Robert. *From Slavery to Affluence: Memoirs of Robert Anderson, Ex-Slave.* Hemingford, Neb., 1927.

Anonymous. *A Narrative of the Life, Capture, Confession and Burning of Enoch and Joseph, A Couple of Runaway Slaves; the Former of, or Near New Orleans.* Mount Carmen, Ill., 1842.

Ball, Charles. *Fifty Years in Chains; or, the Life of an American Slave.* New York, 1858.

————. *Slavery in the United States; A Narrative of the Life and Adventures of Charles Ball, a Black Man, Who Lived Forty Years In Maryland, South Carolina and Georgia as a Slave.* Lewiston, Pa., 1836.

Banks, J. . . . *A Narrative of Events of the Life of J. H. Banks, An Escaped Slave, from the Cotton State, Alabama, in America.* Liverpool, 1861.

Bayley, Solomon. *A Narrative of Some Remarkable Incidents in the Life of Solomon Bayley, Formerly a Slave, in the State of Delaware, North America; Written by Himself and Published for His Benefit.* London, 1825.

Bibb, Henry. *Narrative of the Life and Adventures of Henry Bibb, An American Slave, Written by Himself.* New York, 1849.

Black, Leonard. *The Life and Sufferings of Leonard Black, a Fugitive from Slavery, Written by Himself.* New Bedford, 1847.

Brown, John. *Slave Life in Georgia: A Narrative of the Life, Sufferings, and Escape of John Brown, A Fugitive Slave, New in England.* London, 1855.

Brown, Josephine. *Biography of an American Bondman, by his Daughter.* Boston, 1856.

Clark, Lewis Garrard. *Narratives of the Sufferings of Lewis and Milton Clarke.* Boston, 1846.

Cooper, Thomas. *Narrative of the Life of Thomas Cooper.* New York, 1832.

Craft, William. *Running a Thousand Miles for Freedom; or, the Escape of William and Ellen Craft from Slavery.* London, 1860.

Davis, John. *Personal Adventures and Travels of Four Years and a Half in the United States of America by Mr. John Davis. Being Travels in Search of Independence and Settlement.* London, 1817.

Davis, Noah. *A Narrative of the Life of Reverend Noah Davis, A Colored Man. Written by Himself, at the Age of Fifty-Four.* Baltimore, 1859.

Douglass, Frederick. *Life and Times of Frederick Douglass, Written by Himself.* Boston, 1892.

————. *My Bondage and My Freedom.* New York, 1855.

Fedric, Francis. *Slave Life in Virginia and Kentucky; or, Fifty Years of Slavery in the Southern States of America.* London, 1863.

Gilbert, Olive. *Narrative of Sojourner Truth, A Northern Slave, Emancipated from Bodily Servitude by the State of New York, in 1828.* Boston, 1850.

Grandy, Moses. *Narrative of the Life of Moses Grandy; Late a Slave in the United States of America.* Boston, 1844.

Green, Jacob D. *Narrative of the Life of J. D. Green, A Runaway Slave from Kentucky, Containing an Account of His Three Escapes in 1839, 1846, and 1848.* Huddersfield, 1864.

Grimes, William. *Life of William Grimes, the Runaway Slave. Written by Himself.* New Haven, 1855.

Henson, Josiah. *The Life of Josiah Henson, Formerly a Slave, Now an Inhabitant of Canada, as Narrated by Himself.* Boston, 1849.

Hildreth, Richard. *The Slave; or, Memoirs of Archy Moore.* John N. Easburn, Printers, 1836.

Jones, Thomas H. *The Experience of Thomas Jones, Who Was a Slave for Forty-Three Years, Written by a Friend, as Given to Him by Brother Jones.* New Bedford [Mass.], 1871.

Jefferson, Isaac. *Memoirs of a Monticello Slave, as Dictated to Charles Campbell in the 1840's by Isaac, One of Thomas Jefferson's Slaves.* Ed. Rayford W. Logan. Charlottesville, 1951.

Maddison, Reuben. *Reuben Maddison: A True Story.* Birmingham, n.d.

Northup, Solomon. . . . *Twelve Years a Slave; Narrative of Solomon*

Northup, a Citizen of New York, Kidnapped in Washington City in 1841, and Rescued in 1853 from a Cotton Plantation Near the Red River, in Louisiana. Auburn and Buffalo, N.Y., 1854.

Parker, Allen. *Recollections of Slavery Times.* Worcester, Mass., 1895.

Prince, Nancy. *A Narrative of the Life and Travels of Mrs. Nancy Prince. Written by Herself.* Boston, 1853.

Steward, Austin. *Twenty-Two Years A Slave, and Forty Years A Freeman.* Rochester, N.Y., 1857.

Thompson, John B. *The Life of John Thompson, a Fugitive Slave.* Worcester, 1856.

Williams, Isaac D. *Sunshine and Shadow of Slave Life, Reminiscences Told by Isaac D. Williams to Tege.* East Saginaw, Mich., 1885.

Books

Abrahams, Roger D. *Positively Black.* Englewood Cliffs, N.J., 1970.

Andrews, Ethan Allen. *Slavery and the Domestic Slave-Trader in the United States.* Boston, 1836.

Aptheker, Herbert. *American Negro Slave Revolts.* New York, 1943.

———. *A Documentary History of the American People.* New York, 1951.

———. *Negro Slave Revolts in the United States 1526–1860.* New York, 1939.

Ball, James M. "Resurrection Days." *Lectures on the History of Medicine. A Series of Lectures at the Mayo Foundation and the Universities of Minnesota, Wisconsin, Iowa, Northwestern, and the Des Moines Academy of Medicine, 1926–1932.* Philadelphia, 1933–.

Bernard, Luther Lee. *Social Control.* New York, 1939.

Blassingame, John W. *The Slave Community.* New York, 1972.

Boatright, Mody C. *Folk Laughter on the American Frontier.* New York, 1942.

Bødker, Laurits. *International Dictionary of Regional European Ethnology and Folklore.* Copenhagen, 1965.

Bontemps, Arna. *Great Slave Narratives.* Boston, 1969.

Boskin, Joseph. "Sambo: the National Jester in the Popular Culture." *Fear: Race in the Mind of America.* Eds. Gary Nash and Richard Weiss. New York, 1970.

Botkin, Benjamin, ed. *Lay My Burden Down.* Chicago, 1945.

Bradford, W. R. *The Catawba Indians of South Carolina*. Columbia, S. C., 1946.

Brown, Douglas Summers. *The Catawba Indians*. Columbia, S. C., 1966.

Brown, William Wells. *Clotel, Or The President's Daughter*. New York, 1853; rpt. 1969.

Bruce, Philip A. *The Plantation Negro As a Freedman*. New York, 1889.

Bryan, Wilhelmus Bogart. *A History of the National Capital 1815–1878*. 2 vols. New York, 1914.

Burton, Annie Cooper. *The Ku Klux Klan*. Los Angeles, 1916.

Carroll, Joseph C. *Slave Insurrections in the United States, 1800–1860*. Boston, 1938.

Coleman, J. Winston. *Slavery Times in Kentucky*. Chapel Hill, 1940.

Coulter, E. Merton. *The South During Reconstruction 1865–1877*. Baton Rouge, 1947.

Delano, Judah. *The Washington Directory*. Washington, D.C., 1883–1930.

Dollard, John, and Leonard W. Doob, et. al. *Frustration and Aggression*. New Haven, 1969.

Dorson, Richard M. *American Folklore and the Historian*. Chicago, 1971.

————. *Folk Legends of Japan*. Rutland, Vt., 1962.

————. *Negro Folktales in Michigan*. Cambridge, Mass., 1956.

Egypt, Ophelia Settle, J. Masuoka, and Charles S. Johnson, eds. *Unwritten History of Slavery*. Social Science Documents No. 1, Social Science Institute, Fisk Univ., Nashville, 1945; rpt. Washington, D.C., NCR/Microcard Press, 1968.

Feldstein, Stanley. *Once A Slave*. New York, 1971.

Fisher, Miles Mark. *Negro Slave Songs in the United States*. New York, 1963.

Fleming, Walter L. *Documentary History of Reconstruction*. 2 vols. Cleveland, 1907.

————. *The Sequel of Appomattox*. New Haven, 1921.

Floyd, N.J. *Thorns in the Flesh*. Lynchburg, Va., 1884.

Franklin, John Hope. *Reconstruction: After the Civil War*. Chicago, 1961.

————. *From Slavery to Freedom*. New York, 1967.

Frazier, E. Franklin. *Negro Youth at the Crossways*. Washington, D.C., 1940.

————. *The Negro in the United States.* New York, 1949.

Garner, James Wilford. *Reconstruction in Mississippi.* New York, 1901.

Goffman, Erving. *Interaction Ritual.* Chicago, 1967.

Gottschalk, Louis, Clyde Kluckhohn, and Robert Angell. *The Uses of Personal Documents in History, Anthropology, and Sociology.* New York, 1945.

Green, Constance McLaughlin. *Washington Village and Capital, 1800–1878.* 2 vols. Princeton, 1962.

Green, John P. *Recollections of the Inhabitants, Localities, Superstitions, and Ku Klux Outrages of the Carolinas.* Cleveland, 1880.

Grund, Francis J. *Aristocracy in America.* London, 1839.

Hall, Gwendolyn Midlo. *Social Control in Slave Plantation Societies.* Baltimore, 1971.

Harding, Vincent. "Beyond Chaos." *Amistad* I. Ed. John A. Williams. New York, 1970.

————. "Religion and Resistance Among Antebellum Negroes." *The Making of Black America,* Vol. I (The Origins of Black Americans). Gen. ed. August Meier, New York, 1969.

Haymond, Henry. *History of Harrison County of West Virginia.* Morgantown, W. Va., 1910

Heard, J. Norman. *The Black Frontiersmen.* New York, 1969.

Henry, Howell M. *The Police Control of the Slave in South Carolina.* Emory, Va., 1914.

Hesseltine, William B. *The South in American History.* New York, 1943.

Horn, Stanley F. *Invisible Empire.* Boston, 1939.

Howe, Elizabeth M. *A Ku Klux Uniform.* Buffalo Historical Society *Publications* 25 (1921).

Hunt, Gaillard. *The First Forty Years of Washington Society.* New York, 1906.

Ingle, Edward. *The Negro in the District of Columbia.* Baltimore, 1893.

Johnson, Hayes. *Dusk at the Mountain.* New York, 1963.

Jones, Winfield. *Knights of the Ku Klux Klan.* New York, 1941.

Katz, William Loren. *Five Slave Narratives.* New York, 1969.

Keckley, Elizabeth. *Behind the Scenes.* New York, 1868.

Kittredge, George Lyman. *Witchcraft in Old and New England.* Cambridge, Mass., 1929.

Landis, Paul H. *Social Control.* Chicago, 1939.

Lane, Ann J., ed. *The Debate Over Slavery.* Urbana, Ill. 1971.

Lester, J. C., and D. L. Wilson, *Ku Klux Klan.* New York, 1905.

Levine, Lawrence W. "Slave Songs and Slave Consciousness: an Exploration in Neglected Sources." *Anonymous Americans: Explorations in Nineteenth Century History.* Ed. Tamara Harveven. Englewood Cliffs, N.J., 1971.

Lockwood, Mary S. *Yesterdays in Washington.* Rosslyn, Va., 1915.

Lofton, John. *Insurrection in South Carolina: The Turbulent World of Denmark Vesey.* Yellow Springs, Ohio, 1964.

Lovell, John, Jr. *Black Song: The Forge and the Flame.* New York, 1972.

McColley, Robert. *Slavery and Jeffersonian Virginia.* Urbana, Ill., 1964.

McDougle, Ivan. *Slavery in Kentucky, 1792–1865.* Lancaster, Pa., 1918.

Mecklin, John Moffatt. *The Ku Klux Klan: A Study of the American Mind.* New York, 1924.

Montell, William Lynwood. *The Saga of Coe Ridge: A Study in Oral History.* Knoxville, 1970.

Moody, Vernie Alton. *Slavery on Louisiana Sugar Plantations.* Reprinted from the *Louisiana Historical Quarterly,* April 1924.

Morison, Samuel Eliot, and Henry Steele Commager. *The Growth of the American Republic.* 2 vols. New York, 1950.

The Negro in Virginia. Compiled by Workers in the Writers Program of the Work Projects Administration in the State of Virginia. New York, 1940; rpt. 1969.

Nichols, Charles H. *Many Thousand Gone.* Bloomington, Ind. 1963.

Niebuhr, H. Richard. *The Social Sources of Denominationalism.* New York, 1957.

Olmsted, Frederick Law. *A Journey in the Back Country.* New York, 1860.

———. *A Journey in the Seaboard Slave States.* New York, 1859.

Ordinances of the Corporation of Washington. Washington, D.C., 1836.

Osofsky, Gilbert. *Puttin' On Ole Massa.* New York, 1969.

Patterson, Caleb Perry. *The Negro in Tennessee, 1790–1865.* University of Texas *Bulletin* No. 2205, Feb. 1, 1922.

Phillips, Ulrich B. *Life and Labor in the Old South.* Boston, 1963.

Puckett, Newbell Niles. *Folk Beliefs of the Southern Negro.* Chapel Hill, 1926.

Randel, William Peirce. *The Ku Klux Klan.* Philadelphia, 1965.

Reisman, Karl. "Cultural and Linguistic Ambiguity in A West Indian Village." *Afro-American Anthropology.* Eds. Norman E. Whitten, Jr., and John Szwed. New York, 1970.

Report of the Joint Select Committee to Inquire into the Condition of Affairs in the Late Insurrectionary States. 13 vols. House Report, 42nd Congress, 2nd Session, No. 22. Washington, D.C., 1872. (Referred to in text as KKK Report.)

Romaine, William Bethel. *A Story of the Original Ku Klux Klan.* Pulaski, Tenn., 1924.

Ross, Edward A. *Social Control.* New York, 1922.

Roucek, Joseph S. *Social Control.* Toronto, 1947.

Scaife, H. Lewis. *Catawba Indians of South Carolina.* Senate Document No. 92. 71st Congress, 2d Session. Washington, D.C., 1930.

Scott, Emmett J. *Negro Migration During the War.* Carnegie Endowment for International Peace, Preliminary Economic Studies of the War, No. 16. Washington, D.C., 1920.

Shibutani, Tamotsu. *Improvised News.* Indianapolis, 1966.

Simmons, William Joseph. *The Klan Unmasked.* Atlanta, 1923.

Speck, Frank G. *Catawba Hunting, Trapping and Fishing.* Joint Publications: Museum of the Univ. of Pennsylvania; The Philadelphia Anthropological Society. No. 2. University Museum, Philadelphia, 1946.

Stampp, Kenneth. *The Peculiar Institution.* New York, 1956.

Starobin, Robert. *Denmark Vesey.* Englewood Cliffs, N.J., 1971.

Stearns, Charles Woodward. *The Black Man of the South and the Rebels.* New York, 1872.

Still, William Grant. *The Underground Railroad.* 1873; rpt. New York, 1968.

Stuckey, Sterling. "Through the Prism of Folklore: the Black Ethos in Slavery." *The Debate Over Slavery.* Ed. Ann J. Lane, Urbana, Ill., 1971.

————. "Twilight of Our Past: Reflections on the Origins of Black History." *Amistad 2.* Ed. John A. Williams. New York, 1971.

Swanton, John R. *Indian Tribes of North America.* Smithsonian Institution, Bureau of American Ethnology Bulletin 145. Washington, D.C., 1969.

Sydnor, Charles. *Slavery in Mississippi.* New York, 1933.

Taylor, Joe Gray. *Negro Slavery in Louisiana.* Baton Rouge, Louisiana Historical Association, 1963.

Trelease, Allen W. *White Terror.* New York, 1971.

Trollope, Frances. *Domestic Manners of the Americans.* London, 1832.

Vansina, Jan. *Oral Tradition.* Chicago, 1961.

Weld, Theodore Douglas. *American Slavery As It Is.* 1839; rpt. New York, 1968.

Wiley, Bell I. *Southern Negroes, 1861–1865.* New Haven, 1938.

Williams, Robin M., Jr. *Strangers Next Door.* Englewood Cliffs, N.J., 1964.

Willis, William S., Jr. "Anthropology and Negroes on the Southern Colonial Frontier." *The Black Experience in America.* Eds. James C. Curtis and Lewis L. Gould. Austin, 1970.

Woodson, Carter G. *The Education of the Negro Prior to 1861.* New York, 1915.

Yetman, Norman R. *Voices From Slavery.* New York, 1970.

Articles in Periodicals

Amulree, Lord. "A Strange Affair at Coldingham." *Scots Magazine,* 53 (April–Sept. 1950), 398–403.

Baker, Frank. "A History of Bodysnatching." *Washington Medical Annals,* 15 (May 1916), 251.

Blake, John B. "The Development of American Anatomy Acts." *Journal of Medical Education,* 30 (Aug. 1955), 431–39.

Botkin, Benjamin A. "The Slave As His Own Interpreter." *Library of Congress Quarterly Journal of Current Acquisitions,* 2 (Nov. 1944).

Cade, James B. "Out of the Mouths of Ex-Slaves." *Journal of Negro History,* 20 (July 1935), 294–337.

Chaplin, F. Stuart. "Primitive Social Ascendency Viewed as an Agent of Selection in Society." *Papers and Proceedings, Twelfth Annual Meeting American Sociological Society,* 12, pp. 61–74.

Clephane, Walter C. "The Local Aspects of Slavery in the District of Columbia." *Records of the Columbia Historical Society,* 3 (1900), 224–56.

Culin, Stewart. "Concerning Negro Sorcery in the United States." *Journal of American Folklore,* 3 (Oct.–Dec. 1890), 281–87.

Dorson, Richard M. "Ethnohistory and Ethnic Folklore." *Ethnohistory,* 8 (Winter 1961), 12–30.

Edwards, Linden F. "Cincinnati's 'Old Cunny,' A Notorious Purveyor of Human Flesh." *Ohio State Medical Journal,* 50 (May 1954), 466–69.

————. "The Famous Harrison Case and Its Repercussions." *Bulletin of the History of Medicine,* 31 (March–April 1957), 162–71.

————. "A Ghoulish Tale of Three Cities." In two parts. *Ohio State Medical Journal,* 55 (June–July 1959), 788–90, 946–49.

————. "Resurrection Riots During the Heroic Age of Anatomy in America." *Bulletin of the History of Medicine,* 25 (May 1951), 178–84.

Eliot, Llewellin. "A History of Bodysnatching." *Washington Medical Annals,* 15 (May 1916), 247–53.

Ellison, Ralph. "A Very Stern Discipline." *Harper's* (March 1967), 83–84.

Fauset, Arthur. "Negro Folk Tales From the South." *Journal of American Folklore,* 40 (July–Sept. 1927), 269–70. The article covers Alabama, Mississippi, and Louisiana.

Fleetwood, John F. "The Irish Resurrectionists." *Irish Journal of Medical Science,* Sixth Series (July 1959), 309–21.

Fleming, Walter L. "Prescript of the Ku Klux Klan." *Publications of the Southern History Association,* 7 (Sept. 1903), 327–33.

Franklin, John Hope. "New Perspectives in American Negro History." *Social Education,* 14 (May 1950), 196–200.

Genovese, Eugene D. "On Writing the History of Black Slaves." *New York Review of Books* (Dec. 3, 1970), 34–42.

Goldsmith, Harry S. "Some Historical Aspects of Human Dissection," Part I. *Boston Medical Quarterly,* 11 (June 1960), 58–61.

Goodman, Neville. "Supply of Bodies for Dissection." *The Lancet,* 264 (Jan.–June 1944), 671–72.

Gordon, Susan Joan. "The 'Sack-'Em-Up' Boys." *Journal of the Medical Society of New Jersey,* 57 (May 1960), 263–65.

Guttmacher, Allan F. "Bootlegging Bodies." *Society of Medical History of Chicago,* 4 (Jan. 1935), 353–402.

Hale-White, Sir William. "John White Webster (The Guy's Ghoul)." *Guy's Hospital Reports,* 80, Nos. 1–4, (1930), 4–19.

Hansberry, Leo William. "The Social History of the American Negro: A Review." *Opportunity,* 18 (June 1923), 20–21.

Harris, D. Fraser. "History of the Events Which Led to the Passing of the British Anatomy Act, A.D. 1832." *Canadian Medical Association Journal,* 47 (Winter 1920), 283–84.

Hawkins, John. "An Old Mauma's Folk-Lore." *Journal of American Folklore*, 9 (April–June 1896), 129–31.

Henderson, Donald H. "The Negro Migration of 1916–1918." *Journal of Negro History*, 6 (Jan. 1921), 383–498.

Higginson, Thomas Wentworth. "Nat Turner's Insurrection." *Atlantic Monthly*, 8 (Aug. 1861), 173–86.

Hile, George D. "The Laws Pertaining to Taking Human Bodies for Dissection." *Cleveland Medical Gazette*, 12 (Sept. 1897), 621–26.

Joyner, Charles. "Soul Food and The Sambo Stereotype: Foodlore from the Slave Narrative Collection." *Keystone Folklore Quarterly*, 15:4 (Winter 1971).

Lawrence, D. G. "Body-Snatching in Relation to the Anatomy Act in the Province of Quebec." *Bulletin of the History of Medicine*, 32 (Sept.–Oct. 1958), 408–24.

Lea, Vic. "They Came by Night." *Bedfordshire Magazine*, 5 (Winter 1956), 274–76.

"Letters to the Editor." *The Kourier Magazine*, 1 (Dec. 1924–Nov. 1925), 7.

Lewis, Mary Agnes. "Slavery and Personality." *American Quarterly* (Spring 1967), 114–21.

MacPhial, Alexander. "The After-Math of Body Snatching: A Plea for Anatomy." *St. Bartholomew's Hospital Journal*, 24 (Dec. 1916), 28–34.

McWhiney, H. Grady, and Francis B. Simkins. "The Ghostly Legend Of The Ku-Klux Klan." *Negro History Bulletin*, 14 (Feb. 1951), 109–12.

Milburn, Page. "The Emancipation of Slaves in the District of Columbia." *Records of the Columbia Historical Society*, 16, pp. 96–119.

Mitchell, G. A. G. "The Story of Anatomy in Scotland." *Aberdeen University Review*, 25 (July 1938), 200–209.

Moore, Ruby Andrews. "Superstitions of Georgia, No. 2." *Journal of American Folklore*, 9 (July–Sept. 1896), 227.

Morgan, Kathryn I. "Caddy Buffers: Legends of a Middle Class Negro Family in Philadelphia." *Keystone Folklore Quarterly*, 11:2 (Summer 1966).

Niles, H. (ed.). *Niles' Weekly Register*, No. 26, Vol. IV. Baltimore, Aug. 27, 1831.

Parsons, Elsie Clews. "Lines Between Religion and Morality in Early

Culture." *American Anthropologist*, 17 (Jan.–March 1915), New Series, 51–57.

Peterson, Warren A., and Noel P. Gist. "Rumor and Public Opinion." *American Journal of Sociology*, 57 (Sept. 1951), 159–67.

Phifer, Edward W. "Slavery in Microcosm: Burke County, North Carolina." *Journal of Southern History*, 28 (May 1962). 137–65.

Prasad, J. "The Psychology of Rumour: A Study Relating to the Great Indian Earthquake of 1934." *British Journal of Psychology*, (July 1935), Part I, 1–15.

Randolph, Laura. "Uncle Si'ah and the Ghosts." *Southern Workman*, 32 (Oct. 1903), 506.

Reddick, L. D. "A New Interpretation for Negro History." *Journal of Negro History*, 22 (Jan. 1937), 17–28.

Richardson, Clement. "Some Slave Superstitions." *Southern Workman*, 41 (April 1912), 246–48.

Riezler, Kurt. "The Social Psychology of Fear." *American Journal of Sociology*, 49 (May 1944), 489–98.

Sheeler, J. Reuben. "The Control of the Negro, Body, Mind, and Soul." *Negro History Bulletin*, 21 (Dec. 1957), 67–69.

Shugg, Roger W. "Survival of the Plantation in Louisiana." *Journal of Southern History*, 3 (Aug. 1937), 311–25.

Simkins, Francis B. "The Ku Klux Klan in South Carolina, 1868–1871." *Journal of Negro History*, 12 (Oct. 1927), 606–47.

Stampp, Kenneth M. "Rebels and Sambos: The Search for the Negro's Personality in Slavery." *Journal of Southern History*. 37 (Aug. 1971), 371.

Thorpe, Earl E. "Chattel Slavery and the Concentration Camps." *Negro History Bulletin* (May 1962), 171–76.

Uya, Okon E. "The Culture of Slavery: Black Experience through a White Filter." *Afro-American Studies*, 1, no. 2 (1971), 203–209.

———. "Life in the Slave Community." *Afro-American Studies*, 1, no. 3 (1971), 281–90.

———. "The Mind of Slaves as Revealed in their Songs: An Interpretative Essay," *Current Bibliography on African Affairs*, 5 (1972), Series 11, pp. 3–10.

Waite, Frederick C. "Grave Robbing in New England." *Medical Library Association Bulletin*, 33 (1945), 272–94.

Wish, Harvey. "American Slave Insurrections Before 1861." *Journal of Negro History*, 22 (July 1937), 299–320.

Wood, S. "Exit the Body-Snatchers." *Quarterly Review*, 240 (Jan.–April 1933), 141–50.

Newspapers

The Charleston Mercury, Charleston, S.C., 1837–1839.
The Decatur Daily, Decatur, Ala., Feb. 14, 1965.
The Durham Morning Herald, Durham, N.C., Oct. 24, 1965.
The Evening Star, Washington, D.C., Feb. 13, 1862; July 25, 1972.
The Pathfinder, Washington, D.C., Dec. 17, 1938.
Washington Mirror, Aug. 15, 1835.
Washington Post, Dec. 13, 1964; Jan. 6, 1971.
United States Telegraph, Washington, D.C., Aug. 13, 1835.

Speeches and Papers

Egypt, Ophelia Settle. "An Ex-Slave Oral History Project." Paper read at the Black Oral History Conference, April 20–22, 1972, Fisk Univ., Nashville.
Milner, Duncan C. "The Original Ku Klux Klan and Its Successor." Paper read at Stated Meeting of the Military Order of the Royal Legion of the United States. Commandery of the State of Illinois. Oct. 6, 1921.
Minnis, John A. Address, "Ku-Klux in Alabama," Montgomery, July 1, 1872.
Papers Read at the Meeting of the Grand Dragons Knights of the Ku Klux Klan at their First Annual Meeting Held at Asheville, N.C., July 1923.
Pratt, Daniel D. Speech delivered in the Senate of the United States, May 17, 1872.
Sherman, John. Speech delivered in the Senate of the United States, March 18, 1871.

ACKNOWLEDGMENTS

THIS BOOK is based on a dissertation originally submitted to the Folklore Institute of Indiana University. Professor Richard M. Dorson, my thesis adviser and director of the Folklore Program, saw possibilities in the study from its inception. In the years when few recognized the potential of oral history, he had faith in this venture, and once the dissertation was completed he urged that the manuscript be revised for publication. This book is the result of his promptings. Naturally, Professor Dorson is deserving of very special thanks for his continuing encouragement.

At various stages of interviewing, research, and writing, a number of people have been especially helpful. I would like to single out a group of Black Baptist ministers in Washington, D.C., who took the time (perhaps hoping to save me) to be interviewed and who often gave me names of the parishioners to be used as possible informants. Slavery reminiscences, a kind of "ethnographic dynamite," were not an easy subject matter to collect in the mid-sixties. Without the endorsement of these key church members, much of this material might have remained unrecorded.

Four people either connected in some way with the Federal Writers Project or independently engaged in gathering slave narrative material should also be acknowledged and thanked. Sterling Brown, Lawrence D. Reddick, Ophelia Settle Egypt, and James B. Cade gave me valuable, first-hand information which, in some cases, had not previously been published. Also invaluable to my research in the WPA materials was the cooperation I received from Mrs. Ray Korson, former head of the Folksong Archives at the Library of Congress, and her former assistant and present head of the Archives, Joe Hickerson. Aside from allowing me free access to the WPA supplementary and duplicate materials, they were both generally helpful during my stay at the Library of Congress in May–June 1964.

The revisions, always tedious, have been facilitated by Roger Abrahams, of the University of Texas, and by Okon Edet Uya, of Howard University; both made a number of helpful suggestions. Judith Taggart gave the final manuscript a thorough going-over, and Joan Ruman Perkal provided all of the indexes. The staff of the English Department of the University of Maryland (especially Molly Emler) typed the manuscript uncomplainingly—at least within earshot.

A grant from the Graduate School of Indiana University financed the initial fieldwork. Two awards in the summer of 1970—a National Endowment of the Humanities Summer Stipend and a Faculty Research Award from the General Research Board of the University of Maryland—freed me from academic responsibilities in order to work full time on my manuscript, and a later subvention from the General Research Board at Maryland, this time toward publication costs, was most helpful also.

Although it has not been possible to name each person, my thanks go to all who have been in some way a part of this book. I want to thank especially my family and a longtime friend—John C. Richardson—who have provided tangible and intangible support as the occasion required.

College Park, Maryland
January 1975

INDEX

Abrahams, Roger, 60
Afro-American Bicentennial Corporation, 206
American Indians, 50, 119–22
American Slavery As It Is, 174
Andrews, Ethan Allen, 34, 92
Apparel of night doctors, 188–90
Autobiography of Malcolm X, The, 8

Badgett, Joseph, 157
Ball, Charles, 11, 68–69
Bernard, Luther Lee, 56
Bibb, Henry, 12
Bing, Marie, 36, 105–106
Black connections with Ku Klux Klan, 162–69
Black folk view of Ku Klux Klan, 154–62
Black genealogies, 8–9
Black night doctors, 202–207
Black oral history projects, 28–29
Black population migration to the North, 172–73
Blake, James, 91
Blassingame, John, 27, 28
Blue, Mary, 198
Body-snatching, 29, 36, 52, 170–211
Boston Herald, 201
Botkin, B. A., 21, 24–25
Bowie, Robert, 199, 210
Boyd's Directory of the District of Columbia, 206
Bridges, Francis, 156–57
Brown, Henry Lewis, 60, 70, 98, 180, 188–89, 190, 191, 198
Brown, Jessie, 64–65, 71, 182
Brown, Julia, 60
Brown, Letitia Woods, 34
Brown, Sterling, 20–21, 24
Brown, William Wells, 175–76

Bruce, Philip A., 4, 55
Bryan, Javan, 113–14
Bunche, Ralph, 20
Burke, Russell, 196
Burke, William, 176–77
"Burking," 176–77

Cade, James B., 17–18, 97
Carroll, Joseph C., 48
Catawba Indians, 120–21
Chappell, Samuel, 64, 76, 80–81, 97
Charleston Mercury, The, 173–74, 175, 176
Cherokee Indians, 120–21
Chisholm, Francis White, 70
Cobb, W. Montague, 177–78
Cocletz Clan legends, 119–22
Cocletz, Clopton, 119
Cocletz Indians, 119–22
Coleman, J. Winston, 87, 94–95
Congressional testimony concerning Ku Klux Klan, 14–15, 111, 113–14, 123–24, 132–33, 162, 165, 167
Congressional testimony concerning slavery, 14–15, 30
Conjuring, 54–55
Cooper, Mandy, 100–101
Cooper, William Mason, 97
Craven, Avery, 4
Crawford, Floyd Wardlaw, 49, 99–100, 107–109
Crowley's Ridge, 157
Cunningham, William, 202n
"Curfew Wagon," 199–200

Davenport, Ella, 181
Davis, John P., 20
Dawson, Anthony, 161
Dell, Hammett, 140–41

247

Denmark Vesey Rebellion, 39–40, 41–42, 48
Devil lore, 61–63
Dew, Thomas R., 39
Dickens, Charles, 34
Douglass, Frederick, 11
DuBois, W. E. B., 27
Duke, Alice, 134
Duvall, Alice Williams, 97, 200, 210

Egypt, Ophelia Settle, 18–19, 23
Elkins, Stanley, 4–5
Ellison, Ralph, 4, 28
Evans, James C., 214–15
Evening Star, The, 200
Ezell, Lorenza, 97

Fagin, Gaynelle, 190, 197
Family sagas, 8–9
Feldstein, Stanley, 25
Fisher, Miles Mark, 26
Floyd, N. J., 119–20
Folk history, historical sources, 10–29
Folklore: attitudes concerning Black traditions, 4; psychological uses of, 3, 7, 29, 63, 73–80, 113–14, 152, 168–69, 179–82
Folk narratives: historical sources, 9–10, 17–29; illustrative texts, 58, 74, 77–78, 80–81, 107–109, 115–16, 140–41, 144–45, 186, 198–99, 205
Folk tales, 73–81; Master and John cycle, 60, 101–102; texts, 75–79, 80–81; utilization of, 59–81
Folk tradition, transmission of, 7–9, 212–15
Fountaine, Minnie, 47, 58, 107, 113, 144, 201
Franklin, John Hope, 10–11, 112–13
Franklin, Leonard, 88
Free Negroes in the District of Columbia, 1790–1846, 34
Free Trader, 175

Gabriel, 39–40, 41–42; *see also* Slave insurrections
Ghost Chases Uncle Daniel Home, 80–81
Ghost tales: transmission of, 63–65; utilization in slave control, 59–82
Ghost visits, 71
Ghosts, 61–81; African belief in, 9; encounters with, 74–78; night doctors

Ghosts (*cont.*)
use of, 180–82; of the Confederate dead, 136–37, 141; whites masquerading as, 3, 52, 69–73, 113; viewed as hoax, 79
Gill, Frank, 105
Gilmore, Brawley, 146
Goff, Jim, 72
Graves, Wesley, 152
Green, Mildred, 179, 196
Griffin, Madison, 146–47
Grund, Francis J., 34
Guttmacher, Allen, 177

Haley, Alex, 8
Hansberry, Leo, 16, 27
Harding, Vincent, 27–28
Hare, William, 176
Harrison, The Reverend Earl L., 154, 214
Haunted places, 66–69
Hawkins, John, 4
Haymond, Henry, 62
Hays, Eliza, 158
Henderson, Donald H., 172
Henderson, William, 55, 64, 71, 180, 188
Henry, Julia, 69, 79
Henry, Thomas L., 161, 199
Hesseltine, William B., 49
Higginson, Thomas Wentworth, 174
Hines, Gabe, 135
History of Harrison County of West Virginia, 62
Holloman, The Reverend J.L.S., 47, 66
Hopkins, Louise, 193
Horton, Benjamin, 115–16
Hurley, Matthew, 66
Hutcheson, Alice, 146

Invisible Empire, 112; *see also* Ku Klux Klan (Reconstruction)

Jackson, Fred, 180
Jackson, Solomon, 76–77
"Jayhawkers," 157–58
Jenfier, Rachel, 182, 189, 197, 203
Johnson, Charles S., 18–19
Johnson, John, 193, 202
Johnson, Mary, 179, 189
Johnson, Richard, 74
Jones, Mary Elizabeth, 72–73
Journal of American Folklore, 4, 173
Joyner, Charles, 6

King, Messiah, 191
"Kluxing," 160
Knox, John, 120
Kourier Magazine, 118
"Ku Klux," 157–58, 160
"Ku Kluxing," 160
Ku Klux Klan Act, 14
Ku Klux Klan (Reconstruction), 3,
14, 15, 36, 71, 88, 106, 110–69; Black
activities in, 162–65; Black folk view
of, 154–62; Congressional testimony
concerning, 14–15, 111, 113–14, 123–
24, 132–33, 162, 165, 167; continuation of slave patrols, 113, 147–49;
costume, 122–35; disguised as animals, 142–44; folk names for, 158,
160–61; historical background, 110–
22; in Alabama, 115–17, 145–46; in
Georgia, 122–23; in South Carolina,
134, 159; in Tennessee, 110, 112–13,
128, 142; in Virginia, 160, 181;
intimidation through use of supernatural practices, 135–47; legends
concerning, 115–17; officially dissolved in 1869, 114; origin of name,
117–22, 152; origins in 1865, 110–13;
parades, 145–47; patrols, 147–53;
regional names used by Blacks, 160–
62; use of corporal punishment, 114,
151, 159; use of psychological intimidation, 114, 152

Law, Mamie, 180
Lee, Randall, 156
Legend of Cocletz Indians, 119–22
Legends, 34, 119–22
Lewis, Roscoe, 21–22, 23
L'Ouverture, Toussaint, 43
Lucy Cotton Outruns the Patrollers,
107–109
Lyles, Grace, 69

McDougle, Ivan, 82
McKeever, Armenia, 206
McKeever, Eliza, 206
McKeever, Essie, 207
McKeever, Exter, 207
McKeever, Laura, 207
McKeever, Sam, 202–207
McKinney, Evelyn, 55–56
McLain, C. T., 195, 198
Manassas Gap, 137, 139
Manning, Fred, 186–87

Marshall, Matilda, 54–55
Martineau, Harriet, 34
Master and John tale cycle, 60, 101–
102
Memorat, 9–10
Memphis Appeal, 118
Methodology, 29–31
Mitchell, Ida, 195
Monstrous births, 116–17
Morgan, Kathryn, 8
Morrison, James, 202, 204
Mt. Zion Slave Cemetery, 206
Mounted patrols; *see* Patrol system
Murdock, Lucille, 65, 191

*Narrative of the Life of Frederick
Douglass, An American Slave, Written by Himself, The*, 11
Nat Turner Rebellion, 21
Neeley, Mary Howard, 54, 64
Negro in Virginia, The, 22
Night doctors, 3, 170–211; Black, 202–
207; bled victims, 200–201; as body-
snatchers, 171, 173, 183–88; choice
of victims, 190–92; costume, 188–90;
historical background, 170–78; in
Chicago, 193; in New York, 191; in
rural South, 178–82; in Washington,
D. C., 182–88; locale of, 183–88, 199;
methods of obtaining victims, 192–
97; narrative texts, 180–81, 182, 184,
185, 186; origin of name, 171–72;
relationship to Ku Klux Klan, 180–
81; transport of victims, 197–202;
whites masquerading as, 180–82
Night riders, 3, 73, 75, 113, 160, 162–
69; *see also* Patrol system
Night-riding Blacks, 162–69
"Night thieves," 161
Niles' Weekly Register, 40–41
Northup, Solomon, 11

Olmsted, Frederick Law, 34, 38, 90
Oral history, 16–17
Oral traditions, 103–109; concerning
Sam McKeever, 202–207; night doc-
tors, 171, 173; preservation in Black
culture, 212–15; utilization of, 3, 7–8,
29, 45–58, 59–81
Osofsky, Gilbert, 12

Parker, Eva Francis, 184
Parsons, Elsie Clews, 57

"Paterollers"; *see* "Patterollers"

Patrol system, 82–109; Black folk view of, 102–106; duties, 85–86; evaluation of, 93–109; historical background, 3, 44, 61, 82–85; in Louisiana, 85; in Mississippi, 85; in North Carolina, 84; in South Carolina, 84; in Tennessee, 84–85; in Washington, D. C., 89–92; methodology, 86–89; narrative texts, 87–89, 93–95, 98–102, 104–106, 107–109, 150–52; post-Civil War, 155–57; punishments inflicted by, 92, 96–99; slave-owners opposition to, 96–97, 106; slaves resistence to, 93–96, 100–101

Patroller Taylor Burned with Hot Coals, 107

"Patterollers," 3, 44, 61, 75, 103–104, 157–58

Pattillo, G. W., 99

Peculiar Institution, The, 45–46, 57–58

Phifer, Edward W., 34

Phillips, Ulrich, 39

Postwar patrols, narrative texts on, 156–58, 160–62

Powell, Bruce, 184

Poyas, Peter, 48

Prasad, J., 53

Pugh, Nicey, 127

Pulaski Citizen, 118

"Pulaski Six," 110, 119, 152

Pulaski, Tennessee, 110, 112–13, 119, 138

Randall, James, 4, 39

Randel, William Peirce, 112

Randolph, Perry, 185, 194, 196

Reconstruction Ku Klux Klan, 3, 14–15, 36, 71, 88, 106, 110–69, 195; *see also* Ku Klux Klan (Reconstruction)

Reddick, Laurence, 16, 22, 23, 27

Reed, Mrs. Charles, 54

Reed, Elizabeth, 72

Reed, Laura, 181, 187, 190, 197, 203–204, 205

Returning-dead, beliefs in, 135–41

Richardson, Jessie, 200

Richmond Whig, The, 118

Robinson, Katherine Brooks, 196

Robinson, Mamie Ardella, 93

Romaine, W. B., 119

Roots, 8

Ross, Frederick, 139

Roy, Anna Cooper, 209

Sambo stereotype, 4–6

Scott, Senator John, 14

Scriber, Walter, 192

Sheeler, J. Reuben, 61–62

Shiloh, 137–40

Slave Community, The, 28

Slave control, 38–81; historical background, 38–44; methods of, 45–58; psychological means of, 45–58; religious and educational restrictions, 42–44; role of master and overseer, 59–63; through encouragement of superstitious beliefs, 60–81

Slave informers, 47–49

Slave insurrections, 38–44, 48

Slave Insurrections in the United States, 48

Slave memoirs: abolitionist editing of, 11–12; Congressional testimony, 14–15; printed, 11; recorded, 11–13

Slave narrative collections, 11, 22–25

Slave patrols and Ku Klux Klan, 147–49

Slave Songs in the United States, 26

Slavery, historical sources, 10–29

Slavery in the United States: A Narrative of the Life and Adventures of Charles Ball, A Black Man, Who Lived Forty Years in Maryland, South Carolina and Georgia as a Slave, 11

Slaves as tricksters, 6

Slaves used for medical experimentation, 173–78

Smith, Bessie, 204–205

Smith, Darwin, 183

Smith, The Reverend E. C., 60–61

Snow, Beverly, 91

Souls of Black Folk, 27

South Carolina Patrol Act of 1740, 96–97

Stampp, Kenneth, 25, 45–46, 57–58

Stealey, Jacob, 62

Steward, Austin, 47–48

Still, William, 13, 14

Stillman, Dr. T., 175

Story of My Life and Work, The, 11

Story of the Original Ku Klux Klan, A, 119

Storytelling in Black society, 212–15

Stuckey, Sterling, 27
Supernatural: animals, 65; fear of,
  3–4, 6–7, 10, 45–58; power of ghosts,
  142–45

Taylor, Joe Gray, 102
Taylor, Samuel S., 157–58
Theft of cadavers for medical purposes,
  171–78
Thorns in the Flesh, 119
Tolbert, James, 53
Torrey, Jesse, 34
Trelease, Allen W., 163
Tubman, Harriet, 26
Turner, Nat, 21, 26, 29–40, 41–42, 176
Tuskegee Study, 170–71
Tymes, James Daniel, 192

Underground Railroad, The, 13

Vesey, Denmark, 26, 39–42, 48
Vigilance Committee, 13–14

Ward, Morgan, 194
Washington, Booker T., 11
Washington, D. C.: folk tradition in,
  32–37; night doctors in, 182–88, 202–
  207; patrol system in, 89–92
Weld, Theodore Douglas, 174–75
"What You See, You Don't See," 58
Wheeler, Elizabeth, 189
"White caps," 160–61
White Terror, 163
White, Walter, 20
Williams, Millie, 94
Willis, William, 67–68
Winn, Willis, 147
Witchcraft, 54–56
Work Projects Administration, 11
WPA Federal Writers Project, 19–20

Night Riders in Black Folk History was manually set on the Linotype in eleven-point Times Roman with two-point spacing between the lines. Pistilli Roman, a photo face, was selected as the bold display type.

The book was designed by Jim Billingsley, cast into type and printed letterpress by Heritage Printers, Inc., Charlotte, North Carolina, and bound by The Delmar Companies, also of Charlotte. The paper on which the book is printed is designed for an effective life of at least three hundred years.

THE UNIVERSITY OF TENNESSEE PRESS : KNOXVILLE